SECRET MISSIONS
OF THE
SUFFRAGETTES

Thank you to Raphie for keeping me grounded.

Author Jennifer Godfrey with her dog, Raphie. (© Ruth Jessamine Godfrey)

SECRET MISSIONS
OF THE
SUFFRAGETTES

GLASSBREAKERS
AND SAFE HOUSES

JENNIFER GODFREY

PEN & SWORD
HISTORY
AN IMPRINT OF PEN & SWORD BOOKS LTD.
YORKSHIRE – PHILADELPHIA

First published in Great Britain in 2024 by
PEN AND SWORD HISTORY
An imprint of
Pen & Sword Books Ltd
Yorkshire – Philadelphia

ISBN 978 1 39901 396 3

A CIP catalogue record for this book is available from the British Library.

Typeset in Times New Roman 10/13 by SJmagic DESIGN SERVICES, India.
Printed and bound in the UK by CPI Group (UK) Ltd.

Pen & Sword Books Limited incorporates the imprints of Atlas, Archaeology,
Aviation, Discovery, Family History, Fiction, History, Maritime, Military,
Military Classics, After the Battle, Politics, Select, Transport, True Crime, Air
World, Frontline Publishing, Leo Cooper, Remember When, Seaforth Publishing,
The Praetorian Press, Wharncliffe Local History, Wharncliffe Transport,
Wharncliffe True Crime and White Owl.

For a complete list of Pen & Sword titles please contact
PEN & SWORD BOOKS LIMITED
George House, Units 12 & 13, Beevor Street, Off Pontefract Road,
Barnsley, South Yorkshire, S71 1HN, England
E-mail: enquiries@pen-and-sword.co.uk
Website: www.pen-and-sword.co.uk

or

PEN AND SWORD BOOKS
1950 Lawrence Rd, Havertown, PA 19083, USA
E-mail: uspen-and-sword@casematepublishers.com
Website: www.penandswordbooks.com

Contents

Introduction

This book has two parts, the first dedicated to the detail behind and stories involved in the large-scale window breaking 'Great Militant Protest'[1] of March 1912. This was a Women's Social and Political Union (WSPU) protest led by Mrs Emmeline Pankhurst. She said that the outcome of this protest and the large volume of arrested suffragette glassbreakers or vitrifragists[2] had left the magistrates 'dismayed ... facing, not only former rebels, but many new ones...'[3] Ethel Violet Baldock, whose previously untold story was profiled in chapter one of my first book, *Suffragettes of Kent*, was one of these new rebels hence the interest in this particular protest.

Aged 19 years old[4] at the time of her arrest, Ethel Violet Baldock appears to be the youngest March 1912 glassbreaker with Hilda Brackenbury being the eldest, at 79 years old[5]. Both of their stories are explored further in this book with Hilda smashing windows on 1 March and Ethel glass breaking on 4 March. Hilda was known for her prior involvement in the WSPU whilst Ethel was not. Ethel was a working class maid from Kent. Hilda owned two properties, one in London and another in Peaslake, Surrey, both were used by suffragettes seeking a safe place for rest and recuperation after imprisonment.

The WSPU were convinced that 1912 would be the year that some women would get the vote. In 1910 the Conciliation Bill was designed to placate the women's suffrage movement by giving a limited number of women the vote according to their property holdings and marital status. In July 1910 the Bill was debated and carried by 109 votes and it was sent away for amendment by a House of Commons committee. However, the Prime Minister, Mr Asquith, spoke of shelving the Bill. The WSPU responded on 18 November 1910 with a huge protest, known as 'Black Friday'.

In 1911, the Conciliation Bill was re-introduced and it appeared that it would be given appropriate facilities in Parliament to be discussed, debated and voted on. It was on this basis that the WSPU agreed to a cease fire, stopping their protests. However, in November 1911, 'the Government had broken their plighted word and had deliberately destroyed the Conciliation Bill.'[6] The Government had announced that they would now be introducing and passing through a Bill for enfranchisement applicable to adult males only. They argued that this legislation would be framed in such a way as to make it possible for a women's suffrage amendment in the future. However, the WSPU saw the introduction of such a Bill as entangling the question of women's suffrage with that of universal suffrage.[7]

Mr Asquith accepted requests for a deputation from nine suffrage societies. The WSPU sent Christabel Harriette Pankhurst, Mrs Pethick-Lawrence, Miss Annie Kenney, Lady Constance Lytton and Miss Elizabeth Robins. Christabel was the eldest daughter of Emmeline Pankhurst and a co-founder of the WSPU. Mrs Pethick-Lawrence was a prominent WSPU member and financed and edited the WSPU *Votes for Women* newspaper. Miss Annie Kenney was another prominent WSPU member and paid organiser for London. An influential suffrage activist, writer, speaker and campaigner, Lady Constance Lytton famously used an alias name and disguised herself as a London seamstress when arrested and imprisoned. Miss Elizabeth Robins was an actress, playwright, novelist and suffragette. From the United States of America, Elizabeth moved to England in 1888 and became a member of the National Union of Women's Suffrage Societies (NUWSS) as well as the WSPU. She was a strong advocate for women's rights through her writing. Her country farmhouse in West Sussex was searched by the police in March 1912 when they were looking for Christabel Pankhurst (see chapter thirteen).

At the deputation, it was Christabel who spoke for the WSPU:

> 'We are not satisfied,' she warned him, and the Prime Minister said acidly: 'I did not expect to satisfy you.'[8]

In November 1911, the WSPU's response was the breaking of hundreds of windows, with over two hundred women arrested and around one hundred and fifty of them imprisoned for between one week and two months. The period that followed and led to a further window breaking protest in March 1912 is explained in the words of Mrs Emmeline Pankhurst:

> 'The King's speech, when Parliament met in February, 1912, alluded to the franchise question in very general terms. Proposals, it was stated, would be brought forward for the amendment of the law with respect to the franchise and the registration of electors. This might be construed to mean that the Government were going to introduce a manhood suffrage bill or a bill for the abolition of plural voting, which had been suggested in some quarters as a substitute for the manhood suffrage bill. No precise statement of the Government's intentions was made, and the whole franchise question was left in a cloud of uncertainty. Mr Agg-Gardner, a Unionist Member of the Conciliation Committee, drew the third place in the ballot, and he announced that he should reintroduce the Conciliation Bill. This interested us very slightly, for knowing its prospect of success to have been destroyed, we were done with the Conciliation Bill forever. Nothing less than a government measure would henceforth

satisfy the WSPU, because it had been clearly demonstrated that only a government measure would be allowed to pass the House of Commons. With sublime faith, or rather more, a deplorable lack of political insight, the Women's Liberal Federation and the National Union of Women's Suffrage Societies professed full confidence in the proposed amendment to a manhood suffrage bill, but we knew how futile was that hope. We saw that the only course to take was to offer determined opposition to any measure of suffrage that did not include as an integral part, equal suffrage for men and women.'[9]

Another provocation cited by the WSPU and many 1912 glassbreakers were the speeches of Mr Hobhouse MP in which he proclaimed 'that in the case of the suffrage demand there had not been the kind of popular sentimental uprising which accounted for Nottingham Castle in 1832 or the Hyde Park railings in 1867. There had been no great ebullition of popular feeling.'[10]

The WSPU then began preparations for the 'Great Militant Protest' in March 1912. Set out in Part One of this book are details of the planning and execution of this protest with the profiles of some of the individuals involved and their stories.

The March 1912 glassbreakers had amongst them 'former rebels'[11] some of whom used alias names or pseudonyms when arrested. Others had been under surveillance and photographed by a special branch of the Metropolitan Police. Many had and would continue to escape the police's surveillance operations. Some suffragette prisoners were involved in the smuggling of material both into and out of prison. Others were members of an elite 'security team' that mastered self-defence techniques to protect Mrs Emmeline Pankhurst. Part Two of this book therefore seeks to unpick some suffragette stories involving secrecy around their protests and missions, use of alias names, the security team, surveillance by the police, and the safe houses they could retreat to for rest, recuperation and hiding from the authorities.

Glossary

Each glassbreaker named will have a number included after the first mention of their name. This is their age at the time of arrest at the Great Militant Protest.

Where the term 'glassbreaker' is used, unless otherwise stated it refers to one of the 1912 Great Militant protestors.

A list of known 1912 glassbreaker is included as Annex 1. It is in order of date of offence, location and surname. Where a glassbreaker damaged more than one property there is an entry for that glassbreaker for each location targeted.

The following is an alphabetical list of acronyms/abbreviations used:

AFL	Actresses' Freedom League
IWFL	Irish Women's Franchise League
IWSS	Irish Women's Suffrage Society
MLWS	Men's League for Women's Suffrage
MPU	Men's Political Union for Women's Enfranchisement
NUWSS	National Union of Women's Suffrage Societies
TRL	Tax Resistance League
WFL	Women's Freedom League
WSPU	Women's Social and Political Union

Part One

Glassbreakers. (© Jennifer Godfrey. Image created for author by Daniel Atkinson (Dan Rhys Design))

Chapter 1

A Great Militant Protest

'In her opinion the time was now ripe for women to make the
supreme effort for freedom.'[1]

This first chapter sets out the preparation undertaken to deliver such a large protest and introduces some of those involved.

The first meeting about the Great Militant Protest was in January 1912 at the Savoy Theatre. The manager at the Savoy and the manager from the London Pavilion (another venue regularly used by the WSPU) gave evidence about their interactions with the WSPU in the case against Mrs Emmeline Pankhurst and Mr and Mrs Pethick-Lawrence. As set out in chapter four, these three were found guilty in 1912 of conspiring together to unlawfully and maliciously damage certain property and inciting others of the same. Giving evidence,

> Frank Glenister, manager of the London Pavilion, said that during 1911 and the early part of this year [1912] the theatre was used for meetings of the Union, and produced the agreements under which the place was let. These included undertakings of the Union that the premises should be left in good order after the meetings, and nothing be done or permitted contrary to the terms of the theatre license, and that the proprietors should be reimbursed for any damage resulting from the meetings....... The meetings were very well attended, and quite orderly. We found the Union satisfactory tenants in every way....... It never occurred to me that we were letting the Pavilion as part of the machinery of a great conspiracy. Harry Percival Towers, business manager of the Savoy Theatre, gave similar evidence.[2]

Suffragette and glassbreaker Zoe Proctor, 44, tells of her involvement in the January 1912 meeting at the Savoy Theatre via her autobiography, *Life and Yesterday*. She describes a meeting taking place where Christabel Pankhurst made 'an impassioned plea for more volunteers to commit those symbolic acts of violence, such as window breaking, which could almost certainly lead to imprisonment. She reminded us all that a great many women had served sentences again and again,

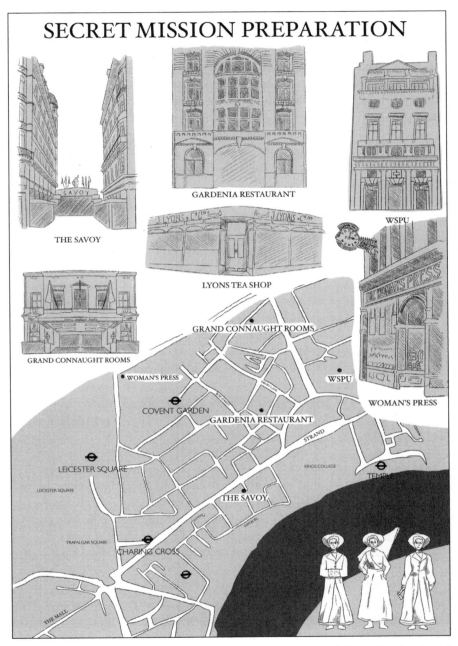

Secret mission preparation. (© Jennifer Godfrey. Image created for author by Daniel Atkinson (Dan Rhys Design))

whereas, if a large number filled the prisons at the same time, it might influence the policy of the Government.'[3]

Zoe said that she decided she must go to prison and along with many others at this Savoy meeting, gave her name in for the demonstration.

On 16 February 1912 Mrs Emmeline Pankhurst hosted a meeting in the Connaught Rooms in Great Queen Street. Mrs Pankhurst welcomed the suffragette prisoners released from Holloway where they had served sentences for window smashing in November 1911. 'Pankhurst proposed the guests of the evening. She reminded her hearers that stone throwing had been their offence. That was a form of argument that seemed to carry more weight with the Government than an appeal for citizenship based on justice and reason. It was the argument she intended to adopt when leading the protest on March 4. She urged all women present to join the protest. In her opinion the time was now ripe for women to make the supreme effort for freedom.'[4]

At this February meeting speeches were heard from released prisoners and Mrs Helen Archdale, the WSPU Prisoners' Secretary. Helen said that 'the time had passed for women to exercise patience. She appealed to those hesitating as to militancy to come forward. They would find the wall of their difficulties diminish as they approached it.'[5] Those present at the meeting included Sir Edward and Lady Busk, Lady Constance Lytton, Mr and Mrs Pethick-Lawrence, the Reverend Hugh Chapman, Lady Muir Mackenzie, Mr and Mrs Cecil Chapman, the Ranne of Sarawak, Lady Brassey, Miss Christabel Pankhurst, and Mrs Cobden Sanderson.[6] All pro-suffrage, these attendees would have been invited to attend this meeting

Mrs Pankhurst speaking at the London Pavilion, flanked by Emmeline Pethick-Lawrence and Christabel Pankhurst, with representatives of WSPU branches also on the platform, 1912. Some of these representatives could have been March 1912 glassbreakers. (© LSE Women's Library Collection)

as special guests. Rev. Hugh Chapman was the Chaplain of the Royal Chapel of the Savoy in London. On 13 January 1912, Rev. Hugh Chapman married suffragette Una Dugdale to Victor Duval, founder member of the MPU. Victor's mother, Jane Emily, and sister, Norah were March 1912 glassbreakers. Another sister of Victor, Elsie Duval, assisted with the escape of suffragette and glassbreaker Lilian Lenton (see chapter thirteen). Mr Cecil Chapman was the chief metropolitan magistrate of London. He had been chairman of MLWS and openly supported the WSPU often speaking at events organised by Mrs Emmeline Pankhurst. Mrs Cobden Sanderson was the daughter of Kate Cobden who had signed the 1866 mass petition for votes for women. Mrs Cobden Sanderson was an ardent life-long suffrage supporter and campaigner, imprisoned in

Victor Duval, c.1910. (© LSE Women's Library Collection)

1906 for protesting in the lobby of the House of Commons. At her trial it is reported that she said, 'I am a law breaker because I want to be a law maker.'[7]

The day after this meeting, 17 February 1912, the following call to action was released to WSPU members:

> MEN AND WOMEN I INVITE YOU TO COME TO PARLIAMENT SQUARE ON MONDAY, MARCH 4TH 1912 at 8 o'clock to take part in a Great Militant Protest MEETING against the government's refusal to include women in their reform Bill. Speeches will be delivered by well-known Suffragettes, who want to enlist your sympathy and help in the great battle they are fighting for human liberty.[8]

Mrs Lillian Ball, a working class dressmaker and married mother with three children, aged 24, 21 and 4 (of 12 Holderness Road, Tooting, London) responded to this 'call to action' stating that she would join 'a great militant protest.'[9] This was despite Lillian's failure to go through with the November 1911 window smashing mission. The following is the extract from a witness statement Lillian made to the police in March 1912:

> In the early part of November last year I received a letter from the Union asking me to join in another deputation. I cannot remember who

it was signed by, but communications of that kind are usually signed by Mrs Pankhurst. It might have been signed by Mrs Pethick Lawrence as Mrs Pankhurst was at that time in America. I replied volunteering for the deputation as I understood it was to be similar to the one I had taken part in during the previous year, and received a further communication directing me to call at the "Woman's Press", Charing Cross Road, at about 6pm on the 21st November. I went there along, arriving about 6pm and was shown to a large room upstairs. I had to produce a card ... several times before I was admitted to the room. I should think there would be quite a hundred women present when I arrived. We were each called in turn into a smaller room, adjoining, and there I saw three ladies who were giving instructions. They were unknown to me. On entering one of them asked me if I had a pocket in my skirt. I replied "No". She then asked me to unbutton a long coat I was wearing. I did so and she then produced the pocket (handed to Police by my brother) containing stones, and I protested against using them saying that I only expected to join a deputation, not to break windows. They got angry and said I should have come prepared to do anything. We had some sort of a discussion and it ended by these ladies tying the bag of stones round my waist. I protested that it was too heavy and they took some out. I was then instructed to go with two other women, whose names I do not know, to the back of the Houses of Parliament and break windows there. I then left with the two other women, whom I had met that evening, for the first time, and we tried to get to the Houses of Parliament, but were unable to do so owing to the Police. We walked about together until about 9pm and the other two women then said they would go to Pall Mall and smash windows there. I had had enough of it so I went home.[10]

There was much correspondence about who could and who could not participate in the March 1912 protest. Some of the letters were subsequently seized by the police in their pursuit of Mrs Emmeline Pankhurst, Mrs Tuke and the Pethick-Lawrences in the case against them for conspiring to cause damage.

The contents of the letters and their back stories demonstrate the level of support for the cause and the Great Militant Protest meeting whilst also highlighting some of the factors that supporters and potential glassbreakers needed to consider before responding or stepping up.

Nurse Ellen Pitfield wrote to Mrs Emmeline Pankhurst addressing her as 'Mrs Pankhurst' saying:

> I am with you heart and soul in the great demonstration on March the 4th 1912. A Soldier to the death.[11]

Nurse Ellen Pitfield acted independently after the preliminary action of 1 March and before the 4 March orchestrated mass window smashing. She was sentenced to six months for her part in the disturbances, having set fire to a basket containing shavings and smashed a window in the Post Office in Roman Bath Street, Newgate Street. Being state owned, the General Post Office became a target for suffragette window breaking. In 1912 many had windows broken during the Great Militant Protest. This line of attack continued beyond this mission. In 1913 attacks on Royal Mail property and the destruction of letters was seen as a turning point in the WSPU use of militant tactics, moving away from the notion of gaining public sympathy in order to obtain equal rights to outright coercion - a government forced to act in the face of public outrage.[12] Ellen had come up to Police Constable Pemmers at about 10pm on Sunday 3 March and said, 'I have thrown a brick through the Post Office window and have done something which I hope will burn the place down.'[13] At her hearing Ellen said that she did it as protest against the Government, saying 'I have been unable to rest since Mrs Pankhurst and the others have been arrested. I came up form Bucks this evening to do it.'[14] She had been diagnosed with terminal cancer prior to participating and was carried from the court to the prison hospital when sentenced. She refused to sign an undertaking against further militant action but expressed that 'it was not in her to offend again.'[15] In her collection of letters[16], suffragette and glassbreaker Mary Ellen (Nellie) Taylor writes that Ellen cries at night and that all the suffragette prisoners wish for her release. She appears to have been released early from her sentence, and died in August 1912.

Another letter was received from Amy Woodburn, 49, dated 26 February 1912 stating:

> Dear Miss Pankhurst,
>
> In reply to your letter received this morning I will just repeat what I have written to your Mother. I am with you heart and mind and fighting for our great cause and will follow whatever lead. I cannot understand the non-militant party. We have tried their methods for years without believing in them and in simple fairness and justice they ought to try ours, whether they believe in them or not. If instead of asking for a sum of £40,000 to carry on the campaign they would resolve to break 40,000 windows they would soon realise who was right. Yours sincerely, Amy Woodburn. Cannot you challenge these ladies to join us for one big protest and prove whether principle or cowardice sways their opinions.[17]

Amy Woodburn of 168 Broadhurst Gardens, West Hampstead, joined the demonstration on 1 March 1912. It is however unclear where she caused damage.

She was sentenced on 2 March 1912 at Bow Street Police Court to fourteen days' imprisonment.

Some were unable to commit to supporting the protest. On 19 February 1912, Lady Constance Lytton wrote on behalf of Miss Avery of Knebworth School. The letter stated:

> In reply to your appeal to join the deputation sent to Miss Avery, The School House, Knebworth.
>
> Dear Mrs Pankhurst,
>
> Miss Avery would consider it the very highest privilege in going to follow you on March 4th. She will not be able. She is a School Teacher, her imprisonment would mean the sacrifice of her economic independence and would throw her on to her family for support.
>
> This fact causes her such bitter sorrow that she could not bring herself to put the refusal into words. I therefore undertook to write to you for her.
>
> She serves our cause in every other way possible to her.[18]

In another letter, Mrs Hetherington wrote to say that she could not join the protest as she had two small children, one only a few months old. A suffrage supporter called Francesca pointed out that she loved the cause better than her life but her fear of defying her mother prevented her from joining the protest. She said: 'The only gift I envy anyone is freedom and I am hoping someday to get mine.'[19]

Mrs Emmeline Pankhurst had been in America when the WSPU undertook their November 1911 window smashing protest and feeling she needed some practice for the March 1912 raid, asked suffragette and English composer, Ethel Smyth, 54, for some tuition. Mrs Emmeline Pankhurst 'went to Ethel's home, Coign Cottage, close to Woking. At dusk Ethel took her on to Hook Heath for tuition (Ethel was a fine sportswoman, who enjoyed a scrimmage[20]). Mrs Pankhurst's first try flew backwards, narrowly missing Ethel's sheepdog, but eventually one stone thudded against a tree and she looked so pleased with herself that Ethel collapsed in the heather, roaring with laughter.'[21]

It is known that other preparation included the collection of missiles outside central London as they 'were not readily available in the well-to-do parts of London where many suffragettes lived, paved forecourts facing parks or squares staffed by gardeners and keepers.'[22] Indeed, according to Mrs Emmeline Pankhurst's second daughter Sylvia Pankhurst, 'suffragettes went by motor-car at dusk to country lanes for flints. Ladies from Peaslake surely gathered them locally and took up to town not primroses, newlaid eggs, or the first green peas, but hard-edged flints that fitted snugly into the hand.... The missiles could be carried in a drawstring bag tied round the waist under the skirt and reached through a pocket with an unstitched seam'.[23] As had been provided to suffragettes on earlier glass-breaking missions these pockets filled with stones were given out in March 1912. One glassbreaker recalled that the pockets 'all appeared to be made out of the same material.'[24] This uniformity of 'equipment' provided to the glassbreakers was used by the Metropolitan Police when they argued that certain WSPU leaders and members were guilty of conspiracy to incite malicious damage. Further details on this are included in chapter four.

Those joining the protests received the following instructions from Mrs Emmeline Pankhurst. These were dated 28 February 1912 and read:

> Instructions to Volunteers. When arrested and taken to Cannon Street or other Police Station, you will, after an interval, be bailed out and then return to your home or hostess. In the morning you should surrender at the time mentioned on your charge sheet, at the Police Court, bringing with you a bag packed with everything you are likely to need during your imprisonment.[25]

As is highlighted in this instruction, to enable the involvement of WSPU members from further afield than London, arrangements had been made for London based members to act as hostesses for this protest. This was necessary as those participating in this protest came from far and wide, including overseas. Also evident from this instruction is how the WSPU took care of bail for the arrested suffragettes.

The following letter was found in suffragette Elsie Duval's possession. Elsie is not listed as arrested at the March 1912 window smashing but could have been there and evaded arrest. Her mother, Jane Emily, and sister, Norah, were both arrested. The letter read:

> Dear Colleague,
>
> Strictly private and confidential
> March 4th Protest
>
> With reference to the above Protest will you make a point of being at the Gardenia Restaurant, Catherine Street, Strand on Monday, the 4th inst., at 6 p.m., where my friends, Mrs. McLeod and Miss Wallace Dunlop, will give you all instructions.
>
> I am enclosing ticket without which you will not be admitted to the Restaurant.

N.B. Please do not mention the contents of this letter to anyone, especially the place and time of meeting. Also note that no one but yourself can be admitted with your ticket.

Yours sincerely

[signed by Mrs Emmeline Pankhurst]

P.S. Please do not wear colours or badge.[26]

The 4 March demonstration had been announced and widely shared

and the announcement created much public alarm. Sir William Byles gave notice that he would 'ask the Secretary of State for the Home Department whether his attention had been drawn to a speech by Mrs Pankhurst last Friday night, openly and emphatically inciting her hearers to violent outrage and the destruction of property, and threatening the use of firearms if stones did not prove sufficiently effective; and what steps he proposes to take to protect Society from this outbreak of lawlessness.' The question was duly asked, and the Home Secretary replied that his attention had been called to the speech, but that it would not be desirable in the public interest to say more than this at present.[27]

It appears that some suffragettes including Lillian Ball were selected to receive a further letter from Mrs Pankhurst:

1 March 1912

Dear Friend, In view of the precautions which the police are likely to take on Monday, and in order to increase the total effect of the protest, I have thought it well that I and several others should take some preliminary action today. The rest of the volunteers and any who, having made their protest today, are still at liberty, will go and make a brave fight on Monday. My thanks and greetings to you. Yours sincerely, (signed) E. Pankhurst.[28]

This letter was Mrs Emmeline Pankhurst's call to those women available to join an earlier protest on the evening of Friday, 1 March, and if they escaped, return on Monday evening (4 March). Lillian Ball did not join the preliminary action, attending instead on 4 March. Glass breaker Zoe Proctor was one of the WSPU members given prior warning of this earlier preliminary attack as she recalls: 'In February I learned where I was to be at six o'clock on the evening of 1st March.'[29]

It seems that glassbreaker Miss Hazel Inglis, 27, was also notified as in her oral history[30] she recalls receiving a piece of paper in the post with 'Regent Street H.M. Post Master General' written on it. She said that this was her instruction to attack those premises with a hammer which she did on 1 March (see Chapter Two).

Glass breaker Kitty Marion wrote in her autobiography:

> On February 26, Mr Lloyd George as principal speaker at an Albert Hall meeting of the National Union of [Women's] Suffrage Societies, the non-militants, made more evasive promises to which we had a ready answer.[31]

The result for the Great Militant Protest was a two-pronged attack, one completely unexpected by the authorities, taking place on 1 March 1912, and the other announced and therefore expected by the authorities, an orchestrated mass window smashing protest on 4 March 1912. In total over 250 women were arrested and charged with causing malicious damage, breaking over 340 windows. Some protestors evaded arrest, like Mrs Leonora Cohen[32] and possibly Elsie Duval. The Metropolitan Police estimated that 270 windows were smashed on 4 March 1912 alone at an estimated cost of £6,600[33] (equivalent to approximately £965,000 today). It is therefore highly probable that the total cost of damage across the two nights exceeded the equivalent of £1m today. There was a span of 60 years age range for those arrested, from 19 to 79 years old. Two of those involved are known to have been under 21, Ethel Violet Baldock, the youngest at 19, and Olive M. Fontaine at 20. Their involvement (see chapter three) is not compliant with Mrs Pankhurst's reported inflexible rule that no one under 21 years old should do anything that might incur a prison sentence.[34]

The next chapters tell the stories of many of those involved as they rose for the cause – fighting to give women a voice through the right to vote.

Chapter 2

Preliminary Action

'We had planned a demonstration for March 4th, and this one we announced. We planned another demonstration for March 1st, but this one we did not announce.'[1]

On Friday, 1 March 1912, the WSPU window smashing began. This was three days ahead of the planned Monday, 4 March protest and called 'preliminary action' by Mrs Emmeline Pankhurst who accounted that:

> Whatever preparations the police department were making to prevent the demonstration, they failed because, while as usual, we were able to calculate exactly what the police department were going to do, they were utterly unable to calculate what we were going to do. We had planned a demonstration for March 4th, and this one we announced. We planned another demonstration for March 1st, but this one we did not announce.[2]

The Metropolitan Police had as suspected by Mrs Emmeline Pankhurst, on 17 February 1912, the day after the WSPU meeting in the Connaught Rooms, filed a Criminal Investigation Department report of the intentions of the WSPU. It read:

> With reference to the Women's Social and Political Union for Women's Suffrage,
> I beg to report having been informed that the leaders of the above Union have decided to demonstrate in the vicinity of Parliament Square, Westminster, during the evening of the 4th proximo. They will be led by Mrs. Pankhurst and stone throwing and window breaking will be their object, and the leader has announced her intention to indulge in this form of violence.
> Government buildings and private addresses of members of the Government will be singled out for special attention but the windows of private houses in the neighbourhood of Westminster and also in other districts will not be allowed to escape. Mrs. Pankhurst boasts of having 5,000 volunteers for this work but this is probably a very

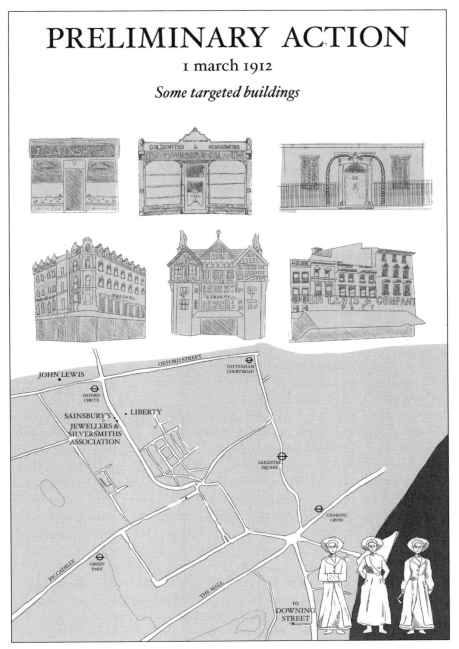

Preliminary Action – 1 March 1912. Some of the targeted buildings. (© Jennifer Godfrey. Image created for author by Daniel Atkinson (Dan Rhys Design))

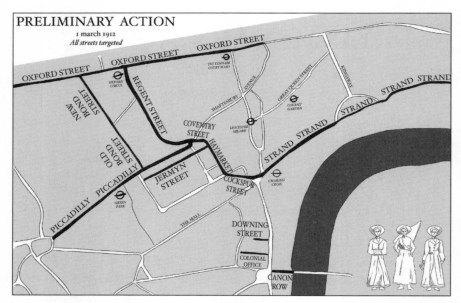

Preliminary Action, 1 March 1912 – All streets targeted. (© Jennifer Godfrey. Image created for author by Daniel Atkinson (Dan Rhys Design))

great exaggeration. I am reliably informed that 300 would be nearer to the correct number. These women will be provided with stones and instructed to break as many windows as possible before giving themselves up to the police.[3]

Volunteers for the 1 March 1912 preliminary action were organised secretly. Leaders warned them that it was 'danger duty' and they could expect arrest, charges of criminal damage and prison sentences. According to glassbreaker Kitty Marion, they were asked not to talk about it until it was completed and then talk about it all they liked.[4]

Leading the preliminary action on 1 March 1912 was Mrs Emmeline Pankhurst with Mrs Mabel Tuke and Kitty Marshall. Mrs Emmeline Pankhurst recalled that:

'Late in the afternoon of Friday, March 1st, I drove in a taxicab, accompanied by the Hon. Secretary of the Union, Mrs Tuke and another of our members, to No. 10 Downing Street, the official residence of the Prime Minister. It was exactly half past five when we alighted from the cab and threw our stones, four of them, through the window panes. As we expected we were promptly arrested and taken to Cannon Row police station.'[5]

14

Emmeline Pethick-Lawrence and Mabel Tuke, c.1907. (© LSE Women's Library Collection)

Mrs Mabel Tuke, 35, nicknamed 'Pansy' because 'she had eyes like pansies'[6] threw one stone through the window at number 10 Downing Street. She was sentenced at Bow Street receiving twenty-one days' imprisonment. Described as a 'very charming person' originating from South Africa, 'a friend of the Pethick-Lawrences and…. devoted to Christabel and her mother', Mabel was known to be 'rather highly nervous.'[7] Her anxiety levels will have significantly increased as she was also charged with conspiracy to cause damage alongside Mrs Emmeline Pankhurst and Mr and Mrs Pethick-Lawrence. These charges were however eventually dropped against Mabel on 4 April 1912.

The other member of the Downing Street party, was Kitty (Emily Katherine) Marshall. She was aged 41 and married to Arthur Marshall, a partner at solicitor firm Bisgood and Marshall who acted for many of the glassbreakers. 'Kitty was familiar with Downing Street. Every Friday she would deliver a copy of *Votes for Women*, hammering with the knocker four times and shouting "Votes for Women" before handing the newspaper to the commissionaire'.[8] According to the archived charge sheets, Kitty threw five stones carrying messages through a window at number 10 and after being arrested, threw a sixth one through a window of the India Office. Like Mabel, she was sentenced on 2 March at Bow Street Police Court and received two sentences to run consecutively for two months and twenty-one days. This sentence was successfully challenged by her solicitor husband, Arthur. Kitty was also one of the WSPU members in Mrs Pankhurst's undercover 'security team' (see chapter twelve).

'Mrs Pankhurst had two tries at Downing Street and missed but was arrested anyway.'[9] She was sentenced at Bow Street Police Court, receiving a sentence of

Bow Street Police Court. (© Jennifer Godfrey. Image created for author by Daniel Atkinson (Dan Rhys Design))

two months in Holloway. She was also then charged and went on trial for conspiracy to cause and incite damage. Kitty's husband, Arthur Marshall, acted on behalf of the WSPU on many occasions and represented Mrs Emmeline Pankhurst and many of the other women at this time (see chapter seven for further details).

The hour that followed this first act of window smashing 'will long be remembered in London. At intervals of fifteen minutes relays of women who had volunteered for the demonstration did their work. The first smashing of glass occurred in the Haymarket and Piccadilly, and greatly startled and alarmed both pedestrians and police. A large number of the women were arrested...'[10]

Another account given by *The Daily Graphic* was:

> The West End of London last night was the scene of an unexampled outrage on the part of militant suffragists.... Bands of women paraded Regent Street, Piccadilly, the Strand, Oxford Street and Bond Street, smashing windows with stones and hammers.[11]

Anti-suffrage comic card depicts a suffragette wielding a hammer and smashing a department store window. (© LSE Women's Library Collection)

17

Believed to be the eldest glassbreaker was 79-year-old Hilda Brackenbury. She owned two properties, one in London and the other in Peaslake, Surrey. Her home in Peaslake was a safe house for suffragettes needing to recuperate after imprisonment and/or forcible feeding. More details about Hilda's properties are included in chapter thirteen.

On 1 March, with a hammer hidden in her muff, Hilda Brackenbury made her way to the United Services Institution and smashed a window. She later cited Mr Hobhouse's speech as provocation. She chose the United Services Institution 'in order to contrast her family's military involvement [two of her sons had died on active service] with her own lack of political enfranchisement.'[12] Hilda served eight days on remand and then a fourteen-day sentence. When she was released, she addressed a large audience at the London Pavilion.[13] The United Services Institution building was targeted again on 4 March (see chapter three).

Also carrying a hammer was glassbreaker Zoe Proctor. To conceal the hammer, Zoe was given a large muff by friend and fellow suffragette, Nina Boyle. Zoe's account of that evening is:

> I was a very frightened woman as I walked past the National Gallery to the Haymarket. I heard the clock strike six and tried to pretend that I had not heard it, but immediately afterwards there sounded the crash of shattered glass from the direction of the Cunard Company's offices, and I hastily turned the corner and swung my hammer against several of the small panes of an old-fashioned silversmith's shop.[14]

This was 4 Haymarket, owned by Hill and Son. It appears from Zoe's account in her autobiography that she was also tasked with breaking windows at the American Express too but she had to abandon this:

> The son of the owner was dressing the window, and hurried out to remonstrate with me; laying his hand on my arm, he said 'You must be mad, madam!' I shook his hand off, and said: 'Don't touch me, unless you have a warrant for my arrest', and went on my way, the man walking beside me, stammering reproaches. Even at that moment I felt thankful that I could now leave the American Express windows unbroken.
>
> As we passed the Haymarket Theatre we gathered a small crowd which formed into a train behind me. At the corner of the next street, a very young Policeman barred the way and asked my captor, 'What's all this?' On being told, he said I must go along with him. I said 'If you get me a cab to take me to Vine Street I will go with you.' He hoped to discourage me by informing me that I would

Nina Boyle. (© LSE Women's
Library Collection)

have to pay for the cab. I replied 'Of course, I have the money.'
I realised afterwards that, being young, he could not understand how
a lady of respectable appearance, could be so knowledgeable about
the procedure. As we, the bewildered shop man, the policeman, and
I drove through Piccadilly I naturally lowered my muff, containing
the hammer, on to the floor of the cab, where I left it. At Vine Street
Police Station I found a large crowd assembled, with the Police
keeping a passage free for the prisoners, who were being brought
in every few minutes. These onlookers pleased my dramatic sense
by howling at the window-breakers, as though 'thirsting for their
blood.' I was thrust into a small, dark room filled with women of
all ages, among whom I soon found friends. After a few minutes,
the door opened and a Policeman stood in the doorway holding up
a hammer, saying 'Who does this belong to?' A shout of laughter
greeted him and he retired blushing. The window sills of the room
were already piled with stones and hammers.

The number of arrests was so great that it was more than an hour before I reached the room where I was charged with an offence of 'malicious damage' amounting to £5.00. Mr Marshall, the lawyer friend of the Union, was getting bail for the prisoners at that Police Station. I was given my charges sheet and told to reappear at Bow Street the following morning. It is difficult to describe what a feeling of relief and peace was mine now that the dreaded ordeal was over.[15]

Zoe was released on bail, ordered to report to Bow Street Police Court the following day. She returned to her home in Chester Terrace, Chelsea and like so many of the other accounts by these glassbreakers described her feeling of relief:

My relief was so great at having accomplished the task which I had been dreading so long that I slept peacefully.[16]

Zoe's acquaintance from the WSPU Chelsea Shop, Miss Charlotte Blacklock, 45, was also arrested on the 1 March. She smashed one window (cost of £210) at 16 Piccadilly, the property of Drew & Co. Zoe and Charlotte (known as Charlie) travelled to Bow Street Police Court together on the morning of 2 March.

Mrs Flora Drummond was amongst the fifty women Zoe reported had gathered in the policemen's billiard room at Bow Street. She had 'acquired the nickname 'General' for riding at the head of WSPU processions dressed in epaulettes and a peaked cap.'[17] The General was not arrested as part of the Great Militant Protest but was likely there to show her support to those that had been. From late 1911 she 'was working from Clement's Inn, put in charge of the organisation of the local WSPU union throughout the country.'[18]

Also waiting at Bow Street Police Court was Violet Helen Friedlander 'seated on a suitcase busy writing.'[19] Violet was a 33-year-old novelist and poet arrested for breaking windows in 38–39 Piccadilly (property of Cook & Sons). Like Charlotte Blacklock, Violet received a sentence of four months and served it in Birmingham prison.

Glass breaker Lily Delissa Joseph, 49, used alias Leah Joseph when arrested for causing malicious damage and was given a custodial sentence of one month. Lily was an artist herself and sister of Solomon Joseph Solomon, a British painter and founding member of the New English Art Club and member of the Royal Academy. Lily had an exhibition of her own paintings planned before the protest and asked to be let out for a day on 15 March 1912 to open it. Unsurprisingly, this was not permitted.

Geraldine Phyllis Stevenson, 37, gave her name as Grace Stuart when she was arrested for smashing two windows at 69 Piccadilly, the property of Houcheron & Co. She received a lengthy six months' sentence and served it at Aylesbury prison. Geraldine's sister Ella was also a suffragette. She used the alias name Ethel Slade. Ella was also arrested on 1 March but where is unknown.

Flora Drummond, 'The General' carrying a travel rug outside Bow Street Police Court, c.1908. (© LSE Women's Library Collection)

Mrs Emmeline Pankhurst accounted that at this stage in the evening's protest, 'everybody thought that this ended the affair. But before the excited populace and the frustrated shop owners' first exclamation had died down, before the police had reached the station with their prisoners, the ominous crashing and splintering of plate glass began again, this time along both sides of Regent Street and the Strand.'[20]

A long line of women, many carrying suitcases, outside Bow Street Police Court, a policeman at the head of the queue, c.March 1912. (© LSE Women's Library Collection)

Kitty Marion smashed two windows of 134 Regent Street (property of Jewellers and Silversmiths Association) and one window at 136 Regent Street (belonging to Sainsbury's) and was sentenced to twenty-one days' imprisonment. Kitty Marion, who sometimes used alias Aunt Maggie 'was given a hammer and told to break windows at 5.45 pm, in the twilight as shoppers were going home.'[21] In her autobiography, Kitty described her experience:

> I arrived at my scene of action, the Silversmiths' Association and Sainsbury's, 134 Regent Street, about five minutes too soon, feeling awful and looked round for encouraging, friendly fellow in the fray. But I seemed to be the only one there. Was I going to be the only one? Had I possibly made a mistake in the day or time? Surely not, whatever happens I must break these windows, those two great ovals at the entrance to Silversmiths and that huge plate glass window of Sainsbury's. I must not fail. Such and similar were my thoughts, and I found later that others had experienced the same; as I walked round the block to the back just in time to see "one of us" a couple of shops ahead, gazing round furtively as I had done. Our eyes met in silent encouragement just as "Big Ben" started to boom three quarters.[22]

Kitty Marion. (© LSE Women's Library Collection)

Kitty described hitting the windows low, as instructed, to avoid glass falling from above. When arrested, she was taken to Vine Street Police Station and it is reported that she sang whilst in her cell.

Barbara Bodichon Ayrton-Gould, 25, nicknamed 'Barbie', was also arrested in Regent Street. She was named after suffragist Barbara Leigh Smith Bodichon and was a university college graduate, having studied chemistry and physiology. She gave up her post graduate research to become a full time WSPU organiser. She was married to Gerald Gould, one of the founder members of the MLWS. Barbara went on to become a member of Parliament for Hendon North from 1945 to 1960.

Two sisters from the Croydon branch of the WSPU, Miss Hazel Inglis, 27, and Mrs Helen Green (née Inglis) (Treasurer), 25, were arrested on 1 March 1912 although not together. From a family of WSPU members and supporters, this was the first time the sisters had been arrested and imprisoned. Both gave alias names. Hazel gave May Morrison and, Helen gave her maternal grandmother's maiden name, Helen Collier. This information is identified by the women themselves in a 1976 oral history project.[23] Hazel smashed windows at the Regent Street Post Office and Helen broke windows in the Strand – she claims Kodak but *The Times* newspaper on 14 March 1912 reported Messrs Downs and Co. outfitters. Hazel recollects that her father had silver hammers made for them especially for the mission. Both chose to be bound over to keep the peace for twelve months (as their mother was taken unwell following news of their arrest) and so only served ten days on remand. Hazel was arrested with another suffragette choosing to use an alias. This was Florence Jessie Hull, 24, from Letchworth WSPU (Honorary Secretary) who gave her name as Mary Gray when arrested. She received a sentence of one-month hard labour and served it in Holloway.

Close by in Regent Street[24], Rosa Leo, 38, smashed windows at 33-37, the property of Drew and Sons. Rosa was a WSPU and AFL member. She 'was 'Honorary instructor in Voice Production' to the WSPU speakers class, which was for a time held in Hertha Ayrton's house in Norfolk Square, at which she instructed women in the skills of outdoor speaking.'[25] Rosa and Hertha were cousins. Rosa also gave lessons to the MPU.

Also targeting shop windows in Regent Street were Helen Creiggs, 27, Edith Lane, 38, and Dorothy Bowker, 26. Together they worked to break windows in Regent Street and Piccadilly. This included the windows at Swan & Edgar's luxury department store. Swan & Edgar regularly advertised in the WSPU's *Votes for Women* paper and yet were still attacked. Information about Helen and Edith has not been found. However, it is known that Dorothy had previously (1910–1912) worked in Leicester with Emmeline Pethick-Lawrence's sister, Dorothy Pethick as a WSPU organiser. She also set up a WSPU shop in Hastings but had left there by April 1912.

The broken windows at the Swan & Edgar luxury department store smashed by glassbreakers Helen Creiggs, Edith Lane and Dorothy Bowker. (© LSE Women's Library Collection)

Miss Rebecca Hyams, 24, gave her name as Janet Green when arrested for smashing windows in Regent Street.[26] She received a sentence of six months' and was transferred to Birmingham.

Two windows were smashed by suffragette Sarah Benett, 62, in Regents Street on 1 March 1912. These were 103 Regent Street, the property of Simpson & London and 105 Regent Street belonging to Sir John Bennett. Sarah received one months' imprisonment for the first offence and a further two months for the second. However, Sarah went on hunger strike and was released early from her Holloway prison sentence. Prior to her involvement with the WSPU, Sarah had been a member and Treasurer of the WFL. However, by 1910 she was involved in the more militant action, participating in Black Friday. In February 1913, Sarah joined a further protest and smashed one of the windows in the department store, Selfridges in Oxford Street. Selfridges had not been targeted in the March 1912 window smashing and according to women's suffrage researcher and author Elizabeth Crawford, this may have been due to Selfridges having suffrage sympathies. 'Many department stores – even those which, like Swan and Edgar, were regular advertisers in *Votes for Women* – were targeted. But

Above left: Jennie Baines, 1907–1912. (© LSE Women's Library Collection)

Above right: Mabel Capper outside Bow Street Court. (Public domain)

Selfridges' windows – 21 in all, of which 12 contained the largest sheets of plate glass in the world – escaped unscathed.'[27] There were several clues to Selfridges' sympathy towards votes for women and suffragettes identified by Elizabeth Crawford. One was *The Suffrage Annual* and *Women's Who's Who*, published in 1913 which included details of the women involved in the suffrage movement. 'It is likely that Selfridges underwrote much of the expense of producing it for… besides its cover advertisement, the store took running advertisements along the foot of every page.'[28] In addition, a Selfridges' employee (from 1908 to 1909) was WSPU suffragette Gladys Evans. In July 1912 Gladys along with fellow suffragettes Mabel Henrietta Capper, Mary Leigh and Jennie Baines set fire to a Dublin theatre where Prime Minister Mr Asquith was due to speak. Whilst serving their prison sentence and being forcibly fed, there were many calls for their better prison treatment and an end to their sentences. 'One of those who wrote on Gladys' behalf was Selfridges staff manager, Mr Best and 253 of the store's employees signed a Memorial sent to the Lord Lieutenant of Ireland pleading for a remission of Gladys Evans' sentence.'[29]

Unlike Selfridges, Liberty & Co, the department store in Regent Street, had windows smashed. Glassbreakers Louisa Field, 28, and Elsie Howey, 27, were arrested for this. Louisa was also charged for breaking a window at Maison Lewis at 210 Regent Street. Accounts of Louisa's life and involvement in the WSPU have not yet been uncovered. However, Elsie Howey's life is well documented as is her commitment to the cause. Elsie was born in Finningley, South Yorkshire, the daughter of a Nottinghamshire clergyman. In 1887 after her father's death, the family moved to Malvern. Elsie's sister, Mary, was also a suffragette, but was not involved in this protest. Emmeline Pethick-Lawrence wrote the following about Elsie in 1909:

> Miss Elsie Howey is honorary organiser in Plymouth. She is the daughter of Mrs. Howey, of Malvern. Mrs. Howey and her two daughters have given generously of all that they have, but the best prized gift is the life work of this noble girl who has undergone two periods of imprisonment for the sake of women less privileged and happily placed than herself. She is one of our most able and successful organisers, and takes all the duties and responsibilities of our chief officers.[30]

Large numbers of women were involved in glass-breaking in Regent Street and the Strand on 1 March 1912. It caused 'A furious rush of police and people towards' it. 'While their attention was being taken up with occurrences in this quarter, the third relay of women began breaking the windows in Oxford Street and Bond Street.'[31]

Suffragettes Ada Cecile Granville Wright and Charlotte Augusta Leopoldine Marsh, 25, were arrested for breaking windows on the Strand including at the premises of pawnbroker Mr C.B. Vaughan. Ada was involved in earlier protests including Black Friday in November 1910. As is told in Part Two, Ada was a member of the elite security team 'the Bodyguard' and helped Mrs Emmeline Pankhurst escape a property in London. Charlotte, or 'Charlie' as she was known, 'with her tall figure and wonderful corn-coloured hair … figured as St. Joan in one of the great Processions for which the WSPU was famous'[32] was another notable suffragette. In a BBC broadcasted recording from 1958, Charlie said, 'I waited for two people to stop looking at the rings and then just banged my hammer through the window. And I continued on down the Strand for quite a way and did quite a lot of damage. Yes, that sort of thing was happening all over London and we had about 200 women arrested that night.'[33] When brought before Mr Robert Wallace K.C. the Chairman and a bench of magistrates at the London Sessions, Charlie said 'that she had had the privilege of being sent to prison on two occasions, and she was prepared to go again and again. No matter how long her sentence might be, when she came out of prison, if she found the Government had not carried out the Bill into law, she would be prepared to go on what they called "active service" again.'[34] Both Charlie and Ada were sentenced to six months' imprisonment and served it at Aylesbury prison. Interestingly, during the First World War, Charlie was Prime Minister Lloyd George's chauffeur. She had applied unsuccessfully to be Mrs Pankhurst's chauffeur, and though Vera Holme got the job, Charlie did occasionally drive the Pankhursts.

Oxford Street was also targeted. Miss Constance Louise Collier, 65, of King Henry's Road, Hampstead, and Miss Margaret Eleanor Thompson, 47, of Stanley Gardens, Hampstead were arrested in Oxford Street on 1 March 1912. Both were members of the Hampstead WSPU. An account of their experience is included in a book written by Margaret Eleanor Thompson[35] (copied from a diary she scribbled on the back of a calendar in prison in 1912):

On Friday, March 1st 1912, Miss Collier and I set out to do our appointed bit of destruction. We got to Oxford Circus a quarter of an hour too soon. We tried to talk about various things—all the other people going about their usual occupation seemed so cheerful and so blissfully ordinary.

When we got to Cavendish Square, Miss Collier remarked, 'I can't do it . . . I'm not going to do it.'

I said I would never speak to her again if she didn't and urged her to think of all that our leaders and others had said about the fight for freedom.

We kept walking slowly on. It had been arranged that she should break the windows in Holles Street that were nearest Oxford Street, and that I should begin mine in Oxford Street at, or almost at, the same time. To my horror, as soon as we came to Lewis' windows in Holles Street I suddenly saw the gleam of the white hammer in her hand and in a second it had crashed through a window. (She had felt she must do it at once, or not at all). I hurried on, fearing I should be arrested as her companion before my work was done. I felt angry too, but also I could have laughed aloud as I heard the dull crack, crack of the windows—five in all—until she was arrested.

Soon I arrived at my windows in Oxford Street and broke three. The pavement was crowded. At one window stood a lady and gentleman looking interestedly at the contents. I gently pushed them aside saying 'Excuse me,' and knocked the window with my hammer. I was going on to the eighth window when a policeman took hold of my arm and said, 'My friend, what are you doing?' A clock was visible a little lower down the street. It stood at 5.48. That piece of destruction had taken three or four minutes. The crowd now began to collect round me. Most of the faces looked scared—some just curious. All of them looked on me as if I were a maniac.

The policeman began to move me towards the shop door. This alarmed me as I thought that if I were taken inside the shop, the owner, Mr. Lewis, might possibly have let me go free and slur over the fact of the damage. So, I said, emphatically, 'I have done this, not against the shop, but against the Government,' and made a few other remarks.

The policeman then began to move me along the street towards Marylebone Police Station. A large crowd followed me at first, then left me, as other arrests were being made all down the street.

At the Station I found several colleagues already there. The usual waiting and preliminaries had to be gone through, then we were taken upstairs and put each into a cell.[36]

Also protesting and smashing windows in Oxford Street on 1 March, were Olive Grace Walton, 25, Eileen Casey, 30, and her mother, Isabella Casey. Olive and Eileen smashed windows at the Marshall & Snellgrove department store (334–348 Oxford Street) whilst Eileen's mother, Isabella, smashed one window at 351 Oxford Street. Olive was from Tunbridge Wells in Kent and estranged from her family due to her involvement in militant activity. Eileen was also heavily involved in WSPU militant activity and although using her real name when arrested on this mission, often used other alias names including Eleanor Cleary and Irene Casey. Another glassbreaker who liked to use pseudonyms was Kate Cardo (alias Catherine Swaine) who was arrested for breaking windows in New Bond Street, specifically number 27, the property of Richard Jules, number 32, the property of Jes Marsus, and number 33, the property of Silver Maker, Alfred Clark. Charges were dropped against Kate for number 32 New Bond Street but she was found guilty of smashing the other windows and sentenced to four months in Holloway.

'The demonstration ended for the day at half past six with the breaking of many windows in the Strand'. *The Daily Mail* gave this graphic account of the demonstration:

> From every part of the crowded and brilliantly lighted streets came the crash of splintered glass. People started as a window shattered at their side; suddenly there was another crash in front of them; on the other side of the street; behind – everywhere. Scared shop assistants came running out to the pavements; traffic stopped; policemen sprang this way and that; five minutes later the streets were a procession of excited groups, each surrounding a woman wrecker being led to custody to the nearest police station. Meanwhile the shopping quarter of London had plunged itself into a sudden twilight. Shutters were hurriedly fitted; the rattle of iron curtains being drawn came from every side. Guards of commissionaires and shopmen were quickly mounted, and any unaccompanied lady in sight, especially if she carried a hand bag, became an object of menacing suspicion.[37]

On the evening of 1 March 1912, Emmeline Pethick-Lawrence's husband, Frederick Pethick-Lawrence (a barrister) 'told a meeting of the MPU that he was a man of law and order, but if women thought this action was necessary for the success of their movement, then they were justified.'[38]

Christabel Pankhurst released the following leaflet to the press for printing on 2 March 1912:

Broken Windows

Every step in the militant campaign, including the first, has provoked at the moment when it was made a new outburst of censure. For practical reasons, it is impossible for us to regret this. It is part of the effect of militancy that it shall excite regret and consternation. Our very definite purpose is to create an intolerable situation for the Government, and, if need be, for the public as a whole.

The attack – not indeed a very serious one, but still an attack on private property – is the latest subject of censure. 'Government property,' say the critics, 'you are justified in attacking, but not private property.' Militant suffragists would, of course, be glad if an attack on Government property were sufficient to attain their purpose.

They would have been yet more glad if the eventless militant action of the earlier days had sufficed. But the present policy of the Government proves that these measures are not powerful enough to produce the effect desired. They have produced only a sham concession to our demand. More drastic measures have been proved to be essential to gain the genuine confession that we seek. That is why private property has now been attacked.

The message of the broken pane is that women are determined that the lives of their sisters shall no longer be broken, and that in future those who have to obey this law shall have a voice in saying what that law shall be.[39]

Chapter 3

Orchestrated Mass Window Smashing

'From in front, behind, from every side it came –
a hammering, crashing, splintering sound unheard in
the annals of shopping.... At the windows excited crowds
collected, shouting, gesticulating. At the centre of each crowd
stood a woman, pale, calm and silent.'[1]

On the night of the publicised 4 March 1912 orchestrated mass window smashing, the police were prepared. However, the timing of the demonstration had not been announced. Mrs Emmeline Pankhurst had invited women to meet in Parliament Square on the evening of 4 March. *The Daily Telegraph* reported:

> By six o'clock the neighbourhood Houses of Parliament were in a stage of siege. Shop keepers in almost every instance barricaded their premises, removed goods from the windows and prepared for the worst. A few minutes before six o'clock a huge force of police, amounting to nearly three thousand constables, was posted in Parliament Square, Whitehall, and streets adjoining, and large reserves were gathered in Westminster Hall and Scotland Yard. By half past eight Whitehall was packed from end to end with police and public. Mounted constables rode up and down Whitehall keeping the people on the move.[2]

The Metropolitan Police were also watching the suffragettes as they dropped bags, congregated at meeting points, dispersed in small groups and started to take action. At the WSPU headquarters at Clement's Inn,

> Sergeant Lionel Kirchner of the C.I.D. stated that on March 4 he and another constable watched No. 4 Clements Inn, and saw about fifty women coming and going, singly or in small batches, some on foot and some in taxis with luggage. The luggage was taken into No. 4, and after a short time was sent off in taxis, sometimes by itself and sometimes with the ladies. About fifteen women arrived with luggage. He saw Miss Christabel Pankhurst leave the offices in

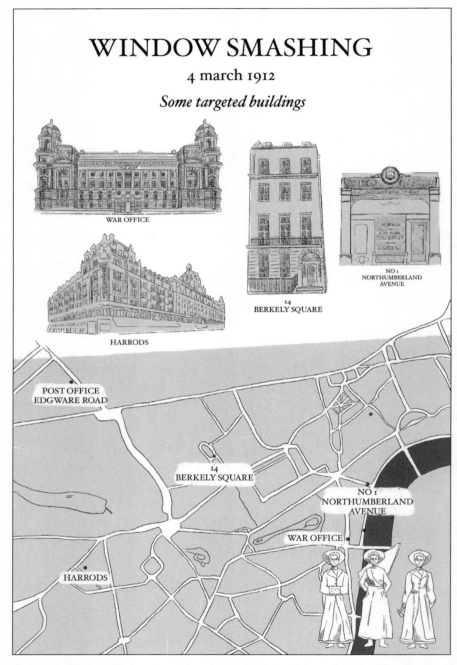

Orchestrated Mass Window Smashing, 4 March 1912 - Some of the buildings targeted.
(© Jennifer Godfrey. Image created for author by Daniel Atkinson (Dan Rhys Design))

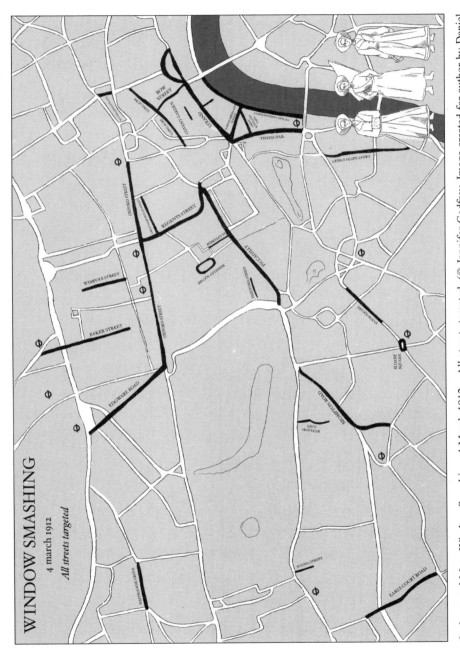

Orchestrated Mass Window Smashing, 4 March 1912 – All streets targeted. (© Jennifer Godfrey. Image created for author by Daniel Atkinson (Dan Rhys Design))

Above: Police outside WSPU headquarters. (© Museum of London)

Left: Clement's Inn, WSPU Headquarters. (© LSE Women's Library Collection)

Clement's Inn, WSPU Headquarters offices. (© LSE Women's Library Collection)

Clement's Inn WSPU Headquarters Information Bureau. (© LSE Women's Library Collection)

Ethel Smyth speaking at the London Pavilion, Emmeline Pethick-Lawrence and Christabel Pankhurst also on the platform, with representatives of WSPU branches behind, 1912. (© LSE Women's Library Collection)

the suffrage motor car about three o'clock with Mrs. Lawrence and Dr. Ethel Smyth. They came back about half-past five and left again about a quarter to six.'[3]

The women were leaving their bags at WSPU headquarters (4 Clement's Inn) and going to the Pavilion Music Hall for a meeting. This would also have been where Miss Christabel Pankhurst, Mrs Pethick-Lawrence and Dr Ethel Smyth were going. 'The police attended the meeting, which was the usual rally preceding a demonstration or a deputation. At five o'clock the meeting adjourned and the women went out, as if to go home.'[4]

According to archived police records, on 4 March, plain-clothed Special Branch police officers were also outside the Gardenia restaurant at 6 Catherine Street. 'The police thought that about one hundred and fifty women congregated there on March 4th.'[5] Detective Edmund Buckley described what was seen from 5.00pm that evening:

> Between [...5.00pm...] and 6:30[pm] a number of women went in, in twos and threes—they went upstairs to the second floor. From about half past 6 to quarter to 7, I saw various small parties of women leaving.[6]

Detective Edmund Buckley followed Alice Agnes Wilson, 41 and Morrie Hughes, 31, as they made their way to Whitehall. Both had travelled from Harrogate where it is known Morrie was a WSPU organiser. They were arrested by another officer for throwing stones at the Agricultural Offices of Whitehall. Alice was photographed in January 1912 with Scottish suffragettes Janet Barrowman, Helen Crawfurd, Margaret McPhun, Frances McPhun, Nancy John and Annie Swan (see chapter five).

At 6.40pm Detective Sergeant Ernest Bowden of New Scotland Yard followed three Nottinghamshire suffragettes, Mary Ellen (Nellie) Taylor, Miss Nellie Crocker and Miss Gladys Roberts

> as they left the restaurant and walked along the Strand towards Charing Cross, accompanied by a crowd of about 20 people including uniformed police. In an evident attempt to throw off their pursuers, the women entered the tube station at Charing Cross and, following a circuitous route, eventually took the District Line to Sloane Square. In what was obviously a well-planned manoeuvre, the three then entered the Court Theatre and went up to the gallery. Just after the performance had started at 8.38 pm, the women left the theatre and, crossing the square walked along Kings Road. Opposite the Post Office the women suddenly ran across and attacked the windows

with hammers. Each of the three windows broken were 9ft by 6ft, and estimates of their financial value tend to vary wildly. Throughout the proceedings the women were shadowed closely by two men – one of whom was identified by police as Mark Wilks, a member of the Men's Political Union, and, of course, Nellie's brother-in-law.[7]

Taken to Gerald Row Police Station, Nellie T., Nellie C. and Gladys were refused bail and after some time on remand, sentenced to three months' imprisonment.

Whilst in prison, Nellie Crocker wrote to Helen Watts (a deaf suffragette from Nottingham) telling her that she was in the company of Louisa Garrett Anderson, Mrs Emmeline Pankhurst and Ethel Smyth.

Another woman from Nottingham was arrested on 4 March (location unknown). Her name was Edith Anne Lees, 32, but she gave a false name, her mother's maiden name, Annie Baker. Edith was married with three children and ran a haberdasher's business at 28-30 Carlton Street in Nottingham. Edith was discharged on 26 March and this may have been because she was pregnant.[8] Also setting off from the Gardenia restaurant in Catherine Street was Mrs Lillian Ball, aged 34, the working-class dressmaker referred to in earlier chapters. Her account read:

> On Monday the 4th March, I arrived at the 'Gardenia' about 6pm and, after being challenged several times for my ticket of admission, I was admitted to a large room upstairs. A number of women were present and I was accompanied by a Mrs. Yorke, who belongs to my branch. There was a smaller room adjoining and after waiting about an hour, a lady, whose name I do not know, came out of that room, spoke to Mrs. Yorke and myself and another woman who was sitting near us, and asked if we were prepared for long or short sentences. I said, 'Mine must be very short' as I had only arranged for seven days absence from my work and home. She then told me to go the United Service Museum, where the windows were small, and gave me directions as to the locality. She then asked if I had brought any implements with me, and upon being told that I had not done so, gave me a new hammer which she told me to put up my sleeve. She further told me that I was to break the windows before 9 o'clock. She was a well-dressed woman of between 25 and 30 years of age, about 5ft 3 inches high, well educated, and very peremptory in her manner, I am not sure that I should know her again.
>
> We then, all three, left together and after having some tea, and walking about a while, we carried out our instructions by each breaking a pane of glass in the windows of the United Service Museum, just before 9pm and were arrested.[9]

The well-dressed woman told the three women that they shouldn't get more than seven days if they only broke one small pane[10]. This woman may have been Mrs McLeod or Miss Wallace Dunlop. Mrs Emmeline Pankhurst had said that these friends of hers would be at the Gardenia on the 4 March to give out instructions (see chapter one). The three women now prepped for their mission took tea at Lyons restaurant, which is interesting because on 1 March Mabel De Roxe was arrested for damaging the Lyons restaurant on the Strand. The three women then broke small panes of glass at the United Service Museum. From archive records it is known that Lillian was with Norah Yorke, 38, whom she knew from the Balham WSPU branch. Both Lillian and Norah were given hammers to use and on Lillian's were written the words: 'Better broken windows than broken promises'. In another account Lillian recollects that she hadn't met the third woman before but thought her name was 'Miss Herrick' and that she had a business in Kensington High Street.[11] It was in fact Miss Elizabeth Herrick, 38, who ran a hat shop called Madame Corelli at 137a High Street, Kensington. Elizabeth had brought her own hammer.

Lillian recalled that:

> I broke one window with the hammer. A man held me first, and then the police took me, I believe to Cannon Row. I broke the window about 20 to 9. I was arrested at once. An ambulance came, as I fainted I believe.[12]

Lillian was bailed out by Mr Pethick-Lawrence and she said:

> I knew he was coming to bail me out, I was told he would do so by the lady of the 'Gardenia' from whom I had received instructions. The next morning I attended at Bow Street Police Court with my change of clothing, and received a sentence of two months' hard labour.[13]

Elizabeth also received a sentence of two months' hard labour, whilst Norah only received 6 weeks hard labour. It was recorded in the *Votes for Women* newspaper at the time that this was because Norah used a small hammer.[14] All three served their sentences in Holloway prison.

Interestingly, Norah's friend, Helen Margaret Spanton, 34, was also arrested that night for breaking a window at the same location but was in a different group of suffragettes. Helen was an artist born in Bury St Edmunds in Suffolk but living at this time in Blackheath, London. Helen was in a group and arrested with middle-class sisters from Dublin, Leila Gertrude Garcias de Cadiz, 25, and Rosalind Mary Garcias de Cadiz, 26. These sisters used pseudonyms Margaret (Maggie) and Jane Murphy respectively when arrested. They were sentenced to two months with hard labour, went on hunger strike and were forcibly fed. They were members of the

Mrs Edith Ruth Mansell-Moullin. (© LSE Women's Library Collection)

IWFL and went on to join in the window smashing campaign in Dublin and serve a further two months' imprisonment.

Helen was related to another artist and March 1912 glassbreaker, Katie Edith Gliddon. Katie, from Croydon, was arrested for breaking the 'post office door glass in Wimpole Street, 7pm. 7.12pm charged at Marylebone Police Court for wilful damage.'[15] When arrested, Katie gave her name as Catherine Susan Gray. She varied the spelling using Catherine and Katherine and used this name to protect the identity of her family. Her brother, Paul, was a member of the MPU and used the pseudonym Charles Gray for the same reason. Katie was arrested with Dinah/Diana Boyle[16], a 28-year-old teacher nicknamed 'Miss Sprott', but whilst at Marylebone Police Court, met other glassbreakers:

> Met Miss Keller in the Police Station. She had just broken Lord Cromer's front door glass. Mrs and Miss Slade sent us in a basket of grapes. PC R.D.16 arrested me. He was charming all the time. Mrs Bennett, Mrs Nesbit also were arrested and taken to Marylebone. All 5 of us were bailed out by Mrs Mansell-Moullin.[17]

Like other WSPU members Mrs Edith Ruth Mansell-Moullin, played her part in this protest without a hammer or stone, paying the bail for glassbreakers. She was a social campaigner, married to surgeon, Charles who was pro-suffrage and a member of the MLWS. Charles condemned the practice of forcible feeding and tried to treat Emily Wilding Davison after she was hit by the King's horse.[18]

In a letter to her mother dated 4 March, 'written on a newspaper wrapper in Marylebone Police Station' Katie described 'her arrest ....with Dinah.....and their detention at the police station' saying they 'are charged with £4.00 worth of damage between' them and so should 'come off very easily' with an exception of 'about 5 days'.[19]

Katie and Dinah/Diana were sentenced to two months' hard labour on 5 March 1912. Katie's diary entry read: 'Stayed in police cell until 4pm. Then went in the Black Maria to Holloway Prison with Constance Moore and Dinah Boyle.'[20] As remembered by a suffragette in her 1974 interview, the Black Maria was the prison van which had cubicles with chairs with 'a bit of a window for ventilation...and there was a little corridor then you were locked in and there was a policeman ... inside... there were no tyres on the Black Maria'[21] and so it rattled terribly on its way to the police station. Kitty Marion described the Black Maria as 'that instrument of torture.'[22]

At Dinah/Diana's court hearing on 5 March in Marylebone Police Court in front of Mr Paul Taylor, it was reported that a 'Sentence of two months' hard labour was passed amid cheers in Court. Diana said that she was incited to do it by Mr Hobhouse's speech.'[23]

Dinah/Diana was not the only glassbreaker claiming to be incited to participate in the Great Militant Protest because of Mr Hobhouse's speech. Mr Hobhouse and

Above left: A pre-First World War photograph of Ethel Violet Baldock. (© Ethel Baldock's family)

Above right: Violet Ann Bland. (© Violet Ann Bland's family)

his strong anti-suffrage speeches had been cited by many of the women involved in the Great Militant Protest as the reason for their action. 'On Saturday, 9 March, Magistrate Mr. Curtis-Bennett heard upwards of fifty cases. Nearly all the women told the magistrate that their conduct was a result of Mr. Hobhouse's speech at Bristol, where he referred to the agitations that led to the burning of Nottingham Castle and pulling down the Hyde Park railings.'[24] This was Mr Hobhouse suggesting that the suffrage agitation was not supported by popular feeling because the women would be doing damage to property similar to that committed by men in the 1832 Reform riots.

Contrary to the reported rule of Mrs Emmeline Pankhurst that under 21 year olds were not to act in a way that would lead to their imprisonment, there were two under 21 year olds known to be arrested on 4 March. Olive M. Fontaine, 20, daughter of an iron founder, an active Newport (Wales) WSPU member was arrested for smashing windows at Marlborough Street Court and Police Station. Olive was briefly co-Secretary at the Newport branch of the WSPU with Margaret Mackworth, otherwise known as Lady Rhondda. It is not known if Olive travelled to London alone but others arrested at the same location were Evelyn Scott, 24, and Mary Fraser, 23. Evelyn and Mary were offered a fine and to be bound over to keep the peace or a prison sentence of one-month hard labour. It is not known what Evelyn chose, but Mary chose the prison sentence and went to Holloway. Olive was sentenced to one-month hard labour and also served her time in Holloway. She was received back in Newport with a heroine's welcome when it is reported she said '... she was glad to be out of Holloway, but gladder still that she went.'[25] The other even younger glassbreaker, and still a teenager, was Ethel Violet Baldock, 19. She was arrested with 49-year-old experienced suffragette Violet Ann Bland (Annie)[26]. They were both charged with smashing windows at 1 Northumberland Avenue, belonging to the Commercial Cable Company.

Their pairing is interesting because it would seem that like many women forming groups on the evening of 4 March 1912, Ethel and Annie did not know each other. They were different in many ways and may have been partnered as 'novice suffragette' (Ethel) and 'master suffragette' (Annie). There is no record of Ethel, aged 19, a working-class maid from Kent, having being involved in women's suffrage or part of any WSPU protest prior to her arrest on 4 March 1912. On the other hand, Annie, more than double her age at 49, was an active WSPU member who had previously been arrested and once owned and ran a Bristol (Henley Grove) guest house frequented by suffragettes. However, there were some similarities, they were both from working class backgrounds with manual worker fathers. Ethel was a maid in 1912 and, in her youth, Annie had worked in domestic service. At the time of her arrest in March 1912 Annie was running a guest house at 22 Old Burlington Street, Piccadilly, London. At her hearing, Annie 'said she was a law-abiding citizen. She had paid rates and taxes to the tune of nearly £1 a week for 20 years, and had been working for her citizenship for a number of years.' She said that 'she did the act in response to a challenge by a member of the Government.'[27] The Government member Annie was referring to was Mr Hobhouse.

Two women even targeted what they believed to be Mr Hobhouse's home in Rutland Gate. Dr Louisa Garrett Anderson, a 37-year-old surgeon, received six weeks hard labour for her part in smashing windows at 47 Rutland Gate, the home of George P. Fuller. Louisa was arrested with Ellen Thomas, 37, as she had smashed windows in the neighbouring property, 46 Rutland Gate, belonging to General Robb. In court both Louisa and Ellen had pleaded guilty and said that they had intended to smash windows of the house belonging to Mr Hobhouse.

Ellen had apologised saying:

I meant it for Mr. Hobhouse's house. I am sorry I made the mistake.[28]

Louisa had reasoned:

It was done as a political protest, and in reply largely to the speech made by Mr. Hobhouse some time ago, in which he did not consider that the Suffrage agitation was supported by popular feeling, because women were not doing the damage to property similar to that committed by men in 1832 in the Reform riots.[29]

When sentencing Louisa and Ellen, Magistrate Mr Francis had said:

> I have this morning sent a man to hard labour for two months for wilfully breaking a public house window. I can see no difference between you and him, and you will be sentenced to six weeks' hard labour.[30]

Dr Louisa Garrett Anderson had her sentence reduced to one month by direct intervention following an appeal from her family. Another female doctor arrested on 4 March 1912 for her part was Dr Alice Jane Shannon Stewart Ker, 58, a widow and the thirteenth woman to be listed on the British Medical Register. With fellow Liverpool WSPU member, Dorothy Foster Abraham, 25, she broke windows at Harrods department store in Brompton Road, Knightsbridge. Alice, born in Scotland but living in Liverpool, was known to be staying in London with Lady Constance Lytton (who was acting as a hostess rather than a glassbreaker for this mission). Lady Constance Lytton was 'out of the ranks of the militants' having never fully recovered her health after being forcibly fed in Liverpool prison in 1910. She maintained her support of the cause in other ways, including hosting those arriving in London for the Great Militant Protest. Suffragette and glassbreaker Zoe Proctor recounted this story in her book, *Life and Yesterday*:

> Lady Constance Lytton on becoming a member, had undertaken, with Miss Annie Kenney, to question a member of the Cabinet Ministers in the North as he got into his car. On asking their question they were arrested, as by that time Cabinet Ministers always travelled with a bodyguard. The two women were sent to prison and examined by a doctor to see if they were fit to receive forcible feeding after the hunger strike, which most prisoners now began as soon as their sentences were pronounced. Lady Constance's heart was found to be weak, and after serving a short sentence, both women were released. A few weeks afterwards, in Liverpool, a certain Jane Wharton, a dressmaker, was arrested for an act of militancy and sentenced to a term of imprisonment. She adopted the hunger strike, and, after a cursory examination by the prison doctor, was forcibly fed. In all cases this operation took place twice a day, and, even if a prisoner submitted without a struggle, the insertion of the rubber tube, in the nostril through which the liquid food was conveyed to the stomach, inflicted such pain that it was no exaggeration to call it torture. I am not sure how Lord Lytton became suspicious about his

Above: Constance Lytton and Leslie McMurdo with other women outside Bow Street Court, carrying suitcases, parcels and rugs, 1912. (© LSE Women's Library Collection)

Left: Liverpool WSPU shop-front. (© LSE Women's Library Collection)

sister's absence, but he finally went to Liverpool and found that Jane Wharton was indeed Lady Constance. Her immediate release and subsequent illness became a scandal, which, for a time, made the authorities very cautious about resorting to forcible feeding.[31]

Lady Constance Lytton is seen in the image opposite (above) with Leslie McMurdo outside Bow Street Police Court. Whilst outside suffragettes reported being subjected to the 'Covent Garden porters all jeering at' them 'and making fun of' them.[32] Suffragette Leslie McMurdo, 42, used alias Leslie Lawless when arrested during the Great Militant Protest. It is unknown where she smashed windows and on which day but she was sentenced to one months' hard labour and served it in Holloway.

Dr Alice Jane Shannon Stewart Ker was sentenced to three months and served it in Holloway. Whilst in prison, Alice wrote the poem entitled 'Newington butts were lively' setting it to the Scottish song, 'Annie Laurie', believed to have been written by William Douglas. The poem tells of Alice's trial by jury, recounting 'the lies piled up like snow drifts'[33] and was included in the booklet 'Holloway Jingles' (see chapter five).

Dorothy Foster Abraham (later Mrs Place) was released from custody after a few days on grounds of insufficient evidence. Dorothy helped look after Alice's two daughters when she left prison whilst Alice remained inside. Alice and Dorothy had travelled to London for the Great Militant Protest with other Liverpool WSPU members, including Helena de Reya, Mary Heliss, Alice Davies and Mary Palethorpe.

Arrested for smashing windows at Harvey Nichols department store in Knightsbridge were Mrs Mary Heliss, 59, and Mrs Helena de Reya, 32. Helena received a sentence of three months. Mary (also accused of smashing windows in Brompton Road) was discharged, 'the magistrate said that there was no direct evidence that she broke a window. Mr. Knight said that she was in possession of a hammer, and when it was stated that she had broken a window with it she did not deny it. Mr Francis – I don't think it is sufficient, and Mrs Heliss is discharged.'[34]

Artist Mary Palethorpe and nurse Alice Davies, 42, Liverpool WSPU branch organiser, were charged with wilful damage but the exact location and date of action is unknown. At her trial Alice said, that 'women were determined to fight for the same human rights enjoyed by men. They were tired of being treated as aliens & would continue their struggle until they had reached their objective'[35]. She received three months' imprisonment, went on hunger strike and was forcibly fed. She served her sentence in Holloway with Dr Alice Jane Shannon Stewart Ker.

Fanny Davison Palethorpe, 39, was the sister of Liverpool artist Mary Palethorpe. She travelled from Ainsdale in Lancashire to participate in the protest and was arrested. At her trial she said that, although she had always worked on constitutional lines, she had come to realise that peaceful protests would be of no avail with the present government. She received a sentence of four months.

Mrs Marie Louise Weller (née Ashby), 33, from 57 Stratford Road, Towcester, Northamptonshire was arrested although the date and location are unknown. It is understood that she received a badge and certificate signed by Mrs Emmeline Pankhurst for her part in the protest. This is interesting as teenage glassbreaker Ethel Violet Baldock's son, Donald, recalled that his mother had these too. Unfortunately, Ethel's were said to be destroyed by her husband when she died. It is likely that the certificates were 'WSPU illuminated addresses'. These were words of gratitude addressed personally to the suffragette and signed by Emmeline Pankhurst. They were designed by Sylvia Pankhurst and incorporated the WSPU colours purple, white and green. Glass breaker Kate William Evans received one in May 1912. The Museum of Wales has the memorandum from the WSPU to Kate confirming this. It may be that Marie and Ethel received a brooch in the shape of a toffee hammer, with the inscription 'Votes for Women'. It is known that such brooches were worn by suffragettes who had taken part in window smashing. The Museum of London holds the toffee hammer brooch owned by March 1912 glassbreaker Agnes Kelly. Agnes was a WSPU organiser in Palmers Green, North London. She broke two panes of glass (location unknown) on 1 March and was sentenced to four months' imprisonment, although was released early after hunger striking.

Also likely to have been involved with the Palmers Green WSPU was Laura Amelia Allan Gargett, 28. Laura had been arrested on 1 March, charged with two counts of malicious damage. When she was released from Holloway, her friend Victoria Summers organised a release party at St John's Hall in Palmer's Green. Sylvia Pankhurst was there and paid tribute to both Laura and Victoria.

Mrs Joan Cather was married to John Leonard Cather, who was supportive of her suffrage campaigning. He was a member of the MLWS. Joan used the alias name Josephine Carter when arrested on 4 March for her part in the protest. She received a sentence of two months' hard labour, serving it in Holloway. She went on hunger strike and her medal is held at the Museum of London.

Miss Rebecca Hyams, 24, used alias Janet Green when arrested for smashing windows in Regent Street. She received a sentence of six months and was transferred to Winson Green.

It is not known which windows Emily Victoria Fussell, 28, smashed on 4 March 1912. She sometimes used the alias name of Georgina Lloyd although did not when arrested on this occasion. She was sentenced to six months' imprisonment which she served in Aylesbury. Victoria's twin sister Maud Fussell was also a suffragette but not arrested in this protest.

Dr Ethel Smyth successfully targeted the house of Colonial Secretary and Liberal Cabinet minister, Lewis Harcourt M.P., No. 14 Berkeley Square. He had apparently said that he would give women the vote were they as intelligent and well behaved as his wife. Arrested, Ethel was bailed by 'wonderful Mr Pethick-Lawrence' and thoroughly enjoyed her trial, catching a 'gleam of amused sympathy' in the judge's eye (she found him rather attractive).' [36]

Dr Ethel Smyth was a significant English composer and became involved in the suffrage movement through her friendship with the Pankhursts. Ethel created 'The March of the Women' piece which was sung by suffragettes everywhere. This quote by Ethel gives an insight into her character:

> Because I have conducted my own operas and love sheep-dogs;
>
> Because I generally dress in tweeds, and sometimes, at winter afternoon concerts, have even conducted in them;
>
> Because I was a militant suffragette and seized a chance of beating time to The March of the Women from the window of my cell in Holloway Prison with a tooth-brush;
>
> Because I have written books, spoken speeches, broadcast, and don't always make sure that my hat is on straight;
>
> For these and other equally pertinent reasons, in a certain sense I am well known.[37]

WSPU waitresses at the Women's Exhibition, 1909. Includes March 1912 glassbreaker Gertrude Golda Lowy, standing third from left. (© LSE Women's Library Collection)

Ethel was sentenced to two months' imprisonment and given the cell next to Mrs Emmeline Pankhurst. It was during this imprisonment that she reportedly beat time to 'The March of the Women' from her cell window using a toothbrush as other suffragette prisoners marched and sang below in the exercise yard. Glass breaker sisters Miss Hazel Inglis and Mrs Helen Green held on remand in Holloway, recounted this story during their interview in 1976[38]. Ethel was released after five weeks owing to her poor mental health, the prison doctor was concerned she would have a severe mental breakdown. On a Home Office file note, the following was written about Ethel (dated 2 April 1912):

> Her mental condition is not likely to improve in a week and as it appears to be the fact that [imprisonment] is in the case of this woman injurious to her health I think it will be better to release her now. She is in some respects an exceptional case and it is by no means unlikely that she may become certifiable whether she remains in prison or not.[39]

Beneath this note was another that read 'Remit as soon as her friends can take her.'[40] Later in the same file it is noted that on 4 April 1912 she was taken to a nursing home at Warwick House in Warwick Square, London to be assessed before going to her home near Woking.

After her release she commented that in England,

> a first offender, who, from personal spite or in a drunken fit, breaks a cheap pane of glass, incurs the penalty of a few days imprisonment with the option of a fine, but we suffragettes - rescue workers, teachers, scientists, missionaries, artists, university graduates, widows of general officers and judges, and so forth, who have done the same thing in order to call attention to a grievance which has been ventilated for forty years, but with which men still refuse to deal, have been sent to prison for two months with hard labour: in some cases the sentences have run to four and six months.[41]

Two other women were arrested for damaging the same property in Berkeley Square as Ethel Smyth and their names were Vera Swann, 38, and Mrs Henrietta Lowy, aged 48. Henrietta was mother to daughters and WSPU members, Ethel and Gertrude Golda Lowy. Gertrude, 24, also participated in this Great Militant Protest on 4 March although where is unknown. She was sentenced to two months' hard labour. Ethel was not involved in this protest.

Lilian Ida Lenton used the alias Ida Inkley when she was arrested at the Great Militant Protest. She was 21 at the time and broke the windows of the Post Office at 70 Oxford Street with accomplice Isabel Inglis, 36, on 4 March 1912. On a 1968 recording, Lilian says, 'We were told that that night they were doing Post Offices. We both had hammers and I'd broken my window, this end one and she'd hit the wall instead of her window and then the policeman got me. I couldn't have only one window between two people so after the policeman had got me I succeeded in pulling away and smashing the other window.'[42]

Also arrested for breaking windows at this Oxford Street Post Office were Edith Prier, 35 and Mary Selkirk, 28. All four women were sentenced to two months' imprisonment.

It was reported by New Scotland Yard that on 4 March 1912 '270 different premises were attacked, the value of the broken glass being very large. A rough estimate on the part of the Police gives this at about £6,600'[43] (equivalent to approximately £965,000 today). The resources required by the Metropolitan Police in order to react to this were described as significant.

Chapter 4

Conspiracy to Incite Others & Christabel Escapes

The similarity of the stones used; the gathering of so many women in one building, prepared for arrest; the waiting at the Gardenia Restaurant; the apparent dispersal; the simultaneous destruction in so many localities of plate glass; and the bailing of prisoners by a person connected with the headquarters mentioned, certainly showed a carefully worked out plan. Only a public trial of the defendants could establish whether or not the plan was a conspiracy.[1]

Husband and wife Emmeline and Frederick Pethick-Lawrence were part of the WSPU for six years providing 'money, time, business skills and contacts.'[2] They edited and financed the WSPU *Votes for Women* newspaper. Frederick was at Clement's Inn working on an article about the window smashing protests late (9.30pm[3]) on the evening of 5 March when the police arrived. They had a warrant for the arrest of Emmeline Pethick-Lawrence, Frederick Pethick-Lawrence and Christabel Pankhurst for 'conspiring to incite certain persons to commit malicious damage to property.' Emmeline was in her flat upstairs in Clement's Inn but Christabel was nowhere to be found.

Accounts by suffragettes show that there was a system in place within the WSPU for each key active member to have an 'understudy'. When a member with a particular role was imprisoned, recovering or in hiding, their understudy would take over their duties.[4] WSPU member and close friend of Emmeline Pethick-Lawrence, Evelyn Sharp arrived just before the police took Emmeline and Frederick away to Bow Street Police Station. A well-known writer, Evelyn had been a regular contributor to *Votes for Women* since the early publication days (began in October 1907). 'In his autobiography Frederick Pethick-Lawrence explains how, providentially, Evelyn appeared just before they were marched off to Bow Street to be charged with conspiracy. He believed that Evelyn was the one person with the requisite technical expertise and political acumen to take over the paper as assistant editor – it was just twenty-four hours away from going to press – and this she agreed to do.'[5] Evelyn proved to be a good choice. Elizabeth

50

Above: Emmeline and Frederick Pethick-Lawrence, arrive in their motor for the Old Bailey trial, 1912. (© LSE Women's Library Collection)

Below left: Emmeline Pethick-Lawrence, c.1910. (© LSE Women's Library Collection)

Below right: Frederick Pethick-Lawrence, c.1910. (© LSE Women's Library Collection)

Evelyn Sharp. (© Museum of London)

Top left: Christabel Pankhurst, *c*.1910. (© LSE Women's Library Collection)

Top right: Annie Kenney, who took charge of the work in London and helped supervise the organisation of the WSPU from 1912. (© LSE Women's Library Collection)

Robins, of the of the WSPU members in the deputation to meet Mr Asquith in November 1911, commented that Evelyn was of 'distinguished ability and rare devotion.'[6]

Christabel was in her own flat. 'It was Evelyn who was indirectly responsible for her dramatic flight since she went straight from the WSPU offices to Christabel's flat to warn her. She got Christabel to sign a cheque transferring WSPU funds so that they could not be confiscated by a court order. Early the next morning she delivered this to the physicist and suffragette Mrs. Hertha Aryton. The money was paid into Mrs Ayrton's account then transferred abroad'.[7] Christabel meanwhile was helped to escape. It is believed that she was hidden at Dorset Hall, Wimbledon by suffragette and WSPU member Rose Lamartine Yates when she fled the police. It is then understood that she was disguised in a nurse's uniform supplied by a suffragette nursing home in Pembridge Villas (believed to be 9 Pembridge Gardens, Notting Hill) and fled to France. She stayed in Paris, from where she directed WSPU affairs, until war broke out in 1914. In Mrs Pankhurst's absence, Annie Kenney took charge of the work in London and helped supervise the organisation of the Union. As Mr Pethick-Lawrence noted, it was curious that the police did not follow Evelyn. Had they done so, the next phase of the suffragette story might have been different.'[8]

The first issue of *Votes for Women* after these arrests included, in place of its usual leader, the words 'A Challenge' followed by a provocatively blank space and Christabel's signature. There were many other blank paragraphs in this issue, signifying the 'suppression by the printers of articles, comments and historical facts considered by them to be inflammatory matter'.[9] The suppressed articles and paragraphs from the 8 March 1912 edition of *Votes for Women* are detailed below:

A Challenge

Gratitude to the women in prison, reverence for their courage and selflessness, these are the feelings that stir the hearts of every one of us. A cause must triumph that is fought by such soldiers as these. Our prisoners in Holloway rank with those heroes and liberators whose names are set like jewels in our national history.

The stupid will exclaim at this. What! The women who broke shop windows! Do you call that action glorious! Why not we answer. The breaking of windows is infinitely less cruel and violent than the acts of destruction to property and even to life which are committed in wars for freedom, whether such wars be international or civil. The statues, standing outside the House of Commons, hand down from generation to generation the memory of a man and a woman. They are Boadicea, who fought for national independence, and Cromwell, who in pursuit of his ideal of freedom, plunged the country into civil war. For their deeds the State itself, which has raised these statues, ask our admiration and reverence. But were these deeds either more dignified or more virtuous than the breaking of windows.

All fighting is ugly, whether of the mild and almost technical kind waged by the militant Suffragists, or whether of the deadly and cruel kind waged by Cromwell, or by Boer and Briton in South Africa. It is only a fine underlying motive that can enable fighting and make glorious what would, without such motive, be squalid and ignoble. The greatest conflicts of history, however worthy their purpose, have been made up of notions which brought death to human beings and devastation to property. Those notions nothing save that purposes could justify. The Suffragettes are happy indeed in knowing that, not only is their object as great as that of any soldiers or militant reformers, but that their notion has been infinitely less harmful to life or property.

The marvel is not that windows have been broken, but that worse has not been done. Successive Governments and the present Government especially, have pursued a recklessly provocative course of action in dealing with the Votes for Women agitation. For half a century has the Women's Movement for the Vote been flouted by the party politicians. More than forty years ago the Liberal Government stifled the first Woman Suffrage Bill. Dishonesty and treachery have been the weapons used by party politicians from that day to this. The Government now in office have outdone all their predecessors. Faced by a franchise agitation unparalleled in real extent and vigour by any of the men's franchise agitations, they have persistently refused to legislate. Had they been dealing with men, they would not have dared to trifle with such a movement. They have deliberately traded upon women's dislike of violence and disorder. Even the militant agitation of the past six years has not been enough to warn this reckless and dishonest Government. Over and over again have Cabinet Ministers jeered at our militancy, in consequence of its restraint. They have derided what they call the policy of pin-pricks, and contemptuously asked why we did not use 'real violence'. Mr Hobhouse, a Minister of the Crown, has actually argued that the woman's demand for the vote need not be conceded because there has not been the kind of popular sentimental uprising which accounted for Nottingham Castle in 1832. Nottingham Castle was, as we know, and as Mr Hobhouse knows, burnt to the ground. It is to the commission of such deeds that a cabinet minister has challenged us. This challenge alone explains and justifies the window breaking. If Members of the Government tell us, as Mr Hobhouse has told us, that nothing but violence can be accepted as a valid demand for the vote, then violence they must expect to have. Mr Hobhouse and the Government, who evidently think as he does, may be thankful that nothing worse than window smashing has happened.

Should they refuse to accept window breaking as a sufficient proof that we demand the Vote, they would make themselves fully and directly responsible for anything more serious which might occur. Considering the direct invitation to violence which he and his colleagues have given by their deeds and words, the Prime Minister's threat of proceedings against the leaders of the WSPU is [amazing] in its effrontery. If the Suffragette leaders are to be attacked, then Mr Hobhouse also must be called upon to face the legal consequences of his inflammatory words. And in this connection, we would urge that two Privy Councillors belonging to the Unionist Party have also put themselves within reach of the law by the incitement which they have given to the people of Ulster to commit breaches of law and order.

Wild and hysterical cries are being raised in newspapers (some of which sympathise with Persian, Turkish, Chinese and Russian revolutionaries whose violence is enormously in excess of ours for a strengthening of the law – for the imposition of heavier penalties.

Repression will make the fire of rebellion burn brighter. Harsher punishment will be a direct invitation to more drastic acts of militancy. If the first mild forms of militancy are to call forth exaggerated punishment, then women will be driven to commit acts commensurate in gravity to the punishment inflicted.

CHRISTABEL PANKHURST[10]

History Teaches

The pages of history all tell the same story. When any section of the community possesses the vote, they can organise and use that vote in order to secure redress of their grievances, or measures of social reform. But when any section of the community is voteless, then the only way in which the bargaining power of the vote can be obtained is by action. When classes of men demanded the vote, they showed far less patience than women have shown. Their methods were far more violent. They broke not windows only, but heads. They burnt the private dwellings of anti-suffragists to the ground. They destroyed property to the value of hundreds of thousands of pounds. Then the Government of the day gave way, because, as the anti-suffrage Prime Minister, the Duke of Wellington, said in 1829, it was a choice between giving the vote or waging a civil war and as the leader of the House of Lords said in 1872 it was impossible to keep peace in the country unless the Bill was passed.[11]

Women's Moderation

Even with these facts staring them in the face, women have been most reluctant to follow the example of the men, and have tried every expedient first. For fifty years they waited in patience, hoping against hope, trusting fair words in spite of often repeated, betrayal, using argument, appealing to justice, relying upon reason and persuasion.[12]

Why Destroy Private Property?

Yes, but why break the windows of the unoffending public? An attack on Government property we can understand, but why this attack on private property? Our answer is that when women realised that even if they lost their health and their lives, the mass of the public remained unaware of the sacrifice that was being made, they determined to make a protest that should bring the matter home to the ordinary citizen, who, so far, had not been directly affected by the attacks upon Government property. There is no danger of personal injury to the shop-keeper in breaking a shop window, and the damage done is in nearly every case covered by insurance. Where this is not so, the owner, in common with the Insurance Companies has the remedy in his own hands. He is an enfranchised citizen; he can go to the Government who are his paid servants, and insist that they shall stop the agitation by rushing a Votes for Women Bill through

Emmeline and Frederick Pethick-Lawrence, Emmeline Pankhurst and Mabel Tuke in court for their conspiracy trial, 1912. (© LSE Women's Library Collection)

Parliament. With those who argue that women's liberty is not worth the destruction of a few shop windows, we have no time to discuss the matter.[13]

Emmeline and Frederick Pethick-Lawrence were charged, along with the already imprisoned Emmeline Pankhurst and Mabel Tuke, with conspiracy to cause damage.

Emmeline Pankhurst, Emmeline Pethick-Lawrence and Frederick Pethick-Lawrence were found guilty of conspiring together and with Christabel Pankhurst (not found so not arrested) 'to unlawfully and maliciously damage and inciting others to unlawfully and maliciously damage certain property'[14] They were sentenced to nine months' imprisonment. The charges for conspiracy against Mabel Tuke were dropped. Frederick and Emmeline Pethick-Lawrence were forcibly fed.

Lillian Ball provided detailed witness statements (extracts already included in earlier chapters) and gave evidence in this trial. At one point Lillian 'was overcome by faintness and ... drank from a bottle which was handed to her by a wardress.'[15] Lillian was questioned by Mrs Pankhurst herself:

> Replying to Mrs Pankhurst the witness said that she went to the meetings willingly.
> Are you here willingly? – Certainly, but if I had known I had to appear against you in Court to give evidence against you I should not have said what I have said.
> How came you to have these questions put to you? – Two gentlemen saw me on Saturday and put several questions to me.
> Did they tell you what they were asking the questions for? – Not until they had taken the answers down. I thought they were either solicitors or detectives.
> You have a little boy, Mrs Ball, about four years of age. Was it suggested that your sentence might be shortened in order that you might see your little boy? – No inducement was held out to me, but of course I want to see my little boy and I thought if I answered the questions my sentence might be shortened, but I did not know I was to give evidence against you.[16]

Following this Lillian was cross-examined by Mr Muir, the solicitor representing Mrs Mabel Tuke and Lillian 'said that her little boy required a mother's care as he was not very strong, but if she had known that this was likely to happen, she would rather have served six months than said anything.'[17]

On 25 March 1912 a Home Office record states 'Ball will be removed to Reading prison tomorrow to get her away from the other prisoners who resent her having given evidence. The D of P P[18] does not think it would be desirable to remit any of her sentence (2 months' H.L[19]) at present as it distracts from the value of the evidence. She is not very well and will probably be treated in the hospital at Reading and will be given the privileges of Rule 243A[20] in the matter of letters, visits, books etc.'[21]

Lillian's sister, Mrs Edward H. Slack, petitioned twice for her early release and questioned the authorities about her removal to Reading. However, despite it being recorded that Lillian Ball would give an undertaking not to offend again, a further Home Office note stated 'I think it is out of the question to release her pending Mrs Pankhurst's trial. She would certainly be "got at" and very likely would be persuaded to keep out of the way. She will be treated kindly at Reading.'[22]

Chapter 5

Scottish Connections & the Holloway Jingles

'I think her fame has gone before her and she must have attracted the attention of the leaders at Head Quarters who frequently visit Glasgow.' [1]

Left to right: Helen Crawfurd, Janet Barrowman, Margaret McPhun, Mrs Alice Agnes Wilson, Frances McPhun and Annie Swan, c.1912. (© Karen Keys, descendant of the McPhun sisters)

This chapter examines 'the Scotch Batch'[2] of women involved in the Great Militant Protest and seeks to tell some of their stories.

There appear to have been a large number of Scottish suffragettes participating in the Great Militant Protest with 23 Scottish women having been identified but there may be more amongst the 273 women arrested.[3]

Beginning with 1 March during the preliminary action, at least six Scottish women were arrested, namely Margaret Macfarlane, Ellison Gibb, Barbara Wylie, Emma Wylie, Alice Maud Shipley and Frances Mary (Fanny) Parker. Margaret (Maggie) Macfarlane, 23, a trained nurse from Dundee who had moved to London, was arrested for glass breaking. At Maggie's hearing at Bow Street Police Court,

> Constable Herbert Tipple, 405c, said at 5.45 he was at Pall Mall, at the junction of Cockspur Street. He found a large plate glass window smashed at 15 and 16 Cockspur Street, the premises occupied by the Hamburg American Line. There was also a very large plate glass window smashed at No 17 and 19. He entered 15 ad 16 and found the defendant (Margaret Macfarlane) being detained by Captain Bax. In the presence of the defendant Captain Bax said 'I saw this woman with a hammer in her hand. I saw her break both the windows.' When the hammer was taken, she said 'I have broken the window as a protest against the government.'[4]

Maggie was sentenced to four months' imprisonment, which she served in Holloway. She went on hunger strike and was forcibly fed.

Ellison Gibb, 32, was from Glasgow and born in Lanark to fish merchant father Peter Gibb and mother Margaret Skirving. Her older sister Margaret was also an active WSPU member although not arrested in the Great Militant Protest. Ellison, Margaret and their mother were all chess players and involved in the running of the Glasgow Ladies Chess Club. In 1910, Ellison was appointed as the Honorary Secretary of the AFL in Glasgow. In 1910 and 1911 she was imprisoned twice in Holloway and Aylesbury and experienced forcible feeding. On 1 March 1912 Ellison was charged with causing wilful damage. The location and number of windows is unknown but she was sentenced to six months' imprisonment and transferred to Aylesbury prison. She would have had her thirty-third birthday (6 March) whilst serving her sentence. Later that same year with fellow glassbreaker Frances Mary Parker, Ellison went on to smash windows in Dundee. Both were arrested and imprisoned again. Frances Mary Parker, 32, known as Fanny, was originally from New Zealand but lived in Scotland. She was a WSPU organiser in the West of Scotland and sometimes used alias name Janet Arthur. She did not however use this name when she was arrested for causing damage on 1 March 1912. Fanny was sentenced to four months' imprisonment. She was the niece of Lord Kitchener and he paid for her education at Newnham College, Cambridge. He was said to have been 'disgusted' by her involvement in the suffrage movement.[5]

Also travelling from Glasgow to participate in the preliminary action on 1 March 1912 were sisters Barbara Franny Wylie, 50, and Emma Wylie, 56. They were arrested for smashing windows at 180 Oxford Street. As is set out in Part Two, chapter twelve, Barbara was a close friend and ally of Mrs Emmeline Pankhurst and acted as one of her bodyguards in an elite security team.

Alice Maud Shipley, 42, a lady's maid to Mrs Margaret Pairman, from Edinburgh, was arrested for smashing windows. Refusing to be bound over to keep the peace, Alice was sentenced to four months in Holloway. She went on hunger strike and was forcibly fed. It is reported that Alice said:

> More than half of my life I have been doing what lies in me to help the poor and unfortunate. I know the condition of our women and girls and the dangers that lie about them and that they have no power to protect themselves. That knowledge has made me take up the attitude I have today. I feel our case is a most urgent one and I feel that only a woman can understand a woman's needs, that women suffer for want and care of men, and that their salvation lies in looking after their needs and demanding the vote.[6]

Alice knew and had been on previous London missions with other women from Edinburgh, including Elizabeth and Agnes Thomson, Edith Hudson and Mrs Grieve. These four women were all involved in the Great Militant Protest although full details are not available.

On 4 March there were at least thirteen Scottish women arrested. Believed to be from near Glasgow, possibly Bothwell (as that was the address of her doctor), was Sara Wilson (also known as Sara Corner). She was arrested on 4 March 1912 for targeting the Lord Chancellor's house. The account of her husband and doctor both writing to petition the reduction of her sentence is set out in chapter seven. Also arrested for targeting the Lord Chancellor's house was Agnes Eleanor Jacobs, 31, wife of novelist William Wymark Jacobs, who received a sentence of one month hard labour.

Married Glaswegian, Helen Crawfurd, 35, attacked the home of Mr Pease, President of the Board of Education. She gave her maiden name, Helen Jack, and was sentenced to one month imprisonment. Helen was married to Reverend Alexander Montgomerie Crawfurd of Brownfield Church. She said of her involvement in the window smashing:

Participation in the raid was right. If Christ could be a militant so could I[7]

Subsequently in 1914, Helen formed part of Mrs Emmeline Pankhurst's undercover 'security team' known as 'The Bodyguard' (see chapter twelve).

Two women preparing for a Westminster meeting, 10 February 1949. On the right is Helen Crawfurd. (© LSE Women's Library Collection)

It is known that on 4 March Elizabeth Thomson, 65, was arrested for throwing missiles. The exact location is not known. Elizabeth's older sister, Agnes Thomson, 67, was also involved (likely also 4 March) but was not arrested.

Edith Hudson, 40, a nurse and member of the Edinburgh WSPU, was also arrested but the date of the offence and location are unknown. The WSPU *Votes for Women* newspaper reported on 8 March 1912 that Mary Brown had been arrested. This was likely Edith Hudson using her alias name. Emily Wilding Davison also used the alias Mary Brown but it could not have been her as she was already in Holloway serving time for an earlier offence in 1911. Edith was sentenced to six months' imprisonment. In April 1913, Edith and a number of other Scottish suffragettes were 'caught attempting to set fire to the new Keslo race course with firelighters and oil.'[8]

Marion Grieve, 63, also a member of the Edinburgh WSPU, was charged with wilful damage but the date of the offence and location are unknown. She was sentenced to two months' hard labour and served it in Holloway.

Other Scottish women arrested where the date of offence is unknown are Theresa Gough and Annie Swan. Theresa Gough, 44, from Glasgow was sentenced to two months' hard labour and served it in Holloway. She wrote the foreword to 'Holloway Jingles', the book of poems written by suffragette prisoners in 1912 and then smuggled out. It read:

> Comrades, it is the eve of our parting. Those of us who have had the longest sentences to serve have seen many a farewell waved up towards our cell windows from the great prison gate as time after time it opened for release. The jail yard, too, where we exercise, now seems spacious, though at first it was thronged with our fellow-prisoners. Yet not one of them has really left us. Whenever in thought we re-enter that yard, within its high, grim walls we see each as we knew her there: our revered Leader, Mrs Pankhurst, courageous, serene, smiling; Dr Ethel Smyth, joyous and terrific, whirling through a game of rounders with as much intentness as if she were conducting a symphony; Dr L Garrett Anderson, in whose eyes gaiety and gravity are never far apart – but we cannot name them all, for there are scores whose brave faces made that yard a pleasant place.
>
> The passing of the weeks was punctuated by the flowers that blossomed in those grim surroundings; sturdy crocuses, then daffodils and tulips, and now the lilacs are in bloom. Always too, we had the sunshine, for the skies were kind.
>
> And within the walls? Ah! there too, the love that shines through the sun and the skies and can illume even the prison cell, was round us, and worked through us and miracles were wrought. We have each been witness of some wonder worked by that omniscient love which is the very basis of our movement.
>
> At these words other faces will rise up before the mind's eye, bruised, perhaps degraded, crushed, sullen, sorrowful, sometime beautiful, but always endeared to use by the thought that it is for their sakes we get the strength to carry on this struggle.
>
> In service to you, O sad sisters, in your hideous prison garb, we gain the supremacy of our souls. And 'we need not fear that we can lose anything to the progress of the soul.'[9]

An Annie Swan, 45, is listed as arrested as part of this mission. She is charged with wilful damage but no location or date of offence given. An Annie Swan was photographed in January 1912 with Janet Barrowman and others. It could be that this was Scottish journalist and romantic fiction writer Annie Shepherd Swan (became Mrs Burnett-Smith) although she was born in 1859 so would have been 53 in 1912 and not 45. However, she, like many, could have given a false age and it is known that Annie S. Swan was a suffrage campaigner and friends with an active suffragette, Beatrice Harraden.

A total of six women were arrested on 4 March 1912 for breaking windows at the Local Government Board in Whitehall. Four of these women had travelled down from Glasgow, one was known to have been Welsh and another from an unknown location. All six women were sentenced on 9 March at Bow Street Police Court to two months' hard labour in Holloway prison. The women were Welsh Kate Williams Evans, Jane Lomax, and Glaswegians, Margaret and Frances McPhun, Janet Barrowman, and Nancy John.

No further details have so far been uncovered about Miss Jane Lomax, 34.

Kate Williams Evans, 45, from Wales was sentenced to two months' hard labour and during her imprisonment went on hunger strike. It is noted that there was also a Scottish suffragette called Kate Williams but also that she was not involved in the Great Militant Protest.[10] Welsh Kate Williams Evans wrote poems that were included in the 'Holloway Jingles' booklet created and sold by the Glasgow WSPU. A full list of the poems are included at the end of this chapter. In 1913 Kate chaired a meeting of the WFL in Llansantffraid-ym-Mechain in Powys. It has been suggested that her movement to the WFL from the WSPU was a result of her experiences in Holloway and wanting to join the less militant league.

Also breaking windows at the Local Government Board on 4 March were two Glaswegian suffragette sisters, Margaret Pollock McPhun and Frances Mary McPhun. Margaret, 35 was a member of the Glasgow WSPU and the West of Scotland WSPU Press Secretary. She gave the alias name Margery Campbell when arrested. Margaret's younger sister, Frances, 32 also gave an alias name when arrested, Fanny Campbell. Frances was the Honorary Secretary of the Glasgow WSPU. Their father, John McPhun, was a timber merchant but also the Police Magistrate of the City of Glasgow and Glasgow East End Councillor who helped to found the People's Palace on Glasgow Green. Both women were educated, holding degrees from Glasgow University. The sisters gave false working-class sounding names as part of their approach to proving that working-class women were treated differently from middle-class ones. This was an approach used by Lady Constance Lytton, the second daughter of Earl Lytton (see chapter three). Both Margaret and Frances received the same sentence, two months' hard labour in Holloway. They both went on hunger strike and were forcibly fed. In a letter to Laura Underwood, the Glasgow WSPU Organising Secretary, Frances said:

> I started a letter to you on the third day of the fast but, when I was in the middle of it, the doctor and nurse and helpers rushed in. A sheet was thrown round me, I was held down in a chair and pints of milk were poured down my throat. Don't gasp with horror, it was only the feeding cup they used. I didn't feel [able to have the] nasal tube. They give you the choice. 'Will you take the feeding cup or must we force it thro' the nose?' they say. I took the cup and

Above left: Frances McPhun. (© Karen Keys, descendant of the McPhun sisters)

Above right: Margaret McPhun. (© Karen Keys, descendant of the McPhun sisters)

> I made up my mind to hunger strike but I wasn't prepared to risk being forcibly fed thro' nose. Margaret took the cup too – I made her promise to take it.[11]

In other letters now treasured by the McPhun sisters' descendent, Karen Keys, Frances writes to Miss Laura Underwood describing her experience in her first week of imprisonment (images of these letters are included at the end of Part One):

LETTER FROM FRANCES McPHUN TO MISS UNDERWOOD SMUGGLED OUT OF HOLLOWAY PRISON.

Sunday

Dear Miss Underwood,

I am feeling quite well and cheerful but isn't 2 months a dreadfully long time to be confined? Some people are still to be tried, so I am sending this letter with one of them. I hear that a lot of the prisoners are getting friends and influential people to write to McKenna, Keir Hardie and others to get sentences reduced. In our case the justice is farcical. Try and do something for us (of course remember our assumed names). It is a pity we hadn't our real names, we could have applied to more people to write about us. Note the damage in all was 9/- (two between us). 4 offenders, all first offenders! We have been here [late] Tuesday and surely that could be made to count. Curtis Bennett the beast says 'no'.

I could stand it quite well by myself and not be very much the worse, but I am afraid of Margaret's health breaking down. Couldn't Dr Chapman write too? You see I am still her patient, please ask her. Of course, I would rather you would try and get Margaret out. Mrs Fairlie should get people to write about Mrs John. Miss Barrowman's employer is already doing his best. It is dreadful for Aunt Mary to think we are in for so long. One month would be nothing. I think they might do away with the hard labour. It means we can't get in books and food, and the food is so dry and uneatable. M. says things are already hanging off her. Mrs Crawfurd did 10/- worth damage and has only one month and no hard labour. The sentences were so unfair.

It was fun to see Dr Ethel Smyth packing away cigarettes in the legs of her combinations! Old Mrs Brackenbury has two weeks. Dr Garrett Anderson is in the cell under me – 6 weeks hard labour!

Love from Fanny[12]

LETTER TO MISS UNDERWOOD FROM MISS FRANCES McPHUN AND SMUGGLED OUT OF HOLLOWAY PRISON – 1912

Holloway Prison
Monday

Dear Miss Underwood,

The last letter was written on Sunday – today is Monday, the sun is shining and here I am in this stuffy den and I had such a night my bones are aching with the plank bed. I was shivering with cold! I asked the doctor this morning if I could have another blanket, so I have got one. I asked if I could send for a cushion and he said 'no'. Nearly everyone has a cushion, they took the precaution of bringing one with them. Mrs Crawfurd sneaked me this writing paper but I am in terror the wardress looks in the inspection hole of my cell and finds me writing and takes it all away. Some of them are callous in the extreme. I was out in the yard today and spied Miss Hudson at her cell window. She is still on remand so is allowed papers. She asked if I would like the Standard and she threw it down to me. Imagine the beast of a wardress saw me saving it and took it away from me.

Oh it seems so long to be here for 2 months – still 57 days to do! The other suffrage prisoners are all so nice, sometimes I exercise with little Mrs Crawfurd. She receives me with tears in her eyes. She is lucky only got one month, and not having hard labour she gets out twice and can get books and fruit sent in. Then she had the satisfaction of doing 10/- worth damage while I only did ¼ of 9/-!

I wish I had smashed the whole place and Mr Curtis Bennett's head! into the bargain. I wish I were near Margaret. She and Mrs John are together in E Wing. I haven't had a bath and no hot water and I have been here one week tomorrow. I have only a few hair pins left and I forgot nail scissors and I shall look quite prehistoric in a few weeks!

I am telling you all the discomforts but to Aunt Mary I write glowing letters pretending we are all having a lovely rest cure! Last time they were all treated quite differently – all out together twice a day – hot water once a day and a bath a day.

Yours much love,

Frances.[13]

LETTER WRITTEN ON ENVELOPE

Tuesday

I found this envelope so I can write a little more. Excuse the dirty look, but I have to carry my paper about with me in my coat pocket in case they find it and take it away.

I have been moved again. This time to wing D. but still I see no signs of M. or Mrs John. I am next door to Mrs Crawfurd which is a blessing! Otherwise my change is for the worse. My other cell was warm at least – this one is damp and icy – I couldn't sleep all night, and to rub myself to try to get some heat all the time. I think the warden must have had instructions to make us as uncomfortable as possible. I haven't had hot water nor a bath since I came here a week ago and the worry is the first 5 days don't count! Mrs Wilson has 2 months hard labour but she is being rather better treated for some reason. She is under the name of Mrs Corner. My hands are frozen, so are my feet. Mrs Crawfurd has just called in from next door to say she couldn't sleep a wink for the cold. It isn't legal for them to freeze us to death. We are all asking to see the Governor to complain but he never turns up. I also want to petition against my sentence. Most of them did so before leaving Bow Street. I have also asked permission to get news from my aunt. I think the chaplain is going to see me about it. He is a nice man. She will know today. I do hope she has gone to Callander to stay till we return.[14]

[Frances would not have known why Mrs Sara Wilson (also known as Mrs Corner) was receiving preferential treatment. As set out in chapter seven, Sara's husband and doctor were challenging her sentence on health grounds].

Glaswegian Clerk, Janet Barrowman travelled in the same glass-breaking party and was also arrested at the Local Government Board in Whitehall. Janet, 32, was highly respected by her manager, David Wilkie, Manager for Scotland of soap manufacturer, Joseph Watson & Sons Ltd, known as 'Soapy Joe's' later purchased by Unilever. Janet had worked for David Wilkie for over eleven years and he wrote a letter of appeal (dated 11 March 1912) to his solicitor, James T. Orr Esq of 174 West George Street, Glasgow. Given its level of detail about Janet, her work, family and involvement in the WSPU it is reproduced in full below:

My Dear Orr,

I am in a serious difficulty this morning. I have a letter from my chief clerk, Miss Barrowman, addressed to me from Bow Street. Kindly refer to this morning's Glasgow 'Herald' under 'Suffragists'.

On Saturday, 2nd inst., Miss Barrowman asked me for two days holiday, Monday and Tuesday of last week, to see some demonstration in London in connection with this confounded movement. I could not very well refuse. We have been very hard pressed with business during the last winter and she has done her full share. She is very sensitive and highly strung and I did think the relaxation of going to London would do her good and she would come back refreshed. I am informed she sent out one of the Juniors to purchase her week-end railway ticket and I certainly expected her return to business on Wednesday morning, 6th inst.

I can only imagine what has taken place in London. I knew she was interested in the movement of Votes for Women and she must have exercised her abilities and resources in connection with that movement somewhat to the same extent as she does in connection with my business. Be that as it may, I think her fame has gone before her and she must have attracted the attention of the leaders at Head Quarters who frequently visit Glasgow. Those leaders I cannot relieve of the responsibility of leading her and others to perform actions which, if they were in Glasgow in their own surroundings, they would have hesitated very seriously in performing. She told me she had never been in London before and I rather think she has been too well looked after by people who ought to have known better.

Now what can you do for me? I am bound, in the interests of the firm, to put the absence that has already taken place against her annual holiday but, as she is only due fourteen days, at the end of that time I must report it to Head Quarters. The consequences may be that I will be instructed to dismiss her from the employment. This would be a very great disadvantage to me as Manager for Scotland. She has been with me for upwards of eleven years and during my frequent absences from Glasgow I can safely leave her in charge of, as you know, a very considerable business. For the girl herself the consequences, as I anticipate, would be very much greater in that it affects not only her own livelihood and future career, but also that of those dependent upon her. She and her sister, who is a Graduate of Glasgow University and a teacher in one of the Schools in Glasgow are the main support of their widowed mother and younger members of the family. Besides that, her own health requires serious care. Her health is affected and she is anaemic. In short, it is with difficulty that I can restrain myself in my expressions concerning the leaders of this movement in how they have behaved towards these young women. Had I suspected anything of the kind, of Miss Barrowman being led so seriously astray, I would either not have given her the leave of absence or have extracted a promise from her that she was only in London as a spectator of what I understood to be on foot, namely, a procession to Trafalgar Square or something of that sort.

I do not profess to regulate the opinions of my staff, be they absurd or otherwise, but I do and will insist that they keep well within the limits of the Law and decency. I do not think that Miss Barrowman, if left to herself, would fall short of this ideal.

I wish your firm would take this matter up for me and lay the whole facts before the proper Authority. Kindly understand, I quite feel the difficulty that presents itself to a Magistrate who has a number of cases before him and, so far as I can read from the report of what took place at Bow Street on Saturday, there has been practically no representation on behalf of Miss Barrowman who received a sentence of two months with hard labour. Surely those who instigated this revolt might have stood by their dupes and explained the circumstances of fairness. I can quite realise that a Magistrate cannot imagine the facts; he must be told them. If you refer to the report in the newspaper, you will find that a Mrs. Brackenbury and her two daughters, said to be the widow and children of the late General Brackenbury, have each received a sentence of fourteen days. I wonder how this came about. I am told that the value of the pane of glass which Miss Barrowman broke was 4/- and if the sentence was in proportion to the damage done, then each of the Brackenburys must have only broken a pane of the value of 1/- each. Surely the sentences could not be meted out in this method of proportion nor can it be on the question of conduct for last week Mrs. W. W. Jacobs, the wife of the Novelist, noted so obstreperously so much so that the Magistrate ordered an enquiry into her state of mind and she received a sentence of one month. In all this I am not minimising the need for this matter being seriously dealt with, but at the same time I do feel strongly that if punishment is to be meted out, it should be so meted out without respect of persons and consideration also should be given to whether the party committing the crime is a principal or only a deluded agent. Could not you put this aspect of the matter before the Authorities in London? Is there not more danger of those young women feeling themselves unjustly treated and leading them to do acts of further violence? I would say that, as a first offender, if Miss Barrowman had got a sentence of fourteen days without the option of a fine, it would have served her right in allowing herself to be mis-led in this matter. You might make this representation on my behalf for if she were able to return to duty by this day [next] week, her situation would be saved to her and I think she will have learned her lesson.

Kindly do me the favour of tackling this matter at once. The poor girl's mother is prostrated with shock and I should like to bring them relief as soon as possible.

Your Aye,
David Wilkie[15]

Janet was not released from her sentence in Holloway early but served her full two months'. It is believed that Janet's hard labour was knitting. Glassbreaker Kitty Marion referred to sewing and knitting being 'associated labour'.[16] Kitty went on to say that she found it soothing for her nerves. Janet lost her position as a clerk at Joseph Watson & Sons Ltd. She found another job as a shipping clerk which she did until she retired. Janet helped Nancy John smuggle out the poems written by suffragette prisoners and made into the 'Holloway Jingles' booklet.

The booklet was advertised for sale in the newspaper *Votes for Women* priced at 1 shilling each, with all proceeds going to the WSPU.

Collecting and editing those poems was glassbreaker Mrs Nancy A. John, 40. Like Janet, she was arrested at the Local Government Board and despite her stone apparently missing the window, she too received a two months' custodial sentence. Nancy was referred to in a letter complaining about the discrepancies between the lengths of sentences given. Dated 16 March 1912, the letter was addressed to the elected Member of Parliament for Glasgow and Aberdeen Universities, Sir Edward Craik, from Una Mackinnon, Jemima Downie, Catherine S. Thomson and S.C. Logan. Also referred to in the letter were Miss Janet Barrowman, Miss Margery Campbell (real name: Margaret McPhun) and Miss Fanny Campbell (real name: Frances Mary McPhun). The letter began with:

> At the present time four women of Glasgow are each undergoing sentence of two months' imprisonment with hard labour in Holloway prison for having among them done damage to the total value of 8/- to Government property in Whitehall – an average of 2/- each. All are first offenders.
>
> At the same time that sentence was passed on these women, we are told, another woman who alone did damage to the extent of 10/- was sentenced to one month, without hard labour, another, who did £2 damage received sentence of one month, with option of a fine. Members of the Brackenbury family, by no means first offenders, were sent to prison for fourteen days, on a charge at least as serious.[17]

The letter concluded:

> We submit that the sentences of these four Glasgow women are absolutely out of proportion to their offence, and ridiculous when compared with the others cited. We feel that great danger lies in allowing such miscarriages of justice. If these women, or others who know the facts should be driven to more desperate deeds, to making the offence at least commensurate with the punishment, we feel that we shall not be without responsibility if we have indifferently allowed such things to pass.[18]

Margaret McPhun was friends with Miss Janie Allan, born into the wealthy Glasgow family that owned the Allan Line Shipping Company. Janie, 44, also a glassbreaker on 4 March 1912, smashed windows in Kensington High Street. She was sentenced to four months'[19] imprisonment in Holloway. One of the 'Holloway Jingles' poems

Smashed windows at Pontings, 123–127 Kensington High Street. (© Museum of London)

entitled 'To a fellow prisoner' was addressed to Janie by an anonymous author. It is believed that Margaret McPhun was the anonymous author. The poem describes the 'tender sorrow' on Janie's face and sets out to explain it, questioning if it could be a reflection of the misery and shame.

Janie apparently made arrangements with her friends to pay the bail of fellow Scottish glassbreakers including Ethel Agnes Mary Moorhead and Florence Geraldine Macfarlane, who like Janie smashed windows in the Kensington area. It is reported that on arrival in London the Scottish women were despatched to different ironmongers to buy hammers. They were then assigned shops in Kensington.

Interestingly, on the back of the above Pontings image[20] is a note identifying Nurse Pine as one of the passers-by. Mrs Pine was a nurse who regularly looked after suffragettes after their release from prison. She nursed Mrs Emmeline Pankhurst and more on this is included in chapter thirteen. Nurse Pine did not engage in militant action and would always comply with the law so perhaps she was just passing.

Ethel Agnes Mary Moorhead, 43, was accused of smashing windows at 19 Kensington High Street, belonging to Messrs Yeats & Company and also the premises of Thomas Cook. This Thomas Cook agent was the one that Ethel's brother, Arthur, used. Ethel was accosted by a male witness (Mr Allen) who took her inside to wait for the police. Ethel was known to use multiple alias names, including Margaret Morrison, Edith Johnson and Mary Hutchinson but when arrested in March 1912, gave her real name. Charged at West London Police Court,

Ethel testified saying. 'I am a householder without a vote. I came from Scotland at great personal inconvenience to myself to help my comrades.'[21] In her memoirs, Ethel described all offenders sitting quietly on benches. She said that they all seemed to know each other whereas she only knew one or two. The police took many notes and worked to identify hammers. Window owners were arriving and giving their accounts of events. One refused to make a charge saying, 'If I had the courage of my convictions I would be sitting with them there on that bench.'[22]

At the sessions hearing, Ethel's case was dismissed as there were no witnesses for the Thomas Cook premises and Mr Allen, the man who held her until the police arrived, muddled his evidence. It is not clear if he did this on purpose.

Receiving a sentence of four months (served in Aylesbury) was fellow Dundee suffragette, Florence Geraldine Macfarlane, 44, (sometimes used alias Muriel Muir). She had been arrested for smashing a window of Messrs Sanders and Company, a Jewellers in Kensington High Street. At West London Sessions when committed for trial, Florence of 61 Nethergate, Dundee, declined the offer of bail and said:

> I wilfully broke the window of my own accord and I should like to
> say I haven't spent my life in window smashing.[23]

Florence had previous experience of militant missions having been arrested with fellow March 1912 glassbreakers Winifred Mayo and Kitty Marshall in the 1910 Black Friday protest. Florence was also younger sister to widowed Mrs Edith Marion Begbie, 46, (see chapters eight and thirteen).

Married suffragette Enid Marguerite Renny, 29, of Broughty Ferry near Dundee, was arrested with two overseas women, Lily Lindsay and Alice Morgan Wright, at the Post Office in Young Street, Kensington. This story is told in chapter six.

Also travelling down from Scotland to participate in this mission was married 56-year-old Caxton McAlpin. She was charged with breaking a small pane of glass at the War Office on 4 March. According to the *Advertiser* newspaper report of 11 March 1912, Caxton said that she was now very vexed with herself for having broken the window, and that she would gladly pay for it. Caxton was however sentenced to two months' hard labour.

Other non-Scots arrested at the War Office that evening included Victoria Simmons, sisters Kate and Louise Lilley, Emma Fowler, Myra Sadd Brown and Katherine Mary Richmond. Describing the scene and how she was caught by a police officer is Victoria Simmons (later Lidiard), 22:

> They did a big smashing crusade. They started at the Marble Arch and
> they were stationed right down from the Marble Arch to Tottenham
> Court Road. And then Bang! Went all the windows in Oxford Street
> but we were doing Whitehall. Well, Whitehall was practically packed

Myra Sadd Brown (second from right, back row) with members of the formal cycling group, c.1890. (© LSE Women's Library Collection)

with policemen each end and they didn't let anybody go through… Well, they let me through and because women had been kicked about rather, I went and stood right near a policeman and I threw one stone through the War Office window and smashed it. Well, the policeman next to me looked at me. He couldn't believe that I'd done it and then farther off another policeman saw that I had done it, and he dashed across the road and then I was led to Bow Street. There was an inspector on horseback, then a policeman behind him, one each side of me and a policeman at the back. And you know, they were mean… I had 8 stones, in case I needed the lot, but I only used one. And so going to Bow Street Police Station, I dropped them gradually one by one and then when I arrived at Bow Street, the policeman said, pulling them out of his pocket, 'She dropped these as well!'[24]

Victoria had been a member of the Bristol WSPU with her mother and sisters since 1907. They were known for disrupting meetings and selling *Votes for Women* in the street. Victoria was sentenced at Bow Street Police Court receiving two months' hard labour with 'the decision… received with cheers'[25] and serving it in Holloway. Later in life, in 1927, Victoria became the first female refractionist.

Myra Sadd Brown, women's rights activist and internationalist, 1937. (© LSE Women's Library Collection)

The Lilley sisters Kate, 38, and Louise, 28, were from Clacton-on-Sea in Essex, daughters of Tom Lilley, co-owner of the shoe manufacturing company Lilley & Skinner. Another interesting link is that the Westbourne Grove Lilley & Skinner shop window was smashed as part of this protest (date unknown) by Ethel Lewis who received a sentence of six months and was transferred to Maidstone prison in Kent.[26] The Lilley sisters were represented at their hearing with Counsel pleading 'for leniency on the ground that this was the first time the prisoners had offended in this way. Mr Curtis-Bennett said it was a bad case. If one of the stones which had been thrown had struck anyone the result would probably have proved fatal.'[27] They both received sentences of two months' hard labour.

Emma Fowler, 50, was sentenced to two months' hard labour for her involvement in window breaking at the War Office.

Myra Sadd Brown, 40, and Katherine Mary Richmond, 50, were defended by barrister, Mr Taylor, who 'asked the magistrate not to impose the full penalty as the prisoners had been led away by speeches they had unfortunately listened to. Mr Curtis-Bennett: 'I can understand a young girl being led away but not a woman of this age. Two months' hard labour.'[28] Whilst in Holloway, Katherine wrote the poem, 'The beech wood saunters idly to the sea', which was included in the 'Holloway Jingles' booklet.

The list of poems included in the 'Holloway Jingles' booklet, and where known, name of suffragette prisoner poet/author are detailed below.

Poem Title	Author
The Women in Prison	Kathleen Emerson Glass breaker
Oh! who are these in scant array	Kathleen Emerson Glass breaker
To a fellow prisoner	To Miss Janie Allan by anonymous, but believed to be created by Margaret McPhun. Both glassbreakers
There was a small woman called G	Anonymous
There's a strange sort of college	Edith Aubrey Wingrove Suffragette but not March 1912 glass breaker
Before I came to Holloway	Madeleine Rock Glass breaker
Full Tide	Alice Agnes Wilson Glass breaker.
Who	Kate Williams Evans Glass breaker
The cleaners of Holloway	Kate Williams Evans Glass breaker
To D.R. in Holloway	Created by Joan Lavender Bailie Guthrie. Believed to be about Dorothea Rock Both glassbreakers

Poem Title	Author
Holloway, 8th March	Alison Martin Glass breaker
The beech wood saunters idly to the sea	Katherine Mary Richmond Glass breaker
An end	Alice Agnes Wilson Glass breaker
L'Envoi	Emily Wilding Davison Not a March 1912 glass breaker but serving time for setting fire to pillar-boxes in Westminster during December 1911.
Newington butts were lively	Alice Jane Shannon Stewart Ker Glass breaker

Chapter 6

Protestors from Overseas

'Lily Lindsay tried to break the window with a hammer and failed.
Mrs Renny then smashed it with a stone and Alice Wright opened
the door and put some stones inside.'[1]

This Great Militant Protest attracted women from far and wide and interestingly one group of three protestors was comprised of Lily Lindsay visiting from Germany, United States citizen Alice Morgan Wright and Scottish Enid Marguerite Renny. Letters were received from Lily's distraught family begging for her to be released so that she could be returned to Germany. Alice's parents and legal representative pleaded for her early release and the American Embassy even involved itself in her case, querying her treatment. Enid's husband petitioned for her release from prison and argued about discrepancies between her sentence and those of other glassbreakers.

It is not clear how all three came to be together in Young Street, Kensington, smashing a window at the Post Office although Enid's fellow Scottish suffragettes were targeting other shops in the Kensington area so that would likely explain why she was there. Having been arrested Lily, Alice and Enid were bailed by John T. Robertson, Lily's brother-in-law. The address used for the bail paperwork (timed at 10.45pm on 4 March) was 90 Regent's Park Road, the home of Lily's sister and brother-in-law.

On Monday, 4 March, the publicised date of window smashing, Lily, Alice and Enid were arrested together for breaking a window at Kensington's Young Street Post Office. A Metropolitan Police Report dated 18 March 1912 read:

> I beg to report that at 7.50 pm 4th. Instant I was on duty at Kensington High Street and was called by some person unknown to Young Street Post Office, where I found a window broken. Standing near the Post Office were Alice Wright of 29 De Vere Gardens, Kensington, Lily Lindsay, 90 Regent's Park Road, and Enid Renny, of 'Ava Bank' of Broughty Ferry, Scotland, who all said 'We did it and will come with you constable to the Station' and they accompanied me there but made no other statement until charged when Lindsay said 'We want bail.'[2]

Lily Lindsay was 35 and married, residing in Germany, but on a six week visit to her sister, Mrs Robertson in London.

Alice Morgan Wright, 30, was an American Sculptor, visiting London.

Enid Marguerite Renny was 29 years old, married and from Broughty Ferry in Scotland. Enid had three children, the youngest of whom was only 13 months old at this time. It seems she had travelled from Scotland with some other Scottish women some of whom attacked windows in Kensington High Street. Chapter five is dedicated to stories of the Scottish suffragettes involved in the March 1912 glass breaking.

The case of Lily, Alice and Enid was heard at the West London Police Court on 5 March 1912 and each were given two months' hard labour. Apparently these three women 'wished to do as little damage as possible and for that very reason selected the glass panel of the door and they all three made their protest on one window.'[3] It seems that 'Lily Lindsay tried to break the window with a hammer and failed. Mrs Renny then smashed it with a stone and Alice Wright opened the door and put some stones inside.'[4]

A letter dated 6 March 1912 was sent to the Right Honourable Reginald McKenna, Secretary of State for Home Affairs from the solicitors representing Lily. It read:

THE HUMBLE PETITION of Mrs. Lindsay of 90, Regent's Park Road, N.W. by her Solicitors Messrs. Watson Sons & Room, of 12 Bouverie Street, Fleet Street, E.C.

Sir,

We beg to apply to you for the consideration of the following facts connected with this case of Mrs. Lindsay who was convicted at West London Police Court yesterday in connection with an attack by suffragists upon the Post Office in Young Street, Kensington, the previous night. Mrs Lindsay was not represented when brought up with others at the Police Court, but her sister, Mrs. Robertson and Brother-in-Law Professor Robertson of the London University were trying to instruct us to appear for her, but were unable to communicate with us in time.

It was desired to lay before Mr. Garrett who tried the case the following facts, but as it is now too late to do so, she now being confined in His Majesty's Prison at Holloway under sentence of two months' imprisonment with hard labour, we beg respectively to address this Petition to you.

Mrs. Lindsay who is a married lady, residing in Germany, has no permanent connection with any suffragist movement, but was on a six week visit to her sister in London. She went out with others on Monday night and did take part in a foolish attack upon the Post Office. She struck at a window with a little hammer which she carried but did not succeed in breaking it (this was admitted by the Police evidence). Her companions who were with her did break the window valued by the Prosecution at 7/6. She was in a very excited state both then and when brought up at the Police Court and had not at that time had proper advice. She has now had such advice both from her relatives and ourselves, and instructs us to say that she regrets what she did and undertakes not to repeat the offence. She has her return ticket to Germany (expiring on Saturday next) and if so fortunate as to receive lenient treatment from you, will undertake to return there immediately. As she was not represented, the Magistrate in passing the above sentence on her and her companions had no reason to suppose that a fine would be paid, but in fact as far as your Petitioner is concerned, she would have been willing to pay a fine.

Her Brother-in-Law Professor Robertson is willing to see that she does return to Germany and to pay the damages and any fines and to be Surety to her future good behaviour. You will readily understand we feel sure, that her foolish conduct has caused very great distress to her relatives and we venture respectively to urge that she might be allowed to leave England under the circumstances set forth upon this expression of regret for her behaviour and undertaking not be repeat is, as this was her first offence.

We have seen Mr. Garrett this morning and are authorised by him to say that none of the above facts which we mentioned in mitigation were before him yesterday when he heard the case, and that should you think well to communicate with him he will place no obstacles in the way of a sympathetic consideration of this Petition.

YOUR PETITIONERS therefore humbly pray that you may in the circumstances shown above exercise your power and reduce the sentence passed on Mrs Lindsay.[5]

Lily's legal representative argued that she had not broken the window but someone else had. Miss Gladys Shedden wrote to the Right Honourable Reginald McKenna on behalf of Alice saying that another girl had done the damage:

Sir,

Are you aware that an American subject … Alice Morgan Wright is undergoing 2 months' hard labour in Holloway Gaol on an unjust sentence? It having been proved in court that although she was present at the Suffragist raid ... she had done no damage at all. She was with a girl who had done damage amounting to 7/6 and she was seen by the policeman to drop a stone with label of protest against manhood suffrage Bill attached – deliberately and with no intent to harm. She had before the raid been frequently heard to say that she would not harm British subjects – though she intended joining the deputation.

Yours faithfully
Miss Gladys Shedden,
3 Cecil Court, The Boltons, S.W.[6]

The author of this letter, Miss Gladys Emily Sophy Compton Shedden, was seemingly connected with the WSPU as she left a small legacy to Christabel Pankhurst's daughter, Aurea.[7] It is likely that she and Alice were connected by 1912 as Alice had been complicit in organising WSPU meetings in Paris and Albany, New York with Mrs Emmeline Pankhurst speaking at both.

Meanwhile, Enid Renny's husband, Mr Henry W. Renny, petitioned for Enid's release, writing to the Right Honourable Secretary of State on 28 March 1912. Mr Renny did not refer to whom did and did not break the window, instead arguing that the sentencing handed out to Lily, Alice and Enid was 'unduly severe when compared with that of other women.'[8] As part of his petition, Mr Renny said:

My wife is 29 years of age and has three children, the youngest of whom is thirteen months old. As she is interested in social work here and seeing much of the hardships that women and children of the working class particularly, have to endure under the law as meted out to transgressing men she became interested in Women's Suffrage and joined as a member the Women's Social and Political Union and as such she desired out of a sense of loyalty to the organisation to take her part in what was considered an effective appeal for the vote. She had no malicious motives and I plead that if this act of hers is to be treated as a criminal offence pure and simple, she has by undergoing over three weeks of imprisonment with hard labour been sufficiently punished and I petition for a remission of the balance of the sentence passed on her.[9]

In the hand written file notes made at the Home Office in response to this petition, it states:

A well argued petition, but the gravamen of the charge was not the actual amount of damage done by the individual offender, but the deliberate participation in an organised scheme for damaging property on a very extensive scale – 'loyalty to the organisation' – when the organisation is of such a character, is hardly an extenuation.[10]

Friends of Alice also requested a reduction in her sentence. Alice studied sculpture and had attended art school in Paris from 1909 and had many friends there. These friends were referred to in a letter from George Montagu Esq. J.P. of 8 Portman Square dated 14 March 1912. George Montagu stated that Alice's American friends in Paris had asked him to help Alice. He commented on the time to appeal her sentence having passed but requested consideration of a reduction in her sentence. Mr McKenna's office replied on 19 March 1912:

> Dear Sir,
>
> With reference to your letter of 14th instant, I am desired by Mr McKenna to say that he has looked carefully into the case of Miss Alice Morgan Wright, and he much regrets that he can find no ground for advising any remission of her sentence. With regard to your remarks as to an appeal to Quarter Sessions, Mr. McKenna desires me to add that if Miss Wright had appealed, she would have been entitled to release on bail pending her appeal. The time for appeal, however, appears now to have gone by.[11]

The American Embassy wrote to Mr McKenna querying the treatment of Alice. After obtaining feedback from Holloway that Alice 'has traces of old-standing weaknesses to the chest but there is no indication of active disease', 'She is otherwise in very fair physical health' and 'Her mental condition appears to be sound'[12], Mr McKenna's office replied:

> Sir,
>
> In reply to your letter of the 15th instant, I am directed by Mr. Secretary McKenna to acquaint you, for the information of the Secretary of State for Foreign Affairs, that Alice Morgan Wright was convicted at the West London Police Court on the 5th instant of committing wilful damage and sentenced to 2 months' imprisonment with Hard Labour. Her offence convicted of taking part with others on the 4th instant in a deliberate and carefully organised scheme to damage property which in fact resulted in extensive damage being done and Mr. McKenna sees no reason to recommend any interference with the sentence passed on her. The Ambassador of the United States of America may be assured that she receives careful medical attention in prison and she is reported to be generally in very fair health.[13]

Towards the end of March 1912, Alice's mother wrote to the Right Honourable Reginald McKenna complaining that she had not been allowed to see or even communicate with Alice. She added 'I have however a letter written by her to a friend after she was sentenced saying she had broken no law and had thrown no stone and it was so found at the trial.'[14]

At the end of March 1912, Alice completes a Petition form stating:

> Sir,
>
> I am informed by my mother that your assistant secretary [Mr] Wall said that I plead guilty to some charge.
>
> I wish to state that I did not plead guilty also that
>
> I did not break any law, as your magistrate knew well when he gave me my sentence, also that
>
> I will not under any circumstances give any promise whatsoever concerning my future action.
>
> Yours Truly
> Alice Morgan Wright[15]

In early April the Acting Governor of Holloway prison reported that Alice's mother had visited with some wording on a slip of paper that she wanted Alice to write. The words read: 'say that "I can certainly promise that I shall not take part in any act of wilful damage."'[16] The Governor's report read:

> Mrs Wright produced the slip of paper attached saying if I can only get Alice to write this she will be released. After some conversation a Petition form was given to Miss Wright but she firmly refused to write anything. She said I have never yet broken windows although I am here for having done so, it is false. The mother pleaded with her daughter and advised her but all to no purpose. Mrs Wright grew impatient and threatened Miss Wright that if she would not obey, she would be cut adrift by her father but the girl remained obstinate. The Matron was present throughout the interview which lasted nearly an hour.[17]

It is reported that Alice used uneaten food to create models of her fellow prisoners and used smuggled modelling clay to form a portrait bust of Emmeline Pankhurst. One of her best-known sculptures called 'The Fist', a clenched fist, is believed to have been to symbolise the struggle of women's voting rights. Alice created and exhibited this sculpture in 1921 and it is now on display in the Albany Institute of History and Art in New York.

It appears that none of these three women were released early from their sentences in Holloway.

Chapter 7

Sentencing and Prison Life
for the Glassbreakers

*'The Women's Social and Political Union, late of Clement's Inn
is now of Holloway Prison.'*[1] *'It is so splendid to be living in the
storm centre of the earth which is at present Holloway gaol.'*[2]

Christabel Pankhurst explained at the January 1912 meeting that one strategy of the Great Militant Protest was to have large numbers of glassbreakers fill the prisons at the same time. The hope was that this might influence the policy of the Government[3]. The glassbreakers were therefore looking to be arrested and imprisoned. However, they were not expecting such lengthy sentences. They ranged from fourteen days to six months and there appeared to be an inconsistent approach applied by the different courts and benches. This is best summed up by glassbreaker Katie Gliddon's rather prophetic comment in her secret prison diary: 'the historian of the future will look upon the March 1912 sentences as curiosities of the English legal administration.'[4]

Interestingly, it was reported by one member of the bench of the first Court with Mr R. Wallace, K.C. that 'after conviction and before sentence, the Chairman went out of his way to induce the women rather than go to prison to enter into their recognisances to keep the peace for 18 months. On the first day about half a dozen took this course, but subsequently it was apparent to the Bench that they had been "got at" and almost without exception they preferred to go to prison.'[5]

Some suffragettes had legal representation. The WSPU solicitor Mr Arthur E.N. Marshall, the husband of glassbreaker Kitty Marshall, represented some glassbreakers. This included his wife, Kitty and Mrs Emmeline Pankhurst.

Late in the evening of 1 March 1912 Arthur was at Marylebone Police Station and visited the cells of suffragette prisoners including Margaret Eleanor Thompson of Hampstead, London:

> At 11 Mr. Marshall came to our cells in turn telling us he would bail us out. How relieved we were, but I was astonished to hear him say that we must turn up at Bow Street next day—Saturday. I felt sure we should not have to go to Bow Street until Monday.[6]

Arthur E.N. Marshall (right) and another man leaving Bow Street Court. (© LSE Women's Library Collection)

Daphne Dorien, 36, and Alison Martin, 50, were also represented by Mr Marshall. Daphne, an artist, and Alison, a widow, were arrested for breaking windows at Westbourne Grove Post Office on 4 March 1912.

Mr Marshall reportedly 'watched the case for'[7] prisoners Catherine Green, Miss Mabel Norton, Ivy Constance Beach and Marie Brown. All four were arrested on 4 March 1912 for smashing windows of the Post Office at 74 Edgware Road. Catherine, 48, was from Reading. Mabel, 32, used alias name Mabel Norton, was a teacher and gave her address as WSPU Clement's Inn. Marie, 42, was married and from Brighton. Ivy, 30, also from Brighton was recorded as having 'no occupation' by *The Times* newspaper[8]. All four 'were committed for trial in each instance bail was allowed in £100, with notice to the police. It was understood, however, that the prisoners decided to await their trial in prison.'[9]

Hampstead WSPU branch member Mrs Lilian Martha Hicks, 54, arranged for a solicitor to represent any Hampstead branch suffragettes. Those members known to have been arrested included Lilian Hicks herself, her daughter Amy Maud Hicks (later Mrs Bull MBE), Georgina Margaret Solomon, Margaret Eleanor Thompson, Constance Louise Collier Amy Woodburn and Alice Singer. Most of them participated in the preliminary action on 1 March 1912. It is not known where Lilian was arrested. Her daughter, Amy, 34, was arrested for breaking the window of Canadian Pacific Railway Company at 62–65 Charing Cross. Sentenced at Bow Street Police Court, Amy received a sentence of four months, was transferred to Aylesbury where she went on hunger strike and was forcibly fed. In 1913, Amy worked with Sylvia Pankhurst to found the East London branch of the WSPU.

Reading WSPU shop-front. Glass breaker Catherine Green was from Reading. (© LSE Women's Library Collection)

Suffrage demonstration in Brighton. Marie Brown Ivy Constance Beach and Dinah/Diana Boyle were from Brighton. (© LSE Women's Library Collection)

Aged 67, Georgina Margaret Solomon was arrested as a glassbreaker on 4 March and served one month imprisonment for her part in the protest. It is not known where Georgina was arrested but notably, she had been involved previously in the 1910 Black Friday action. In a letter to *The Times* Georgina had claimed 'to have been seriously assaulted by police officers when she was grabbed by the breast, thrown to the ground and crushed.'[10]

Amy Woodburn, 49, was arrested on 1 March and sentenced to fourteen days' imprisonment.

Mrs Alice Singer, 30, of 18 Reynolds Close, Golders Green, had two children, an adopted daughter called Mary and 2-year-old daughter, Emmeline Christabel Kenney. Alice broke windows at the West Strand Telegraph Office. As this was her first offence, she was offered the option of being bound over to keep peace for 12 months which she accepted. Elizabeth Crawford researched and reported[11] on a unique story about Alice Singer buying a suffragette doll dressed in a prison uniform in 1908/9. The maker of the doll was suffragette Edith New (Edith was not a March 1912 glassbreaker). Interestingly, in a 1931 diary entry, Alice noted that at a suffragette party she had met the maker of her doll again.

For many suffragette prisoners the lengthy sentences were problematic to their jobs, roles at home, health and families. Of particular note were those who had left behind children, sometimes very young. Lillian Ball left at home three children, the youngest being just 4 years old who was not very strong and needed her.[12] Partners Frances Outerbridge and Caroline Lowder Downing were both imprisoned for four months and had an adopted daughter aged about 14 years. Evelyn Hudleston, sentenced to six months in prison, had a daughter, Joan, aged 5 years. Joan was looked after by her aunts much of the time anyway as Evelyn was a very active WSPU member and divorced from Joan's father. Enid Marguerite Renny was 29 years old, married and from Scotland. She had three children, the youngest of whom was only 13 months old when she was sentenced to two months' hard labour. Winefride Mary Rix, 36, mother to a 12-year-old daughter, was sentenced to two months' hard labour. Winefride 'smuggled a letter to her daughter, 'her precious lamb', signing it from 'your hugely loving old mum'.[13] Agnes Eleanor Jacobs was the mother of five children, two sons and three daughters. During her hearing her husband said 'that his wife had taken up this attitude because she conceived that it was her duty to the children that she should support the movement.'[14] Nellie Taylor was another mother leaving behind three children ranging in age from 8 to 20 years. Myra Sadd Brown 'discovered in her bag a photograph of her children and … kissed them every night.'[15] She wrote a letter to them on dark brown lavatory paper which read:

My three little Darlings & Mlle

Mummy thanks you ever so much & also Mlle for the letters – they were such a joy & I wanted to kiss them all over – but I am going to kiss all the writers when I see them & I don't think there will be much left when I have finished. I have got such a funny little bed, which I can turn right up to the wall when I don't use it. I am learning French & German so you must work well or Mummy will know lots more than you. Next time you see Granny I want you to give her a big kiss and hug from me with lots of love – Now 1. 2. & 3 it is Mummy's bed time – so goodnight ... Lots of love & kisses Mummy[16]

Prison life clearly involved rules and routine. Political prisoners were held in the first division whereas suffragettes were placed in either the second or third division and treated like ordinary criminal prisoners. By 1912 however Rule 243A had been introduced (passed in 1910 by the then Home Secretary, Winston Churchill). This rule meant that suffragette prisoners could be given much the same comforts as those in the first division but were not awarded political status and so denied any rights as such. The following table[17] shows the differences:

DIVISION 11	DIVISION 11 (Rule 243A)	DIVISION 1
SEPARATION FROM OTHER CLASSES OF PRISONERS		
Kept apart from others.	Kept apart from others.	Kept apart from others.
BATH		
To be taken on reception, unless considered unnecessary by Governor or M.O.[18] (all Suffragette prisoners have been exempted).	Not required on reception.	Not required on reception.
SEARCHING		
Yes: subject to general prison rules.	Special search by a special officer.	Special search by a special officer.
SPECIAL CELLS		
Must occupy cell assigned.	Must occupy cell assigned.	Must be placed in room or cell appropriated to Division 1, unless suffering from an infectious disease.

DIVISION 11	DIVISION 11 (Rule 243A)	DIVISION 1
SPECIAL ROOMS (OR CELLS)		
None.	None.	(1) May occupy, on payment, specially fitted cell or room with suitable bedding &c. (2) May have, at own cost use of private furniture & utensils suitable to habits. (3) May have, on payment, assistance relieving him from performance of unaccustomed tasks or office. (Only a limited number of rooms available).
APPLICATION OF PRISONERS' PRIVATE MONEY		
Not allowed.	Not allowed.	Money may be applied for making provision in respect of which payment is required.
FOOD		
As prescribed for these in Division 1. Who do not maintain themselves.	As in Division 11, but prisoner may receive parcel of food once a week not exceeding 11 lbs. M.O. may prescribe diet suitable to age, condition and health.	May supply own food: not permitted to receive prison food at any meal for which he procures or receives food at own expense.
RESTRICTIONS AS TO SUPPLY OF FOOD		
—	—	Only to be received at certain fixed hours. To be inspected; subject to restrictions preventing luxury or waste.
RESTRICTIONS AS TO SUPPLY OF DRINK		
No intoxicating liquor.	No intoxicating liquor.	Shall not during 24 hours receive or purchase more than 1 pint of liquor &c or, if an adult, ½ pint of wine.

DIVISION 11	DIVISION 11 (Rule 243A)	DIVISION 1
CLOTHING		
Prison dress or different colour (but this is not enforced in case of suffragette prisoners).	May wear own clothing.	Own clothing, if fit. Prison dress, if worn of different colour.
DISINFECTION OF CLOTHING		
—	No special provision but the rule for Div. 1. would be applied if necessary.	M.O. may order disinfection of own clothing, prison clothing to be worn meanwhile.
PROHIBITION OF SALE OF PROPERTY		
—	—	Sale or transfer of any article introduced prohibited.
HAIR CUTTING		
Not compelled to shave or have haircut, except on medical grounds.	As in Division 11.	As in Division 11.
CLEANING OF ROOMS		
To be swept and cleaned by themselves; also, furniture and utensils.	May be relieved from this duty if desired – to have on payment, services of someone to perform it.	As in Division 11. (Rule 243A).
BOOKS AND NEWSPAPERS		
Books from prison library.	Books at own expense, not bearing on current events, and unobjectionable.	Books and newspapers or other means of occupation, at own expense, as are not objectionable.
EMPLOYMENT		
To be employed at work of industrial or manufacturing nature to be afforded means of earning remission of sentence and gratuity.	To be employed only on lighter forms of labour and thus afforded facilities to earn remission and gratuity.	Not required to work: permitted (a) to follow trade or profession if practicable and to receive earnings: (b) by consent employed on prison industries, and thus entitled to earn remission and gratuity.

DIVISION 11	DIVISION 11 (Rule 243A)	DIVISION 1
VISITS AND LETTERS		
Visits once a month by not more than three friends for ¼ hour. Write one letter and receive one letter each month.	Visits once a month by not more than 3 friends for ¼ hour, in place provided for Div.1. offenders. Write one letter & receive one letter on private matters in each fortnight, such visits and letters depend on industry and good conduct.	Visits once a fortnight by not more than three friends for ¼ hour. May write one letter & receive one letter each fortnight. Visits may be prolonged by V.C. or additional visits or letters granted to a reasonable extent. Not to receive visits in same place as other prisoners if other place can be provided.
EXERCISE, ASSOCIATION AND CONVERSATION		
Exercise once a day. Conversation during exercise not allowed.	To exercise in forenoon and afternoon; to associate & converse during this time, so long as they behave.	No special provisions. Reasonable opportunities of exercise allowed.
RELIGIOUS SERVICES		
Same as Division 1.	Same as Division 1.	If attended or visited by Minister of any other persuasion than the established church they shall not be compelled to attend any religious service. Otherwise, attend ordinary services.
APPLICATION OF GENERAL RULES		
Subject to general prison rules except as far as they are inconsistent with special rules of this Class.	As in Division 11.	As in Division 11.

Winston Churchill's successor to the position of Home Secretary, Reginald McKenna was questioned in Parliament on 21 March 1912 about the application of Rule 243A for the glassbreaker prisoners and responded:

Suffragette prisoners convicted summarily and sentenced to imprisonment.... are receiving the modified treatment specified in Rule 243A. Those convicted on indictment whose offences are more serious, and those sentenced to imprisonment with hard labour, are being treated under the ordinary rules, with some slight modifications in their favour in the matter of prison clothes and bathing which I have authorised.[19]

The conditions in prison for the 1912 suffragette glassbreakers are well documented in many forms: contemporaneous diaries and subsequent personal accounts, letters, petitions, reports and drawings. These next accounts also give an insight into the rules broken by suffragette prisoners and the resulting revocation of Rule 243A privileges. For example, Zoe Proctor describes being 'shoved' into 'cell No. 1.22 ... on the ground floor of Ward D.X., the best and most modern ward in Holloway.'[20] Her description of her new surroundings included:

It gave me a good stretch of sky to look at and when I stood on the hot water pipes I could see out of the window and catch a glimpse of the Exercise Yard and the coal heap. The window was wide and narrow, consisting of 40 small square panes, four of which could be pushed aside to give scanty ventilation we were allowed. In the corner of the cell, near the window, were two shelves, on which were placed the Bible and 'The Narrow Way' and a copy of the prison regulations, 28 in number. In the mornings, the cell doors were opened and you received the order to pass out to fetch water, to take in your breakfast, and then you 'passed along' to Chapel......Chapel was a grim business. The Sanctuary and Altar were properly fitted, but hope remained at that end of the building. The prisoners sat in rows at the front, and there was a space left between them and the Suffragettes, presumably to prevent our corrupting the normal captives. There were four raised seats, two on each side, where four wardresses stood sideways, with whistles hanging at their waists, in order to overlook and control the behaviour of the congregation......Every morning before Chapel a wardress went round the cells asking each occupant 'Any complaints-Governor, Matron, Doctor?' Demands for the doctor from the Suffragettes soon convinced him that the lack of fresh air and exercise was having a bad effect, and he must have advised that we should be given an extra hour each afternoon...... The prison rule that one walked in single file, with a definite space between each two women, round and round the Exercise Yard, was soon done away with by the Suffragettes. We walked in twos and threes and some days a small group of us would sit upon the ground on my rug, which my pet wardress, Miss Jones, allowed me to carry out with me. We told each other stories of our lives, for we came from far off places......During my six weeks I had one visit from my sister, as only one visit a month was allowed. I wrote two letters which were, of course, censored before being sent out.... I spent a great deal of my time looking out of the window, as did most of the prisoners. Much conversation was held between the watchers at the windows.[21] [Lights were turned out at eight o'clock each night].

March 1912 glassbreakers secretly wrote diaries whilst in prison. Katie Gliddon wrote hers in a copy of Shelly's poems. An extract that started with Katie being held in a police cell after sentencing at her trial on 5 March at Marlborough Police Court, reads:

March 5th ... Stayed in police cell – there until 4pm. Then went in the Black Maria to Holloway Prison with Constance Moore and Dinah Boyle. Had tea at 10 o'clock. Dinah Boyle in next cell. But as window did not open could not talk to her. Phyllis Keller in cell underneath. Miss Whitlock near. Saw doctor. Lay down on bed. At about 4.30 next morning was measured, weighed and had to answer questions. Then undressed and went to bed...

March 6th Got up. Saw sunrise and the pattern of the prison window in sunshine on my wall. No service. Lay down all morning, felt very rotten as had practically not slept and feared the hard labour part of my sentence would mean the hunger strike. The chaplain came and told me there was no hard labour in the prison. I was able to eat my dinner and felt a different being.... Exercise – no one I knew was there at the same time. Miss Brackenbury had heard from Mrs Marshall that Mr and Mrs Pethick Lawrence had been arrested the night before and Clement's Inn ransacked. The warrant was out for Christabel but she could not be found.... Read Shelly. Pigeons came and ate the crumbs on my window sill. Someone... walked down the corridor singing 'O, rest in the Lord'. It was ...and I loved the singer for her courage. Those things make one feel the togetherness of it all. We are all looking after one another's interests. E. yelled from window. Sang to myself 'March of the Women' and Marseillaise. Read Shelly aloud and went to bed about 8pm. Slept all night. I want to sit still and think not even to read. But I am not strong enough to think of people outside who matter or of the spring

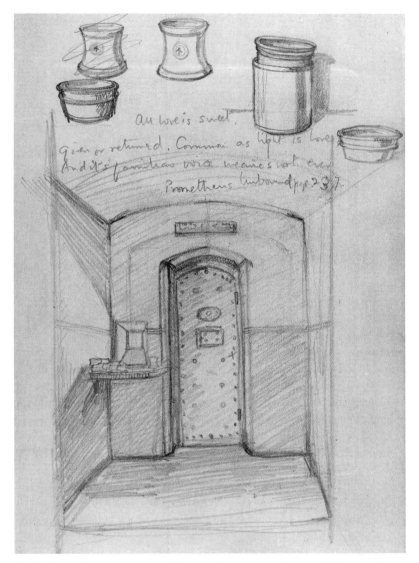

all love is sweet,
given or returned. Common as light is love
And its familiar voice wearies not ever
Prometheus Unbound p 337

Sketch of prison cell by glassbreaker Katie Gliddon. (© LSE Women's Library Collection)

I shall miss. I only think of things in here. We look towards the part of the building where Mrs Pankhurst is with great affection and extraordinary fury. My brain refuses to believe that she is actually shut in there and cannot get out any more than I can. We cannot shout to her when we are out to exercise as we are too few at a time and too far off…

March 7th Got up early. No chapel. Asked to see Governor. Yelled from window to Constance Moore and Miss Keller. Governor yelled from garden to shut up so as I had hopes about my artist materials I obeyed. They can't find Christabel. But then she is magic. The Women's Social and Political Union, late of Clement's Inn is now of Holloway Prison. But is very much alive. I have no idea how many of us there are. We are all wondering what will happen at the London Opera House tonight. O I do want my 'Votes for Women' so badly… I wish we had been able to go to chapel so that I could see who is here. They are only letting a few out at a time because they are afraid of a mutiny.[22]

As indicated by Katie in her diary, a mutiny was feared at Holloway and further sanctions were placed on the suffragette prisoners with privileges such as visits and letters revoked as a result of disruptive behaviour. Fellow glassbreaker Kitty Marshall already on remand having been arrested with Mrs Emmeline Pankhurst and Mabel Tuke at Downing Street on 1 March, describes the chaos in Holloway, how the prison system creaked at having to cope with an influx of more than a hundred women, and a mutiny breaking out when the suffragettes were told that women who had been convicted were not allowed to mix with prisoners being held on remand. As the women on remand milled about outside their cells where Mrs Pankhurst – who had already been convicted – would not be allowed to join them, they were pushed back into their cells and the doors were locked. 'Everyone began banging on their doors and singing *The Marseillaise* to the words of a suffragette song and broke panes of glass in the windows of their cells to let in the fresh air. I believe the row we made could be heard some miles away.'[23] 'Kitty broke all forty panes in her cell and had to spend five days in solitary confinement, 'in an underground cell with no hot pipe, an iron bedstead…. there was snow on the ground and it was bitterly cold. I kicked the bedstead and sang *The March of The Women*… A mattress was thrown in towards evening, which I tried to fold round me.' Kitty was severely depressed and 'cried all the time' and was taken to the hospital wing after five days. She was released from Holloway on 12 April.'[24]

Another glassbreaker's account of this evening was Zoe Proctor:

The wardresses were taken by surprise and the prisoners shouted 'We want Mrs. Pankhurst'. A message was sent to the Governor, who arrived at the far end of the first gallery, looking rather frightened, and begged us to go back to our cells. The demand for Mrs Pankhurst continued and the Matron came forward while the Governor disappeared. She was a woman of great character and remonstrated with us as human beings. Finally, she said, 'I will ask Mrs. Pankhurst to speak to you, and then you must behave yourselves.' A cell door was opened in the gallery and Mrs. Pankhurst stood and looked down on us. Somebody called out – 'How are you? Are you well? Are you being properly treated?' Mrs Pankhurst said 'As you know, I ought not to be here. I have done nothing to justify my arrest, and I do not ask you to return to your cells.' She disappeared, and I realised that there was going to be trouble.[25]

Right: Charlotte Marsh, 1911. (© LSE Women's Library Collection)

Below: Three women, including glassbreaker Charlotte Marsh (centre), holding copies of *Votes for Women* newspaper, Southampton, 1911. (© LSE Women's Library Collection)

When the prisoners had been locked in cells, they began to smash their tin utensils and break panes of glass in their windows whilst shouting to be let out. Zoe Proctor recorded: 'I found myself beating on my cell door in what was, I suppose the result of mob hysteria. I was terribly ashamed of this loss of self-control.'[26]

Zoe Proctor's account also covered the antics of fellow suffragette Charlie Marsh:

> When we were next told to leave our cells, certain well-known Suffragettes gave the order not to 'pass-along', but to mass ourselves at the back of the ward in rows...Two or three wardresses advanced and tried to catch hold of the front row of prisoners. They were resisted, and I saw some painful scenes, such as a prisoner being forcibly separated from her companions and carried by four wardresses holding her arms and legs, and thrown into a cell. I learned later, from Charlotte Marsh, that she was one of the last to be captured, and was carried in this fashion face downwards, with her long hair sweeping the floor, until they reached the iron staircase, when she feared her face would be bumped along the steps. At that moment a wardress, who had known her in Birmingham, called out 'Marsh, what are you doing here?' Charlie gasped 'What are you doing here?' whereupon the Birmingham wardress said—'. If she says she will walk, she will', and Charlie cried 'But I won't.'[27]
>
> Charlie was a very well-known suffragette and according to Mary Ellen (Nellie) Taylor, 'Charlie Marsh has not a single pane left'[28] in her cell.

Charlie had single-handedly smashed at least nine windows in the Strand and was sentenced to six months' imprisonment and as reported by Zoe Proctor, 'several of the Suffragettes were transferred at intervals to other prisons. Charlotte Marsh and several who were considered ring-leaders were sent to Aylesbury where they had a sympathetic and understanding Matron who allowed them, until the Hunger-Strike began, to play games. Charlotte made a cricket ball out of rags wound round a stone'.[29]

There were rumours of further demonstrations and the authorities responded with an assurance that they could cope with any such further misconduct:

> On Thursday last I had a long interview with Mr. Marshall, Solicitor to the W.S.P.U. and in the course of conversation about Mrs Pankhurst's defence, he told me that he had private information that the prisoners in Holloway intended another mutiny unless concessions were made; that we should be unable to cope with it

and that even if we did, a hunger strike would ensue. I told him that he was strangely misinformed as to the resources of the Prison Commissioners; that we were perfectly capable of dealing not only with the present batch of mutinous suffragettes, but with practically any number that might come to prison and that we are also prepared to feed them all in the event of a hunger strike.

This morning he called again to say that he had seen Mrs. Pankhurst last night, that he had told her how futile it was to run her head against a stone wall and strongly advised her to give no more trouble in prison. He said that he found her very low in spirits: she admitted that they had made a grave mistake and said that it was her wish which was to be communicated to suffragettes both inside and outside the prison that all militant action was to be stopped and not again resumed. He took down the message in writing as her dictation; communicated it to both the Governor and the Matron, and, subsequently, to suffragette prisoners whom he had to see as appellants, all of whom he spoke to acquiesced in the decision.

I told him that satisfactory as his statement was, no action could possibly be taken on it as present; that, as he already knew, 53 prisoners were punished by the Visiting Committee yesterday and these punishments would have to be served; that in view of a threat of mutiny in the Chapel tomorrow, the suffragettes would have to be kept from Chapel; that in fact we wanted 'deeds, not words'; before we could relax our precautions.[30]

Many of the suffragette prisoners petitioned against the denial of their privileges and rights. Henrietta Helen Olivia Roberts Fargus (Olive), 32, was one of these women. She had been imprisoned for breaking six windows at 76–78 Regent Street, the property of Packer and Co. on 1 March 1912. She wrote 'Sir, I am writing to ask you to give instructions that suffragist prisoners in Holloway shall be accorded the rights and privileges such as are allowed to men political prisoners. Also that we may have direct information from Mrs Pankhurst and Miss Emily Davison that they are both well and being treated as political prisoners.'[31] A well-known figure in Kensington society, Olive went on to marry solicitor, John Durand-Deacon. Sadly, Olive was murdered in 1949 when she became the sixth and final victim of John George Haigh, commonly called the Acid Bath Murderer.

Professional dancer and glassbreaker, Phyllis Keller, 23, from Woking, found the 'supply of sanitary towels was inadequate' with 'none available and so her mother sent to her some of "the old fashioned, washable sort" while also using the opportunity to

Mr Asquith walking along a street accosted by two suffrage supporters. On the reverse it names Miss Fargus and Miss Ida Corbett. (© LSE Women's Library Collection)

hide in the box a small ball with which the women would play.'[32] Phyllis had broken a window at 36 Wimpole Street, the house of Lord Cromer, on 4 March.

Genie Sheppard, 48, arrested 1 March 1912 for breaking one window at 157 Piccadilly, property of Barret and Sons, wrote a letter to the Right Honourable R. McKenna whilst appearing at Bow Street Police Court:

> Sir, I am a prisoner on remand charged with damages of not more than £3 value. While in Holloway Prison since Saturday last, I have done no damages and given no trouble but have been kept in solitary confinement, been allowed no exercise nor attendance at chapel though I expressed a desire to attend both services on Sunday last. My writing materials were taken away from me and some of my meals were served to me without a plate or other table conveniences. From about 9.30 on Sunday morning I had no means of communication with the wardresses as my bell did not act and every time I put my flag down it was put up again from outside without my cell door being opened. As a matter of fact I was only out my cell to fetch water once on Sunday and once on Monday. As I know that this is directly contrary to the prison regulations for the treatment of prisoners on remand. I shall be glad to hear from you immediately on the matter. Yours faithfully Genie Sheppard.[33]

A handwritten note from James Scott, Governor at Holloway dated 9 March 1912 is in the National Archives and responded stating that the mutinous conduct of the majority of the suffragette prisoners, rendered it absolutely necessary to take strong precautions and made it quite impossible to carry on the ordinary routine of the prison as regards them. 1./ This prisoner was not confined to her cell as a punishment for misconduct here, but because we could not send any of these prisoners to exercise or chapel while there was risk of further disturbance. 2./ Writing materials are prohibited. 3./ While so many of these prisoners were deliberately breaking plates, mugs etc. we had to exercise caution in giving earthenware dishes and on that day, it was thought scarcely safe to trust them with knives. 4./ For some hours there was a continuous singing of electric bells - these gave out after a time and some of the wires etc. were deliberately broken. There was also a continuous hammering at the doors. This rendered it impossible to tell if any quieter prisoner was making a legitimate application. It was also unsafe to let more than one or two of them out of their cells at a time. It has been necessary since to limit the numbers going out to exercise at any one time and Chapel attendance has not been considered safe. Some of them have threatened another combined disturbance....'[34]

Sara Corner (also known as Sara Wilson), 58, was arrested on 4 March 1912 when she had targeted the Lord Chancellor's house. She was sentenced to two months' hard labour and served it in Holloway. Sara asked for: '(1) a reduction of sentence (2) for permission to receive letters and papers; in particular letters from my husband. It is perhaps useless to add that, being married, I am urgently required at home; while my degree of strength makes it extremely difficult for me to work so long a sentence. My motive was purely political, to help to call attention to a deep political grievance: and there was no intention to harm anyone. It was done in pursuance of the policy pointed out to us by Mr Hobhouse.'[35]

Sara's husband, J.T. Wilson, wrote to the Governor at Holloway prison saying that Sara was 'of a feeble and fragile constitution and in my opinion physically unfit for hard prison labour....'[36]

Although there were initial concerns for Sara when she arrived in Holloway the following report written by the Governor on 18 March 1912 concludes that early release is not necessary:

I5395 Sara Corner. This prisoner is of frail physique, and is a very emotional and nervous woman. She was rather depressed for some days after reception, and did not take her food well. Since she has been occupied with work in association with other suffragette prisoners she has appeared more cheerful, and she tells me that she now feels quite in her usual health and spirits. She does not sleep very well, but this, according to her account, is an ordinary trouble with her. In view of her neurotic tendencies I have allowed her an additional period of exercise in the open air.[37]

Kathleen Warne, mother of glassbreaker Mrs Marie Harrison, petitioned for her case to be reconsidered and subsequently for permission to visit her in prison. Kathleen Warne argued that as a first offender, the sentence handed to her daughter was too harsh given that she'd only broken one window at the Home Office valued at £9. From her home at 39 Doughty Street, London, Kathleen Warne also wrote to the Right Honourable Home Secretary again in April:

> I have applied to the Governor for permission to visit my daughter, also to send her in things such as fruit and books, and to write and receive letters. To the first question I received a reply from the deputy Governor stating that during her sentence she could receive no visitors. To the second question there was no reply.[38]

Also arrested at the Home Office were Mrs Kathleen Marie Anstice du Sautoy-Newby, Jeanie Brown, Caroline Morris and Winefride Mary Rix. Kathleen, 32, was from Ilfracombe, and sentenced to two months' hard labour. She is said to have been inspired by glassbreaker Helen Millar Craggs. This followed spending time with Helen when she worked in North Devon as a paid WSPU organiser. Jeanie, 35, was sentenced to one-month hard labour and served it in Holloway. At her trial she reportedly said that if the leaders were punished, the women would do 'worse and worse.'[39] Caroline, 40, was sentenced to two months' hard labour, again serving it in Holloway. Winefride, 36, living in Tonbridge, Kent, married to a solicitor and mother to a 12-year-old daughter, was sentenced to two months' hard labour. This was her only militant protest.

Mrs Katey Mills, 25, was imprisoned for causing wilful damage (location and date unknown). As set out in this report written by the prison's Deputy Matron, Katey was released early:

> She now gives an unconditional promise not to break the law again. She is physically frail and in a nervous condition and she wants to be out of prison before her husband returns from sea. Discharged today 22.4.12.[40]

Glass breaker, Katherine Gatty, 41, a nurse, journalist and lecturer, of 96 Churchfield Road, Acton, London, was a good friend of Emily Wilding Davison. At her trial said that men were allowed to break women's hearts and homes without punishment and contrasted her six months' sentence for minor property damage to the two months' sentence an Edinburgh man received for breaking his wife's skull. In Holloway,

Winefride Mary Rix. (© Museum of London)

Katherine was 'initially placed in E block which "was ghastly!" The lavatory accommodation was absolutely inadequate. The whole block was infested with mice & co. – there was no heating apparatus at all'.[41] She was transferred to block D which was the area usually used for suffragette prisoners. Katherine went on hunger strike and was forcibly fed. After she was taken to the prison hospital, her friend and fellow suffragette, Alice Maud Arncliffe-Sennett (also known as actress Mary Kingsley), tried to visit her. However, she was told that because it was a prison hospital this would not be possible. Mrs Cobden Sanderson who had attended the February meeting at the Connaught Rooms (see chapter one) had written to Alice Maud Arncliffe-Sennett on 29 June 1912 explaining that she couldn't visit Katherine Gatty as she was on TRL business in Southend-on-Sea.

" VOTES FOR WOMEN.'

MRS. ARNCLIFFE-SENNETT.
MEMBER OF NATIONAL EXECUTIVE COMMITTEE WOMEN'S FREEDOM LEAGUE.
1, ROBERT STREET, ADELPHI, LONDON, W.C.

Alice Maud Arncliffe-Sennett, c.1908. Alice Maud tried to visit glassbreaker Katherine Gatty when she was in the prison hospital but was refused entry. (© LSE Women's Library Collection)

Persistent complaints were made about the Holloway prison cell Emmeline Pankhurst was being held in. Sir Frederick Crawley raised with the Secretary of State and Home Department 'whether Mrs Pankhurst was on her recent committal to prison at first put in a cell half underground, in which drainage from the ground above flowed in the direction of her cell; whether there were cockroaches and other abomination in it; and; if so, whether steps will be taken to prevent such conditions in future.'[42] To dispose of these allegations the Assistant Surveyor Colonel Winn was sent to inspect the cell and submitted a detailed report refuting all allegations and stated 'that it is 9 feet 9 inches high, 12 feet 6 inches long, 7 feet broad. It has wooden floor, ventilated underneath, as in ordinary houses.'[43]

Also complaining about her cell in Holloway was glassbreaker Mrs Mary Nesbit, 53. She had been arrested with Blanche Bennett, member of the IWSS, for smashing two glass panels (£2 damage) at Baker Street Post Office on 4 March 1912. On one of the cell walls had been written 'Thank God I am going out in two days – had a month for soliciting in Hyde Park'. Refusing to stay in a room that had been occupied by a prostitute, her request to transfer was 'given without delay'.[44] When she left prison, Mary said 'I was deeply impressed by the wonderful spirit of loyalty and love for the cause and for our leaders – all irrespective of class, creed or age, were unwavering.'[45] This is explored further in Chapter Eight.

Chapter 8

Spirit of Loyalty and Love for the Cause

*'I was deeply impressed by the wonderful spirit of loyalty and love
for the cause and for our leaders – all irrespective of class, creed
or age, were unwavering.'* [1]

There is much evidence of the suffragette prisoners' unwavering strength and defiance whilst serving their prison sentences. As explored in chapter seven, the suffragettes demanded to hear of and see their leader Mrs Emmeline Pankhurst whilst in Holloway prison. They were eventually granted this wish and continued to demonstrate their defiance to their treatment with prison protests. This spirt of loyalty and love for the cause and their leaders did not waver. Instead, they all pulled together to use communication tactics and develop 'social activities' to remain strong.

Communication was key to the emotional and mental wellbeing of the prisoners as well as the continuation of the WSPU's work. The WSPU's sophisticated approach included 'a system of communication with the prison, carried on from a window overlooking Holloway.' [2] The window was on the top floor in a house (12 Dalmeny Avenue) rented by the WSPU for housing and interviewing suffragettes who had just left the prison. This house was 'near enough to the prison that suffragettes could shout out messages from their broken cell windows, wave handkerchiefs and *Votes for Women* badges.' [3] Suffragette Winfred Adair-Roberts (known as Winks) told of going with her mother to this house when her sister Muriel Adair-Roberts was imprisoned in Holloway:

'We weren't allowed in [Holloway] but the WSPU took a top room in a lodging house opposite the yard … The landlady must have been a supporter…the friends of the prisoners could go … up to this top room and see the prisoners walking about in the yard. That was the nearest we could get to them'. [4]

Imprisoned glassbreaker Katie Gliddon said in her secret prison diary: 'saw our tricolour flag in a window on a house roof overlooking the exercise yard.' [5]

The WSPU had codes for use in messages. Examples of some codes are shown below:

Code for Action	Meaning
Wool	Telegram
Woolly	Wire back
Woollen	I am telegraphing
Mix	A letter
Mixture	Letter follows, do nothing until you hear again
Woollen-mixture	I am telegraphing, a letter follows, do nothing till you hear again
Hare	Can you go at once?
Tortoise	Don't do it, wait
Fox	Are you prepared for arrest?
Foxes	How many are prepared for arrest?
Goose	Don't get arrested
Duck	Don't get arrested unless success depends on it
Bird	At once, immediately
Silk	Will you go to protest meeting?
Cotton	Meet
With	At
Without	Wait at, or, wait for

Code for Cabinet	Name of Cabinet Minister
Thistle	Asquith
Lilly	Birrell
Dock	Burns
Daisy	Buxton
Firs	Carrington
Holly	Churchill
Elm	Crewe
Nettles	Lloyd George
Thorns	Gladstone
Ash	Gray
Oak	Haldane
Birch	Loreburn

Roses	McKenna
Beech	Morley
Pansy	Runciman
Violets	Samuel
Trees	Cabinet Ministers

Code for WSPU	Name of WSPU Member
A	Drummond
B	Kenney
C	Hambling
D	Mrs Lawrence
E	C. Pankhurst
F	Mrs Pankhurst
G	Organisers
H	Men
I	Women

Code of Places	Place Name
Kew	Clement's Inn
Potters Bar	House of Commons
Henley	Downing Street
Balham	Whitehall
Oxshott	St James' Hall
Purley	Queen's Hall
Gatwick	Caxton Hall
North	63 Chancery Lane, W.C.
South	147 Harley Street

Code for Stations in London	Name of Station
Gold	Cannon Street
Silver	Charing Cross
Lead	Euston
Iron	Fenchurch Street
Brass	Great Central
Steel	Great Northern

Code for Stations in London	Name of Station *(Continued)*
Tin	Holborn Viaduct
Zinc	Liverpool Street
Pewter	London Bridge
Metal	Paddington
Ore	Victoria
Platinum	Waterloo

Code for Other Actions or Timing	Action or Timing
Oil	Departs
Vinegar	Arrives or arriving
Paper	This morning or morning
Book	This afternoon or afternoon
Review	This evening or evening
Pens	Tomorrow
Ink	Today (sometime)
Stamp	Come

Code for Kind of Meeting	Type of Meeting
Almonds	Public Meeting
Raisins	Dinners
Nuts	'At Homes'
Oranges	Exhibitions (openings, laying stones etc.)
Apples	Lectures
Pears	Out of doors
Grapes	Free
Lemons	Pay
Coffee	Local Post Office
Tea	Tickets

Example
Silk thistle almonds}
Pens review duck Woolly}
E.Kew. }

Will you go to protest at Asquith's public meeting tomorrow evening but don't get arrested unless success depends upon it. Wire back to Ch. Pankhurst, Clement's Inn.

Example 2

Mix with coffee … Letter at Local Post Office[6].

Notes were hidden in stockings and passed between prisoners secretly in chapel. When a prisoner was due for release, they got as close to other prisoners as they could so as to learn anything that needed conveying to the WSPU outside. Nellie Taylor gave an account of doing this by talking to Mrs Sadd Brown just prior to her release in early April 1912. Zoe Proctor said that the day before her release when she went out to exercise she had prisoners to whom she had never spoken approaching her 'with tiny rolled up pieces of paper and instructions and addresses to which they were to be sent.'[7] She said that she could not refuse them and concealed them in her shoes and elsewhere.

Suffragette prisoners passed information to visitors by smuggling and passing notes on toilet paper. Nellie Taylor's sister wrote to another woman intending to visit Nellie saying, 'Remember to shake hands with her in case she wants to give you a note.'[8]

Toilet paper was also used by suffragette prisoners to write diaries, draw sketches, write letters home and even create sculptures. Glass breaker, Florence Jessie Hull's diary, written on toilet paper, from a later term in prison is held by the Museum of London. 'Alice Morgan Wright, the American sculptor, who fashioned a small figure, and sketched on lavatory paper the prison yard and the interior of a cell.'[9] Myra Sadd Brown wrote a letter home on 'dark brown lavatory paper.'[10]

A Minister would also be asked to deliver letters and give reports on the suffragette prisoners. Mr Taylor explained this in a letter to Mr Edwin Richmond, husband of suffragette prisoner Katherine Mary Richmond:

> If your wife is in Holloway will you write to Rev. Fred Hawkinson, 60 Haverstock Hill, Hampstead, London, N.W. He is a Unitarian Minister who visits the convicted prisoners every Monday and Friday, and is allowed to reach each time one letter to the prisoner. My method is to send to him a joint letter from myself, children, and friends (as many pages as you like!). I would suggest sending to him some stamped envelopes addressed to you for the reports which he will gladly send after his visits.[11]

Rev. Hawkinson also visited other prisoners, including Elsie Howey, 27, whilst she was serving four months in Aylesbury prison. However, this means of communication was blocked in mid-April when Rev. Hawkinson was refused access to Holloway. This was a decision made pending enquiries to a mass march and demonstration in Aylesbury prison. Commenting on this, Mr Taylor said:

> The Home Secretary and his Chief Officials not only fail to volunteer information, but employ lying methods to mislead. They seem off

their heads, and evidently are afraid of the pluck, determination and resource of these brave voteless women.[12]

Other acts of support were displayed in gifting food to suffragette prisoners. Zoe Proctor refers to her Chelsea friends Lillian Shepherd and Janet Stratton bringing her food:

> When I received my sentence of six weeks in the Second Division, my sister or friends used to send in to me occasionally fruit and cheese. Two of my Chelsea artist friends, Lillian Shepherd and Janet Stratton, adopted me as their prisoner, and from them, I received the most expensive and marvellous fruit. I was able to distribute as much of this as my coat pockets would hold, to the Hard Labour prisoners during 'Exercise'. Only Second Division prisoners could receive food, and the distribution had to be secret.[13]

Another glassbreaker receiving fruit was Grace Tollemache, 40, of Bath WSPU. Mary Blathwayt of Eagle House near Bath was Grace's friend and sent her oranges. Eagle House was nicknamed the 'Suffragette's Rest' and features in chapter thirteen. Activities that lifted the spirits of the suffragette prisoners included football. Emily Wilding Davison apparently demonstrated especial vigour becoming hot and tired.[14] Glass breaker Sarah Benett, 56, was good friends with Emily and 'caused considerable amusement in the Home Office by having the temerity, at her age, to request that gymnastic appliances such as skipping ropes and balls should be made available in Holloway in order that the suffragette prisoners might keep fit.[15] A 'sports day was held, complete with prizes, and considered by Margaret Thompson as more enjoyable than Vera Wentworth's impersonation, with a button in her eye, of Lord Cromer'.[16] It seems

2WNA/D/04

THE

DANGER of WOMAN SUFFRAGE

LORD CROMER'S VIEW:

I object to granting the Suffrage to Women ———

BECAUSE I consider the measure fraught with DANGER TO THE BRITISH EMPIRE;

BECAUSE it would be subversive of peace in our homes ;

BECAUSE it FLIES IN THE FACE OF NATURE, which has clearly indicated the spheres of action respectively assigned to the two sexes ;

BECAUSE those who make the laws should have the physical force to enforce them, and this women do not possess ;

BECAUSE the measure now before Parliament will almost certainly lead to a strong demand for granting VOTES TO ALL WOMEN ; and

BECAUSE if this is done, the sovereignty of the British Empire will pass FROM THE HANDS OF MEN TO THOSE OF WOMEN, for the reason that the numbers of women in this country are largely in excess of the numbers of men.

ANTI-SUFFRAGE CAMPAIGN.
PALACE CHAMBERS, BRIDGE STREET, WESTMINSTER, S.W.

Published by ANTI-SUFFRAGE CAMPAIGN, Palace Chambers, Westminster, S.W.—22174.

Anti-suffrage league leaflet with Lord Cromer's views on women's suffrage. (© LSE Women's Library Collection)

that the prisoners' played everything imaginable, 'like a lot of small children & sometimes as roughly that now & again someone gets rather badly hurt, with a sprained wrist or ankle.'[17]

Plays were put on in Holloway and included a scene from Shakespeare's *The Merchant of Venice*. In it, Miss Grey was the Duke. Listed below are the other prisoners with parts.

Evaline Hilda Burkitt, 35, a paid WSPU organiser for the Birmingham and Midlands WSPU branch, played the part of Shylock. Evaline gave her real name when arrested but was known to sometimes use the alias name Byron. She was arrested on 1 March 1912 for smashing two windows at 102 New Bond Street, belonging to Long and Sons, two windows at 103 New Bond Street, property of Archibald Ramsden and one window at 105 New Bond Street, owned by W. Coulsen and Son. She was imprisoned for four months, went on hunger strike and was released on medical grounds.

Married glassbreaker Doreen Allen, 33, was Nerissa in the play. Doreen was arrested for causing wilful damage on 4 March 1912 and sentenced to four months. She went on hunger strike and was forcibly fed. Doreen was born in Dartford, Kent as Edith Doreen Allchin and in 1905 married Melville Hodsoll Allen who worked at the Stock Exchange in London. In later years, Doreen lived in Brighton.

Mrs Louisa Field, 28, who had been arrested with Elsie Howey in Regent Street on 1 March performed as Gratiano.

Miss Lilias Mitchell, 27, was Antonia. She had been arrested on 1 March for wilful damage and sentenced to four months' imprisonment was Antonia. Lilias was the organiser in Aberdeen. She became the Newcastle and District WSPU organiser in September 1912 when Laura Ainsworth resigned from the WSPU on account of the Pankhurst Pethick-Lawrence split. Lilias went on hunger strike and was released early.

Kathleen Blanche Bardsley, 41, took the part of Bassanio. Kathleen was arrested for wilful damage although it is not clear on which date or where. She gave her name as alias Kate Bard and was sentenced to four months.

As explored in chapter five, poetry was written by glassbreakers whilst they were in prison. These campaigners were so defiant they smuggled the poetry out of prison and published them to raise awareness of and funds for their cause. One such poem described the strengthening of the women's free, unconquered will was called 'The Women in Prison'. Written by glassbreaker prisoner Kathleen Emerson, 27, from Dublin, Ireland, the poem referred to the Holloway walls being strong but women's free, unconquered will being stronger and that the lonely hours in prison were stepping stones to liberty. Kathleen was a member of the IWFL and whilst serving two months' hard labour for smashing windows at Customs House in Lower Thames Street, she wrote two poems. In her second poem, 'Oh, who are these in scant array', Kathleen outlined 'the various characters in Holloway Prison, including the wardresses, the governor, the chaplain, the doctor, the matron, and [of course] the suffragettes. Several figures are mocked – the chaplain is described as a 'sanctimonious drone' – but the matron is one 'we'll ne'er forget' because 'we feel she is a Suffragette.'[18]

Another interesting insight into some of the suffragette prisoners' characters and personalities serving time in Winson Green prison, Birmingham for smashing windows is a poem written by glassbreaker Kathleen O'Kell, 62. She had been imprisoned for four months for breaking windows at the property of Scotts Ltd at 1 Old Bond Street. The poem spoke of ten other glassbreakers (whose stories are expanded on below) and read:

THE SUFFRAGETTE ABC
A is Miss Aitken, whose friends call her Vi:
Yet here she's named Satan: I can't tell you why
A's Archibold, and from Richmond is she:
She looks upon prison as one endless spree
B's Mrs Begbie, who though she looks frail
Hops about with quiet vigour in Winson Green Jail
B is Miss Blacklock with very much fag
She edits for us girls, the '*Hammeress*' mag
B's Miss Bowen who's just 'sprung' a bed
Out of M.O. who gave it and fled
B is Miss Bray who the violin plays
B is Miss Bray […] of music and art
Alas that she here should be wasting her days
For the expert suffrage movement she has played a good part
B's Constance Bryer but here we've the habit
(O strange time it is!) to call her Brer Rabbit
C stands for Carwin from fear she's exempt
All the rules of the prison she treats with contempt
C's [Mrs/Miss] Cook whose real name is Grace
And yet she's called Adam right up to her face!
D is Miss Downing who sews many shirts
And sometimes knits socks – just by fits and by spurts![19]
A is Miss Aitken, whose friends call her Vi:
Yet here she's named Satan: I can't tell you why[20]

Aitken was Violet Aitken (born Marion Violet Aitken), 26, editor of the WSPU magazine, *The Suffragette*. Together with Clara Giveen, 24, she smashed twelve windows at 245–247 Regent Street, belonging to Jays Ltd, a clothing shop. Both were given four months' imprisonment and after their initial period in Holloway prison, were transferred to Winson Green. Clara (known as Betty and later Mrs Betty Brewster) wrote on WSPU letter headed paper to the Right Honourable Reginald McKenna MP. It read:

> Dear Sir, As a Suffragist Prisoner on remand I wish to draw your attention to the fact that we are not receiving the privilege to which we are entitled. I have been to Holloway since Monday March 4th. I have only been out to exercise once. I have not been to Chapel, neither have I received any of the other usual privileges granted to remand prisoners. We are here for a political offence and if we are not granted the privileges of a political offender we shall take steps to secure our rights. Yours faithfully Clara Giveen.[21]

Violet was born in Bedfordshire, the daughter of Canon Hay Aitken of Norwich Cathedral. A diary entry from Violet's father shows the family's reaction to her involvement in this protest:

> She has been again arrested and this time for breaking plate glass windows, I am overwhelmed with shame and distress to think that a daughter of mine should do anything so wicked.....But my poor wife! It's heart breaking to think of her being exposed in her old age to the horror.... God help us![22]

Violet was released from her sentence early for medical reasons after hunger striking and being forcibly fed. A report from the prison set out: 'Vomited considerably. Nervous anaemic state – continued forcible feeding would endanger health.'[23]

> A's Archibold, and from Richmond is she:
> She looks upon prison as one endless spree [24]

Louise Archibold (possibly spelt *Archibald*), 45, was married and from Richmond. She smashed windows (unknown location) and was sentenced to four months' imprisonment. It seems that she went on hunger strike because a medal with her name engraved on it was sold at auction (Bonhams) in 2017.[25]

> B's Mrs Begbie, who though she looks frail
> Hops about with quiet vigour in Winson Green Jail [26]

Edith Marian Begbie, 46, of 107 Ridgeway, Wimbledon, was charged with three counts of malicious damage on the Strand, and given four months' imprisonment.

Edith was born Edith Marion Macfarlane in Leith in Midlothian in Scotland. At the time of her arrest in 1912, she was living in London and a widow and mother of four children (aged approximately 15 to 23). Edith was a member of the Wimbledon branch of the WSPU. Her sister, Florence Macfarlane was also a glassbreaker and her story is explored further in chapter five. Both went on hunger strike. It is believed that the photograph included in chapter thirteen was taken of them subsequently when they (and glassbreaker Gertrude Wilkinson) required recuperation at the home of Rose Emma Lamartine Yates, the Organising Secretary and Treasurer of the Wimbledon branch of the WSPU.

> B is Miss Blacklock with very much fag
> She edits for us girls, the '*Hammeress*' mag [27]

As set out in chapter two, Miss Charlotte Blacklock (Charlie), 45, was arrested on 1 March. She smashed a window at 16 Piccadilly (property of Drew & Co.) and was sentenced to four months' imprisonment but moved to Birmingham prison to serve it.

> B's Miss Bowen who's just 'sprung' a bed
> Out of M.O. who gave it and fled [28]

Miss Bowen was the alias name used by Mrs E. Bodell, 45. She had been arrested for breaking a window at 160 New Bond Street, owned by Messrs Hudson Brothers, provision merchants. She was sentenced to four months' imprisonment, went on hunger strike and was forcibly fed. Glass breaker, Caroline Downing, reported that she had been companions with Mrs Bodell during their hunger strikes. Caroline had reported that although the Government argued that forcible feeding by tube was only painful when a victim struggled, Mrs Bodell, who was quite passive, still experienced pain. She also referred to a Miss Farmer saying that she suffered a great deal.[29] Miss Alice Farmer, 45, had been arrested for breaking a window at 68 Piccadilly, belonging to Randall Ltd, on 1 March, and sentenced to four months.

> B is Miss Bray who the violin plays
> B is Miss Bray [...] of music and art
> Alas that she here should be wasting her days
> For the expert suffrage movement she has played a good part [30]

Miss Winifred Edith Bray, 32, served her four months' sentence in Winson Green prison. She had broken a window at 106–108 Regent Street, belonging to The London Stereoscopic Company. Winifred worked as a soprano soloist and violinist hence the poem's reference to music. She was a member of the Willesden and Kensal Rise WSPU which she had founded with her sister, Constance, and Louie Cullen. Her sister, Constance, 35, was also a glassbreaker arrested for causing wilful damage and given the option of release and keeping the peace for twelve months or one month imprisonment. It is not clear which she chose.

> B's Constance Bryer but here we've the habit
> (O strange time it is!) to call her Brer Rabbit [31]

Constance Bryer, 29, the Islington North WSPU Honorary Secretary smashed windows in Regent Street on 1 March. Further details are included in chapter nine. A poem, Constance wrote whilst in prison was:

> Suffragettes we sit and sew
> Sew and sit and sit and sew
> Twenty five are we:
> Making shirts and socks for men
> Cannot get away from them [32]

> C stands for Carwin from fear she's exempt
> All the rules of the prison she treats with contempt [33]

North Islington WSPU procession. Glass breaker Constance Bryer was Honorary Secretary. (© LSE Women's Library Collection)

Sarah Jane Carwin, 46, a nurse from 11 Tavistock Mansions, London, smashed eleven windows in Regent Street on 1 March. She received a sentence of six months but was released in June on grounds of ill health after hunger striking and forcible feeding.

> C's [Mrs/Miss] Cook whose real name is Grace
> And yet she's called Adam right up to her face! [34]

Grace M. Cook, 31, was arrested with Chelsea WSPU branch member Winifred Mayo.

> D is Miss Downing who sews many shirts
> And sometimes knits socks – just by fits and by spurts! [35]

Cloth embroidered with signatures, including those of glassbreakers, held by the LSE Women's Library. (© LSE Women's Library Collection)

Janie Terrero. (© Museum of London)

Two Downing sisters were arrested, Caroline and Edith. The Miss Downing in this poem was Caroline Lowder Downing as she had been transferred to Winson Green prison whilst Edith had remained in Holloway. Their story is explored in greater detail in chapter ten.

In addition to poetry, handkerchiefs and cloths were secretly embroidered with the signatures of suffragette prisoners. Annex 2 includes the names of those women who were the March 1912 glassbreakers and signed the three pieces of embroidery work. One is held by the LSE Women's Library and has seventy-nine signatures.

It is understood that one handkerchief with sixty-six signatures embroidered in various colours was started by experienced militant suffragette and glassbreaker Mary Ann Hilliard, 46, whilst she served her sentence in Holloway. It is not known which windows Mary Ann had broken. She kept the handkerchief and as a nurse, bestowed it as a gift to the British College of Nurses in 1942. The British College of Nurses closed in 1956 and during the 1960s the handkerchief was found in a jumble sale in West Hoathly, East Sussex.

Mrs Janie Terrero (née Beddall), 53, was a member of the Pinner WSPU branch and for a period was the Honorary Secretary. Her husband, Manuel, was a member of the MLWS. Two other glassbreakers were arrested for breaking glass at the same location (240 Oxford Street) namely Alice Green and Eveleen Boyle Anna Arton. Their stories are captured in chapter ten.

Janie wrote accounts of her time in Holloway where she went on hunger strike, was forcibly fed during two periods, and released a few days early on health grounds:

> I was in close confinement for twelve days, was in two hunger strikes and was forcibly fed in April and again in June. To those who intend to be actively militant, I want to say this: 'you cannot imagine how strong you feel in prison. The Government may take your liberty from you and lock you up, but they cannot imprison your spirit'.[36]

Janie embroidered twenty signatories onto a handkerchief whilst in prison. These belonged to the women who had endured hunger strike with her in Holloway (see Annex 2).

Chapter 9

Concerned Relatives, Hunger Striking & Forcible Feeding

'It was believed that she was in the early stages of pregnancy
which the prison medical inspector said "would further
aggravate her mental instability." '[1]

Many relatives were extremely concerned about their loved ones being involved in the mission and the lengthy imprisonment particularly as privileges had been reduced and even completely removed. Some suffragette prisoners joined in with planned hunger striking and many were forcibly fed. This chapter explores this providing an insight into more stories of those involved in and impacted by this particular WSPU mission.

One suffragette prisoner who was released early was Ida Cairns, 33. She had been arrested and charged with wilful damage carried out on 4 March and sentenced to six weeks' imprisonment. She was held in Holloway but her health, particularly her mental health deteriorated rapidly. It was believed that she was in the early stages of pregnancy which the prison medical inspector said 'would further aggravate her mental instability.' He continued that

> Under these circumstances I should recommend that she be discharged and handed over to the care of her friends. I have interviewed the prisoner's husband and understand from him that when she is discharged, whether on expiration of sentence or otherwise, he will be in a position to send her away for rest under conditions that will obviate the risk of any impulsive conduct on her part. I have thought it proper to warn him on this point, as the woman may, in my opinion, become suicidal and also because she appears to be morbidly vindictive towards the magistrate who sentenced her and towards other people.[2]

Further information about Ida and her life subsequently has not yet been uncovered. Another glassbreaker known to be pregnant when arrested was Edith Anne Lees. Her story is set out in chapter three.

A parent writing to request a visit to see their imprisoned daughter was father of first-time offender, Constance Moore, 28, a student from South Croydon. She had been arrested on 4 March 1912 for breaking windows at Westbourne Grove Post Office. It is known that once sentenced at Marlborough Police Court, Constance travelled to Holloway prison in a Black Maria with Katie Gliddon and Dinah Boyle.[3] Mrs Dora Beedham (née Spong), 32, from Knebworth was arrested with Constance. 'A poker was found on Moore and a hammer on Beedham.'[4]

They said in conversation that they had been asked to sign to do this damage, and also to sign to do bodily harm if anyone should interfere with them, but they declined to do the latter at the instigation of their friends.

Rabbi Cohen wrote to the Rt. Hon. R. McKenna about suffragette Mrs Lily Delissa Joseph saying 'Her term of imprisonment is to expire on Tuesday, April 2nd, which is the first day of the Jewish Festival of Passover. Mrs Joseph, who is an observant Jewess is very anxious to be liberated on the day before – Monday 1st – so that she may be with her family that evening to observe the Festival In accordance with the Jewish rites.'[5]

The niece of Dame Millicent Fawcett, President of the law-abiding suffragist society, NUWSS, was glassbreaker Louisa Garrett Anderson. It is evident that Louisa's mother, Elizabeth, and brother, Alan, felt that she was influenced

Dr Louisa Garrett Anderson with her dogs William and Garrett, c.1915. (© LSE Women's Library Collection)

by the WSPU and that they were seeking to distance her from the union. They successfully secured her release, just a few days early and took her to their family home, avoiding the other suffragettes as they left prison and gave 'her a few days of quiet with her mother in the country before she could resume her work and as the halo of martyrdom faded she would be helped to gain her mental balance.'[6]

Organised hunger striking was planned and enacted. Some suffragette prisoners were identified and transferred out of Holloway. Nellie Taylor said in one of her letters home, 'I hear it is the mutineers who are being sent to other prisons. They are afraid of a hunger strike starting.'[7] However, the WSPU communicated instructions about the planned hunger striking in many ways. One was via Helen Archdale (née Russell), the WSPU Prisoners' Secretary, visiting the suffragettes. Kitty Marion recalled Helen visiting Winson Green with instructions to stop the hunger strike until Mrs Pankhurst, Mrs Pethick-Lawrence and Mr Pethick-Lawrence were sentenced and imprisoned for conspiracy. Helen apparently confirmed that all suffragette prisoners in all prisons would then only be asked to hunger strike if these three prominent prisoners were not granted 'political prisoner' status. Helen reportedly had a close relationship with Mrs Emmeline Pankhurst. She had spent two months in prison for smashing windows and then played her part in the February meeting in the Connaught Rooms on Great Queen Street where prisoners released from prison for their part in the November 1911 window smashing were welcomed. She spoke at this meeting 'saying that the time had passed for women to exercise patience. She appealed to those hesitating as to militancy to come forward. They would find the wall of their difficulties diminish as they approached it.'[8]

Ongoing exchanges about the hunger strike continued through the developed communication tactics (see chapter eight). For example, when Zoe Proctor was released from prison, she 'brought out the code, which enabled'[9] those outside to learn the state of the hunger strikes. The shared code was used by those still in prison to communicate to WSPU members based in the rented house overlooking Holloway, 12 Dalmeny Avenue. Another more conspicuous method of communicating was via a megaphone from outside the prison!

Forcible feeding was used on glassbreaker suffragette prisoners in Holloway, Winson Green – Birmingham, Aylesbury, and Maidstone prisons. Many had gone on hunger strike and been forcibly fed before. Indeed, two glassbreakers, Evaline Hilda Burkitt, 35, and Charlotte (Charlie) Augusta Leopoldine Marsh, 25, had been amongst the first suffragette prisoners to be forcibly fed in 1909. In 1912, Charlie and fellow glassbreaker Ada Cecile Granville Wright were transferred to Aylesbury, went on hunger strike and were forcibly fed. They were both released early due to ill health. They were sent to Switzerland to recuperate.

Margaret Eleanor Thompson went on hunger strike but because of a facial disability (the result of a car accident) the doctors decided to feed by cup rather than tube.[10]

Scottish suffragette and glassbreaker Margaret Macfarlane was forcibly fed until her release from Holloway at the end of June. Her weight dropped from 7st 5lb when she entered prison to 6st 6lb on her release.[11] Below is an account she gave of her experience:

> People imagine that there is a nurse sitting kindly by the bedside stroking the prisoner's forehead, and the prisoner is sipping from the feeding-cup. Instead of that, I was lifted into a chair and tied with a strong sheet to the back of the chair. As far as I can remember, my arms were held on each side on the arms of the chair. There was a wardress with a feeding cup (this wardress was 5 ft. 10 ½ in height, and very strong) and one behind my chair, making a gag for the mouth with her fingers. Another held my knees. I told them that I would not swallow a drop of the gruel voluntarily. When they found that I did not retain any of the food, the one who was gagging me egged the others on to tickle me, to hold my nose to make me swallow, and to grip me on the throat, which to me is the cruellest. The pressing of the throat to make one swallow gives a fearful feeling of suffocation. When they got my feet up, my head was hanging right over the back of the chair, which added to the choking sensation... When the doctor came to pay an official visit afterwards, I made a strong complaint to

Released suffragette prisoners. (© LSE Women's Library Collection)

him on the way I have been treated. I asked him if he thought I was going to gain by those two thimblefuls of gruel that I had taken after having a quarter of an hour's horseplay from four wardresses? [12]

When they became too weak from the hunger striking and/or forcible feeding, the authorities released the suffragette prisoners.

Groups of glassbreaker prisoners left prison together. One group from Aylesbury prison were released early after hunger striking and being forcibly fed. They had all been involved in the preliminary action on 1 March. Mrs Grace Branson, 35, had smashed a window at 11–12 Haymarket (property of Dewer and Sons) and at No. 24 belonging to Randall Ltd. Miss Margaret Haley, 30, smashed one window at 3–4 Old Bond Street, belonging to Hill Bros., and, two windows at 6 Old Bond Street, property of Hummel & Co. Nurse, Miss Annie Humphreys, 46, broke one window at 47 New Bond Street, property of Maison Pinett, one window at 51 New Bond Street belonging to Whitehouse Linen Specialists and one window at 126 New Bond Street, property of Aerated Bread Co. Dr Frances Ede, 59, smashed windows at 198 and 200 Piccadilly. Agnes O'Kell, 48, alias Miss Oonah Caillagh, broke one window at 43 Piccadilly, property of Sotheran and Co., and two windows at 44–45 Piccadilly belonging to Thomas Wing.

According to an account by Leonora Tyson, leaving Holloway together were herself, Mrs Yorke, Miss Crawley and Miss 'Follitt'. Beatrice 'Follit' (note the different spelling) is listed as having had her signature embroidered on one of the cloths (see Annex 2). No records have been discovered about her involvement in this protest but like others she could already have been in prison having undertaken an earlier suffragette mission. Miss Crawley is deemed to be Miss Ethel Crawley, 31, using alias Mary Carlyn, believed to be a member of the Balham WSPU. Mrs Yorke will have known Norah, also from the Balham WSPU. When released, they were 'given a hearty welcome'. They were greeted with cheers and were given silver medals, bearing on one side their prison letter and number and on the reverse each prisoners' name and date of imprisonment. Rose Lamartine Yates was there and gave short speeches. The speakers declared that the result of Holloway experience was an increase in militancy, for only by that means could any rights be gained or maintained in prison and the lesson could equally be applied to the political struggle outside. [13]

The March 1912 glassbreaker prisoners adversely affected the health of the Holloway prison Governor, Dr James Scott. He retired in 1912 on medical grounds and the 'press explained that "owing to the suffragettes" behaviour in prison' which had 'caused him much worry' he 'had just had a physical breakdown.' [14]

Chapter 10

Friendships and Connections

'We have each been witness of some wonder worked by that omniscient love which is the very basis of our movement.' [1]

There were clearly many existing connections and friendships prior to March 1912. Like other protests and missions, many more were created from women's participation in the Great Militant Protest.

On her release from prison for her part in a 1908 protest known as the 'pantechnicon raid', suffragette and March 1912 glassbreaker Florence Eliza Haig said that it was 'wonderful how each woman who acts influences their own circle. Friends who before may have been but mildly in favour, are converted into active and eager workers for the cause. Coming out is so delightful that the stupidity of the time in Holloway is forgotten.' [2]

Suffragettes waiting for the boat. The only glassbreaker is Maud Joachim. (© LSE Women's Library Collection)

Florence's words voiced the importance of the friendships and connections in the suffrage movement and this resonates with the Great Militant Protest. There were many stories of friendship circles and connections generating influence that were in play at the time of and as a result of the March 1912 glass-breaking.

Florence Eliza Haig, 56, had her own circle to influence and be influenced by. The cited example of the 1908 'pantechnicon raid' used a pantechnicon (furniture van) as a 'Trojan Horse' to transport twenty hidden suffragettes to the House of Commons. Two other women in the pantechnicon were her artist friends, the Brackenbury sisters, Marie, 45, and Georgina, 40. They were also arrested at the Great Militant Protest, charged with obstructing the police. Marie was arrested in Palace Yard, a paved open space between the Palace of Westminster and Westminster Abbey. It is believed that Georgina was arrested at Bow Street Police Station when she protested at not being permitted entry to see her mother, Hilda Brackenbury. Another glassbreaker arrested in the Palace Yard was active Axminster (Devon) WSPU member and Honorary Secretary, Edith Clarence, 35. She 'had carried a banner into Palace Yard on Monday evening, was charged with insulting behaviour, and ordered to find sureties. She said she would have been maltreated by the crowd had it not been for a police-constable' and magistrate Mr Curtis-Bennett replied, 'I hear all sorts of good things about the police.'[3]

Florence Haig was sister to suffragettes Louisa Evelyn Cotton Haig and Cecilia Haig. In 1908, Florence and Louisa Evelyn set up the Edinburgh WSPU branch. When Florence moved to Chelsea she joined the Chelsea WSPU and became the Honorary Secretary. She spent most of 1911 looking after her sister Cecilia who had been trampled and seriously injured at the Black Friday demonstration in 1910. After Cecilia's death in January 1912, Florence became involved in the Great Militant Protest and was arrested with her cousin Janet Augusta Boyd, 61. They were both charged and found guilty of breaking windows in Oxford Street including two sets of windows at D.H. Evans. Florence was released early on medical grounds:

> Elderly woman presenting some indication of cardiac enlargement. Resists forcible feeding. Process caused shock, and food was vomited. Not prudent to have recourse to this method again. Showing signs of suffering in health.[4]

Janet was also released early and described as 'senile, eccentric and weak-minded. Resists efforts to feed her with spoon or cup. In view of age and particularly of arterial degeneration not prudent to feed by tube. Shows signs of mal-nutrition in condition of tongue and increased frequency of pulse.'[5]

Other glassbreakers who were members of the WSPU's Chelsea branch were glassbreakers sisters Caroline and Edith Downing, Charlotte Blacklock, Zoe Proctor and Maud Joachim.

Sisters Caroline Lowder Downing, 56, and Edith Elizabeth Downing, 55, were arrested in Regent Street on 1 March 1912. Edith was a friend of Marion Wallace Dunlop, the first suffragette to hunger strike in 1909, and one of the WSPU members greeting and instructing glassbreakers for this mission. She had smashed three windows at 227 Regent Street, the property of Elphinstone and Co., and one window at 227a Regent Street, belonging to Gladwell and Co. She was sentenced to six months and served it in Holloway. Nearby in the same street, older sister Caroline, 56, smashed No. 221 belonging to Tiffany and Co. Caroline, a nurse, refused bail and at trial received a four months' sentence.

Also arrested in Regent Street during the preliminary action was nurse Frances Olive Outerbridge, 66. Frances had smashed a window at No. 211, the property of trunk makers, Messrs Pound and Company. She was a member of the Sydenham and Forest Hill WSPU and lived with Caroline Downing at 286 Devonshire Road, Forest Hill. When arrested, Frances used her mother's maiden name, Williams. She also 'complained that she was seized by a shop-assistant, who took her inside the shop and kept her there until a policeman arrived.' From this hearing it seemed that several other glassbreaker cases involved the defendants threatening to prosecute civilians 'who seized them after they had committed damage. The magistrate said that some stupid person appeared to have talked a great deal of rubbish about the law to these women. He pointed out that anyone could detain a person who had committed damage.'[6]

Frances went on hunger strike, was forcibly fed and released early:

> Over 65 years of age and presented indication of arterial degeneration. Would not be fed without considerable resistance involving some danger. Refused food. Likely to suffer from continued abstinence.[7]

Charlotte Blacklock, 45, worked at the Chelsea WSPU shop with Zoe Proctor. On 1 March 1912 Charlotte smashed a window at 16 Piccadilly, owned by Drew & Co. Zoe had smashed the window of a silversmiths in Haymarket on the same night. They were both bailed that evening and instructed to return on Saturday, 2 March, Charlotte and Zoe travelled together to Bow Street Police Court:

> The next morning Miss Blacklock, from the Chelsea Shop, called for me and we drove to Bow Street together. As we passed through the Mall she mourned that we should miss the almond blossom, which was nearly out.[8]

Maud Amalia Fanny Joachim, 42, another member of the Chelsea WSPU branch and niece of composer and violinist, Joseph Joachim, was sentenced to six months' imprisonment for smashing two windows belonging to Callard & Co. at 74 Regent Street on 1 March 1912. She was transferred to Maidstone prison in Kent because she was considered 'a person of some influence' with the others and is fomenting trouble in Holloway.'[9] Maud had been imprisoned previously for the cause, including in 1908 after demonstrating outside the Houses of Commons and 1909

Women with WSPU sashes and megaphone advertising their meetings, manuscript inscription on reverse identifies them as Mrs May, Miss Maud Joachim (glassbreaker), Miss Dallas (with megaphone) and Miss Kerr. (© LSE Women's Library Collection)

in Dundee when she interrupted a meeting held by Winston Churchill. After her release from prison in 1908, Maud published an article in *Votes for Women*:

> What one finds on joining the WSPU is, that one is brought into contact with a great number of people whose ideals are the same as one's own, and that the isolation and the reproach are things of the past.[10]

Maud went on hunger strike whilst in Maidstone prison and was forcibly fed. Zoe Proctor said that it was through meeting Maud that she became attached to the Chelsea branch of the WSPU. Zoe joined the Chelsea branch in 1911 and said about her experience:

> I found as hundreds of others had done already, that Mrs. Pankhurst's personality deepened our enthusiasm for the cause. She had a gracious presence, a beautiful voice and such dignity that it was easy to trust to her leadership. I do not think there was very much sentimentality among her followers, although, while we admired Christabel, we loved Mrs. Pankhurst.[11]

Also sharing her opinion on Mrs Emmeline Pankhurst was Kensington WSPU branch member Winfred Mayo. In an interview in 1958 she said of Mrs Pankhurst that she 'had a tremendous admiration and affection for her' and that 'she was personally an amenably loveable woman'. Winifred said that Mrs Pankhurst 'carried immense audiences with her' and that she'd 'heard her speak in the Albert Hall before the days of microphones and her voice carried to the farthest seat. She filled the Albert Hall.'[12]

Winifred Mayo, 33, broke two windows at 73–81 Regent Street, the property of Stewart Dawson and Co. She was the daughter of Alice Monck-Mason, also a March 1912 glassbreaker. Alice, 68, was also arrested on 1 March. She was charged with breaking windows at 205 Regent Street (Burgess & Dercy). Her sentence is unknown. Both mother and daughter were members of the Kensington WSPU and Winifred a founding member of the AFL.

Another mother and daughter duo involved in this mission was Jane Emily Duval, 48, and Norah Duval, 21. Both broke windows on 1 March but again not in the same location. Jane Emily was arrested in Regent Street, sentenced to six months' imprisonment and taken to Winson Green where she went on hunger strike and was forcibly fed. She was released at the beginning of July and taken to a nursing home. Norah smashed windows at the Strand offices of the London and North-Western Railway Company. She received a prison sentence of four months.

Kensington WSPU shop-front, Mary Sinclair standing outside shop with 'Victory Through Prison' poster together with children and other suffragettes, leaflets, flags and an image of Emmeline Pankhurst in the shop window. 1912 glassbreakers and mother and daughter duo, Alice Alice Monck-Mason and Winifred Monck-Mason Mayo were Kensington WSPU members. (© LSE Women's Library Collection)

'They snatched friendships as they rushed past on mad quests.'[13] Companionship and drawing on each other's similarities was an important part of surviving in prison and three women that achieved this were Janet Augusta Boyd, 61, Mary Ann Aldham, 54, and Gertrude Jessie Heward Wilkinson, 60. They were all grandmothers serving time together in Holloway. It is documented that on 10 June 1912 they sang together. As documented above, Janet was arrested with her cousin Florence Eliza Haig. Mary Ann Aldham, 54, sometimes used Mary Wood but gave her real name in the Great Militant Protest. She participated in the preliminary action, smashing windows at 163–165 Regent Street, the property of an International Fur Store and 167 Regent Street, the property of Isadore Goss. She was sentenced to six months' imprisonment and served it in Holloway. Gertrude Jessie Heward Wilkinson gave alias Jessie Howard when arrested on 4 March for smashing window at the Post Office, 30a Dover Street. Gertrude was in the Sheffield WSPU and from 1913 held position of Literature Secretary for the WFL. Gertrude went on hunger strike and was later photographed with glassbreaker sisters Edith Marian Begbie and Florence Macfarlane (see chapter eight).

Audrey Aimler, 28, was arrested at the same property as Gertrude but received a lesser sentence, two months' hard labour.

Kate Williams Evans, 45, from Wales was arrested with Scottish suffragettes so that part of her story is told in chapter five. Whilst in Holloway, Kate met Sarah Benett and an agreement was made that should Kate be released before Sarah then she could go to Sarah's Finchley house to recuperate. Kate stitched the following letter addressed to Sarah's maid, Jane, into her skirt hem:

Dear Jane

Miss Evans will be my guest till she is a little stronger - she has been starving so treat her as an invalid. Get her to stay in bed a make [fully] for her of vegetables, rice, fresh chicken and anything else she fancies. I know you will be just as careful of her as I should. She loves dogs and I dare say Garth will sit with her.

Yours truly, Sarah Benett[14]

Kate had written on the back of the letter:

Miss Benett wrote this in person when the hunger strike began in case I should be discharged suddenly before my time was up on account of my health. Instead of which she was sent out and I was left. I had it stitched in my skirt hem to give to her maid when I turned up suddenly from the sky as it were.[15]

Glass breaker Alice Green was Emily Wilding Davison's landlady.[16] On 4 June 1913, Emily 'left Alice's house, 133 Clapham Road, Lambeth and walked to Oval to catch a train to Victoria station, she told Alice what she was going to do. She pinned a purple, white and green flag inside her jacket and took her latch key, a small leather purse containing three shillings and eight half-penny stamps and a notebook. Another suffragette flag was tucked up her sleeve.'[17] In March 1912, Emily was already in Holloway serving a sentence for her part in an earlier mission. Alice Green, 40, was there for smashing windows at Nos. 236, 238 and 240 Oxford Street and Nos. 255 and 257 Regent Street with Eveleen Boyle Anna Arton, 24. Also charged with smashing a window at No. 240 Oxford Street was fellow glassbreaker Janie Terrero (her story is covered in chapter eight). 'Mr Saunders prosecuted for the Commissioner of Police, and Mr F. C. Bennett defended Mrs Arton. Both prisoners were committed to the Sessions. Mr. Bennett applied for bail on behalf of Mrs. Arton, saying that she was in a delicate state of health. The magistrate declined to grant bail.'[18] Alice refused to be bound over to keep the peace and said, 'Let me tell you what I have gone through lately on behalf of the cause. I have given up my home, my husband and my child, and I shall not go back until women get the vote.'[19]

There were some suffragette glassbreakers who formed lifelong relationships after meeting on this mission or in prison. Zoe Proctor described her first interaction with Dorothea Rock at Holloway prison in March 1912 in her autobiography:

> As I walked along the passage a girl ran out of her cell and thrust a bunch of primroses and violets into my hand saying "Wouldn't you like some flowers?" It was such a wonderful thing in that grim atmosphere that it seemed as though spring had burst into Holloway. It was a glad encounter leading to a friendship which was to last a lifetime.[20]

Zoe smashed windows on 1 March 1912. The Rock sisters, Madeleine, 27, and Dorothea, 30, a hospital nurse, together with Grace Chappelow, 28, and nurse Fanny Pease, 33, joined the mass orchestrated window smashing (4 March) and were charged with breaking windows at the Lord Mayor's residence and the Swordbearer's Office, Mansion House. Pease complained that they had been roughly arrested like pickpockets. Sir George Woodman said 'that they must go to prison for two months with hard labour'.[21]

Madeleine, Dorothea and Grace Chappelow lived in the county of Essex and were friends. Fanny Pease was a nurse like Dorothea which is likely how they connected.

Madeleine was a poet and whilst serving her time in Holloway wrote poetry that was included in the 'Holloway Jingles' booklet (see chapter five). Her poem was called *Before I came to Holloway* and describes the noise and constant routine of prison life.

It is believed that the poem entitled '*To D.R.*' was about Dorothea Rock. It was written by Joan Lavender Bailie Guthrie, known as Lavender, who used the alias name of Laura Grey. This was also Lavender's stage name as she was an actress. Lavender smashed a window at Garrard & Co., the jewellers, 178 Regent Street and was sentenced to six months in Holloway. She went on hunger strike, was forcibly fed and being very unwell, was released early. According to suffrage research expert Elizabeth Crawford, on 8 June 1914, Lavender was found unconscious in her flat at 111 Jermyn Street, having taken an overdose of a drug she had been using for the symptoms experienced since being forcibly fed, and had become addicted to. Lavender could not be revived. She was pregnant and had left a suicide note for her mother. As Elizabeth Crawford explains in her research, the Coroner cited her involvement with the suffragettes and 'temporary insanity' as the cause but in her suicide note Lavender had said that 'Of course the kindly Coroner will call it temporary insanity, but as a matter of fact I think this is about the sanest thing I have yet done. I am simply very, very tired of things in general.'[22] In May 1914 Mrs Guthrie had been concerned about her daughter and sent two doctors to visit Lavender. One was glassbreaker Dr Louisa Garrett Anderson. According to Elizabeth Crawford's work *Suffrage Stories – 'Laura Grey': Suffragettes, Sex, Poison And Suicide,* 'The doctors, however, had not found Lavender suffering from any delusions that warranted restraint.'[23]

There were other glassbreaker prisoners forming lifelong relationships after meeting in prison. For example, Constance Bryer with Olive Wharry. Constance, was the Honorary Secretary at the Islington North WSPU branch living at 49 Tufnell Park in London. She had broken a window at 189 Regent Street belonging to A.E. Hawley & Co., and a further window at 195–197 Regent Street, the property of Raoul Shoe Co. She received a sentence of four months and was sent to Birmingham where she served her time with Olive Wharry. Artist, Olive, 26, was an active militant suffragette who often used alias names (including Joyce Lock(e) and Phyllis North) although not at this protest. She was arrested with others for smashing ten windows at the property of Robinson and Cleaver, 156–170 Regent Street. Olive was also sent to Birmingham but with a longer sentence of six months. Constance was to become Olive's executor in later life and their hunger strike medals (both went on hunger strike in 1912) are now in a private collection.

Arrested with Olive in Regent Street were Isabella Potbury, 22, and Molly Ward, 22. Isabella was a student at the time but went on to be a portrait artist. She was sentenced to six months' in Holloway. Meanwhile, Molly was discharged at their first hearing. Also targeting the same property was Evelyn Hudleston. Evelyn received a six months' sentence and served it in Birmingham. It is believed that Evelyn had a relationship with glassbreaker Bertha Ryland. It is not known when this relationship started. Bertha (19 Hermitage Road, off Hagley Road, Birmingham) was the daughter of suffragette Mrs Alice Ryland. Mother and daughter had switched allegiance from the Birmingham Women's Suffrage Society to the WSPU in 1907. Bertha was a paid organiser for the WSPU Birmingham branch (97 John Bright Street, Birmingham). She smashed a window at 22 Bond Street, the property of Phillips Morris on 1 March and was sentenced to six months which she served in Birmingham.

Other WSPU Birmingham members arrested at this protest include Dorothy Elizabeth Evans, May Riches Jones, Evaline Hilda Burkitt and Adeline Redfern-Wilde. All suffragettes active in Birmingham identified at this protest took part in the preliminary action on 1 March 1912. Dorothy Elizabeth Evans, 23, was an organiser at the Birmingham WSPU. When she was arrested in New Bond Street and imprisoned in 1912, Miss Grew succeeded her. Dorothy went to Aylesbury prison and spent between March and July in the feeble-minded inebriate block having gone on hunger strike and been forcibly fed twice. May Riches Jones, 22, was also arrested in New Bond Street but for 'attempting to break a window'. She received a sentence of two months, went on hunger strike and was forcibly fed. Evaline Hilda Burkitt was also in New Bond Street and imprisoned in Holloway. She was released on medical grounds after hunger striking. Mrs Adeline Redfern-Wilde, 38, set up the Stoke-on-Trent WSPU but was also active in Birmingham. She was arrested for breaking windows in New Bond Street and said 'It was one more blow for freedom.'[24] Adeline had two sisters, Emily and Elizabeth and they were both also active WSPU members although not involved in this protest. An autograph book containing poems, quotations and signatures of many suffragettes, including some March 1912 glassbreakers was found. It is believed that its owner was one of the Redfern sisters. Evaline Hilda Burkitt's signature features in the book with two arrest dates, 1909 and 1912, under the following entry:

> She sits within a prison cell
> Despised and splendid, great, defamed
> Shame close about her and with all
> Shameless and unashamed.[25]

Helen Millar Craggs, 24, sometimes called herself Helen Millar but when arrested for her part in the Great Militant Protest gave her real name. She was arrested on 1 March but it is not known where. She was acquitted. Previously, Helen had worked as a paid WSPU organiser and met and campaigned with Kathleen Marie Anstice du Sautoy-Newby whilst working in north Devon. Helen became Mrs McCrombie when in 1914 she married Duncan Alexander McCrombie. She was widowed in 1936 and in 1957 she married Lord Pethick-Lawrence (his first wife, Emmeline had died in 1954).

Lettice Annie Floyd, 46, was arrested for smashing windows on 4 March 1912. She'd worked in Coventry as children's nurse, 'I was there some years, but as most of the cases seemed to be due to bad housing, bad feeding and immorality, it was not entirely satisfactory work and did not go to the root of the matter.'[26] She was arrested with her romantic partner Annie Williams, 52, (appointed WSPU organiser for Wales in 1912), and was carrying a leather flail which is now held in the Museum of London. Annie gave her sister WSPU member Edith William's address of Glanafon, Devoran, Cornwall. Edith was also a WSPU member but not involved in this protest. Another WSPU member and friend of Edith's was Anne Rachael Perks and she was also arrested at the Great Militant Protest.

Also travelling from Cornwall to participate was Constance I. Craig, 40. In 1910 it was reported that Constance had 'been putting copies of Votes for Women in the shelters, on the tables in the Public Library, and in station waiting rooms. Whenever she went for a ride on her bicycle, or on excursions she took a few copies with her and left them where she had lunch or tea, or gave them away as she passed through some little isolated village. She got to be known as "The Suffragette!"[27] Constance obviously progressed to London based militant action as in March 1912 she received a sentence of two months' hard labour for breaking windows. It may be that she travelled to the protest with Anne Rachel Perks.

Frances Mary (Fanny) Parker (alias Janet Arthur), 32, and Ethel Moorhead, 43, became lifelong friends, living together until Fanny died in 1924. Ethel described Fanny as 'small and looked innocent and disarming with her charming looks, brown eyes and silky hair. But she had an exquisite madness – daring, joyous,

Ethel Violet Baldock during the First World War. (© Ethel Baldock's family)

vivid, strategic.'[28] Fanny was described by fellow glassbreaker prisoner, Margaret Eleanor Thompson as 'A very determined personage and amusing too.'[29]

With so many existing and new connections and friendships surrounding the March 1912 glass breaking protest one pairing that continues to intrigue is Violet Ann Bland (Annie) and Ethel Violet Baldock. At the time of arrest, Annie was nearly 50, the owner of a boutique hotel although she started life in domestic service like Kent teenage maid, Ethel, 19. Annie was an experienced militant WSPU member with connections to many other similar women. Ethel had not been involved before and it has not been possible to discover any further connection details about how she became involved. She travelled from Tunbridge Wells in Kent to take part in the mission. The only other Tunbridge Wells based suffragette found to be involved in the Great Militant Protest was Olive Walton. In contrast to Ethel who was not previously involved in WSPU activity and certainly never previously arrested, Olive was well known to the authorities and had been arrested multiple times. It may have been that Ethel knew Olive. Ethel may have seen glassbreakers Kitty Marion and Alice Lilla Durham with Olive Walton in Tunbridge Wells in December 1911 and early 1912. Kitty spent Christmas 1911 with Lilla at her cottage in Hartfield, Sussex and whilst there went to Tunbridge Wells to sell *Votes for Women* and *The Suffragette* newspapers. Ethel may have been at the Tunbridge Wells meeting in February 1912 when anti-suffrage Mr Hobhouse spoke. It is unlikely that Ethel travelled with either Olive or Lilla to London as both participated in the 1 March 1912 preliminary action and Ethel in the 4 March 1912 orchestrated window breaking. The intrigue surrounding the story of the youngest March 1912 glassbreaker, 19-year-old teenager and first-time offender Ethel Violet Baldock therefore continues.

Additional Images

Left: Edith New and Mary Leigh released from prison where they had been on hunger strike each carrying a bunch of flowers, stepping down from a WSPU carriage for a reception and breakfast at the Queen's Hall London, 1908. (© LSE Women's Library Collection)

Below: Prisoners' breakfast for Mary Leigh and Edith New, 1908. (© LSE Women's Library Collection)

136

Group at Chelmsford by-election, 1908. Kern, Keegan, 'The General' Flora Drummond, Gye, Bray, Flatman, Joachim. Glassbreakers Constance Bray and Maud Joachim are in this group. (© LSE Women's Library Collection)

Janet Barrowman (glassbreaker), Helen Crawfurd (glassbreaker), I.H. McLellard, Hilda M. Monaghan, Mrs Billington-Greig and Miss Helen Tainsh. At a meeting of the 'Women of Westminster', in the women's conference club Glasgow, on the twenty-first anniversary of The Representation of the People (Equal Franchise) Act, 1928. (© LSE Women's Library Collection)

Unveiling of the bronze scroll memorial to suffragettes, Westminster, 14 July 1970, Lilian Lenton. (© LSE Women's Library Collection)

Letters from glassbreaker Frances McPhun to Miss Laura Underwood, the Glasgow WSPU Organising Secretary dated March 1912. These letters were smuggled out of Holloway prison. (© LSE Karen Keys, descendant of McPhun sisters)

Letters from glassbreaker Frances McPhun to Miss Laura Underwood, the Glasgow WSPU Organising Secretary dated March 1912. These letters were smuggled out of Holloway prison. (© Karen Keys, descendant of the McPhun sisters)

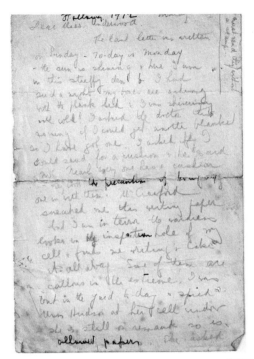

Letters from glassbreaker Frances
McPhun to Miss Laura Underwood, the
Glasgow WSPU Organising Secretary
dated March 1912. These letters were
smuggled out of Holloway prison.
(© Karen Keys, descendant of the
McPhun sisters)

Above left, above right and below: Frances McPhun's WSPU Hunger Strike medal. (© Karen Keys, descendant of the McPhun sisters)

Right and below: Margaret
McPhun's WSPU Hunger
Strike Medal. (© Karen Keys,
descendant of the McPhun
sisters)

PRESENTED TO

MARGARET McPHUN

BY THE WOMEN'S SOCIAL & POLITICAL UNION
IN RECOGNITION OF A GALLANT ACTION,
WHEREBY THROUGH ENDURANCE
TO THE LAST EXTREMITY
OF HUNGER AND HARDSHIP,
A GREAT PRINCIPLE OF POLITICAL JUSTICE
WAS VINDICATED.

Part Two

Glassbreakers. (© Jennifer Godfrey. Image created for author by Daniel Atkinson (Dan Rhys Design))

Chapter 11

Alias Names

'Both gave alias names, Hazel gave May Morrison as her name,
and, Helen gave Helen Collier because it was her maternal
grandmother's maiden name.'[1]

Those fighting for women's suffrage sometimes used an alias, pseudonym or false name. Some used it to protect their family name, others as a form of disguise and disruption to the authorities arresting and processing them.

Of the women arrested for their part in the Great Militant Protest, at least thirty-nine used false names at some point during their fight for votes for women. At least twenty-three gave an alias name when arrested for their part in the glass breaking in March 1912. The other thirteen used their real names when arrested in March 1912 but had used and/or went on to use an alias when arrested at other protests. For example, Mrs Emmeline Pankhurst travelled to France under the name of Mrs Richards when she went to see her daughter Christabel after her release from Holloway in June 1912. Another 1912 glassbreaker using an alias name was Emily Victoria Fussell, 28. In 1913, she wrote to US President Woodrow Wilson saying,

> I write to say how very much I appreciate the kind and just manner in which you have treated Mrs Pankhurst. England has indeed disgraced itself by its vindictive treatment to the best and finest women here.[2]

The stories of each of these glassbreakers has been included throughout the book but a full list of them and their alias names is included below.

Those women who used an alias when arrested at the Great Militant Protest in March 1912:

Real Name	Alias Used March 1912
Kathleen Bardsley	Kate Bard
Mrs E. Bodell	Miss Emma Bowen
Kate Cardo	Catherine Swaine
Joan Cather	Josephine Carter

Real Name	Alias Used March 1912
Helen Crawfurd	Helen Jack
Ethel Crawley	Mary Carlyn
Leila de Cadiz	Margaret (Maggie) Murphy
Rosalind de Cadiz	Jane Murphy
Katie Edith Gliddon	Catherine (or Katherine) Susan Gray
Helen Green	Helen Collier
Joan Lavender Bailie Guthrie	Laura Grey
Florence Hull	Mary Gray
Miss Rebecca Hyams	Janet Green
Hazel Inglis	May Morrison
Lily Delissa Joseph	Leah Joseph
Edith Ann Lees	Annie Baker
Lilian Ida Lenton	Ida Inkley
Leslie McMurdo	Leslie Lawless
Frances Mary McPhun	Fanny Campbell
Margaret McPhun	Margery Campbell
Miss Mabel Norton	Miss Mabel North
Agnes O'Kell	Oonah Caillagh
Frances Olive Outerbridge	Frances Williams
Ella Stevenson	Ethel Slade
Geraldine Stevenson	Grace Stuart
Gertrude Jessie Heward Wilkinson	Jessie Howard

Those women who used their real name when arrested at the Great Militant Protest in March 1912 but either had previously or went on to use an alias:

Real Name	Alias Sometimes Used
Mary Ann Aldham	Mary Wood
Evaline Hilda Burkitt	Byron
Eileen Casey	Eleanor Cleary; Irene Casey
Helen Craggs	Helen Millar
Emily Victoria Fussell	Georgina Lloyd
Edith Hudson	Mary Brown
Florence Macfarlane	Muriel Muir
Kitty Marion	Aunt Maggie

Real Name	Alias Sometimes Used
Ethel Agnes Mary Moorhead	Margaret Morrison; Edith Johnson; Mary Humphreys
Emmeline Pankhurst	Mrs Richards
Frances Mary (Fanny) Parker	Janet Arthur
Mary Ellen (Nellie) Taylor	Mary Wyan
Olive Wharry	Joyce Lock(e); Phyllis North

Chapter 12

Jujitsu and Security Team called 'The Bodyguard'

'It is the Japanese fine art of jujitsu or self-defence that has proved more than a match for mere brute force, and is, therefore, not only a good accomplishment, but a necessary safeguard for the woman who has to defend herself through life.'[1]

Some of the glassbreakers arrested in the March 1912 Great Militant Protest were trained in self-defence with six of them known to be part of a group of up to thirty women on a security team called '*The Bodyguard*'. This group, nicknamed *The Amazon* by the press, took on dangerous duties and could be called upon to act immediately to assist with protection and escapes. As revealed in a 1974 interview with suffragette and Bodyguard member Grace Roe, this was 'a special group, some older, some very young', selected for their 'courage and capacity to be able to act quickly' as they were 'called out at a moment's notice and couldn't tell anybody.'[2]

Edith Margaret Garrud (née Williams) (1872–1971) was a martial artist, playwright and suffrage campaigner, a member of the WFL. The first British female teacher of jujitsu, Edith and her husband, William, were first introduced to it in 1899. Images exist of staged jujitsu moves. These were included in magazines and sometimes used in suffrage theatre performances.

Edith, standing only 4ft 11 inches or 150cm tall, was responsible for training the members of the WSPU Bodyguard in jujitsu self-defence techniques. Putting this into perspective, Metropolitan police officers had to be at least 5ft 10 inches or 179cm at the time. 'As Edith demonstrated... jujitsu was based on the principle of using the enemy's weight and strength to one's own advantage and causing the assailant to submit by applying a lock so as to render it impossible for the opponent to move the locked limb without injuring themselves.'[3]

Edith also said about jujitsu:

> It is the Japanese fine art of jujitsu or self-defence that has proved more than a match for mere brute force, and is, therefore, not only a good accomplishment, but a necessary safeguard for the woman who has to defend herself through life.... physical force seems the only

Edith Garrud and a volunteer dressed as a policeman demonstrate a number of the positions Garrud teaches as an instructor. (© Mary Evans Picture Library)

thing in which women have not demonstrated their equality to men, and whilst we are waiting for the evolution which is slowly taking place and bringing about that equality, we might just as well take time by the forelock and use science, otherwise ju-jitsu.[4]

As with the *Daily Mail*'s previous coining of the term '*suffragette*', the press soon introduced the term '*suffrajitsu*'.

In 1914 the WSPU's annual report included reference to the Metropolitan Police Force's Special Branch and The Bodyguard:

> Police Methods. – The past year has seen an important and dangerous development of the Political Police force which was created by a Liberal Government in 1880, and has been by the present Government very much extended mainly for the purpose of dealing with the militant suffrage agitation. The Political Police force has lately been recruited by men of a low type, prepared as it would seem to put their hands to any scandalous method of coercion which the Government may prescribe. This force principally consists of plain clothes detectives who wear no mark of identification such as, for the protection of the public, is worn by the ordinary uniformed constable, and they are therefore able to commit unchecked, and do commit, serious acts of violence against Suffragists with whom they are deputed to deal.
>
> The Women's Bodyguard. – A women's bodyguard, destined it would seem to expand into a veritable army, has been formed in order to protect Suffragists in danger of arrest and torture. Before the year ended, the Bodyguard had achieved two conspicuous victories, and in both cases were successful in preventing the arrest of Mrs Pankhurst. An important characteristic of the Bodyguard is that it consists entirely of women and makes no appeal to the aid or protection of men. It is increasingly felt that the Government, so long as they see women relying, even where physical conflict is concerned, upon the aid of men, will not realise the true seriousness of the Women's Movement, and will continue to hope that they may subdue it by dint of terrorising or in some way buying off the men connected with the movement. Experience proves that Suffragists will, politically speaking, never stand on firm political ground, until they are able, whether on the platform or on the militant battlefield, to make themselves independent of the help of men. Apart from this, the fact that a Bodyguard consisting entirely of women can hold its own against the police is an education to women in general, and perhaps even more to men.[5]

At least six of the March 1912 glassbreakers were known to be members of this elite group, *The Bodyguard*, namely Mrs Kitty (Emily Katherine) Marshall, Ada Cecile Granville Wright, Mrs Helen Crawfurd (née Jack), Janie Allan, Barbara Franny Wylie and Leonora Cohen. There may have been others not yet identified.

Scottish March 1912 glassbreakers, Helen Crawfurd, Barbara Wylie and Janie Allan were members of The Bodyguard. Barbara was quoted during a tour of Canada in 1913 as saying: 'Abandon ladylike constitutional methods. Don't be docile, don't be ladylike. Don't dread being conspicuous. Now is the time for deeds, not words.'[6]

Preparations were made by The Bodyguard members prior to any mission. Suffragette Grace Roe spoke of them coming to her South Kensington flat, 'they

Barbara Wylie on a train, shaking hands with Mrs Emmeline Pankhurst, 1912. (© LSE Women's Library Collection)

all used to sit round and decide what to do,'[7] working out how they would get a suffragette out and away. Protection measures were taken for themselves too. For example, according to Bodyguard member Leonora Cohen, they put corrugated cardboard in their sleeves to stop people being able to pinch them[8].

On 9 March 1914, during the '*Battle of Glasgow*', Mrs Emmeline Pankhurst was at a public meeting in St Andrews Halls in Glasgow when the police attempted to arrest her. Helen Crawfurd attacked the police officers and was arrested herself. She was released later that night without charge. Barbara Wylie, a close friend and ally of Mrs Pankhurst, was also involved in the scuffle, and was injured as a result. Janie Allan 'went prepared with a pistol, a Scheintod, meaning apparent death. With her fingers around the distinctive motif on the grip cartouche, she fired two blank shots into the face of a constable. The idea was to scare and stall but not to injure the officer on duty. Although these "gas pistols", as they were sometimes known, were non-lethal, they were designed to project a type of pepper spray.'[9] Mrs Pankhurst was roughly and violently removed from the halls and because she refused to sit on a seat in the taxi, laid on the floor. Meanwhile back in the halls, Flora Drummond and Barbara Wylie tried to restore order.

Author Emelyne Godfrey gives 'an insight into the campaign for women's suffrage from both angles'[10] in her book, *Mrs Pankhurst's Bodyguard: On the Trail of 'Kitty' Marshall and the Met Police 'Cats'*. This book includes Kitty's eyewitness accounts, *Kitty's Suffragette Escapes and Adventures*,[11] and Detective Inspector Ralph Kitchener's autobiography, *Memoirs of an Old Detective*. 'During the course of her story, it becomes apparent that Kitty's role as a soldier within the elite Bodyguard accords her a unique place, not only in the story of the suffrage movement but within the history of martial arts, of women's empowerment and their emergence into male space.'[12]

Kitty Marshall was central to many protection and escape missions. One escape mission regarded as highly successful, involved Mrs Pankhurst and Hilda Brackenbury's home at 2 Campden Hill Square, London, nicknamed 'Mouse Castle'. Mrs Pankhurst was due to make a speech from Mouse Castle but the house had been placed under surveillance some days before. After she'd spoken, Mrs Pankhurst looked like she was leaving from the front of the building. However, Kitty had dressed suffragette Florence Evelyn Smith in Mrs Pankhurst's coat and hat. Mrs Pankhurst was dressed in a different hat and veil. Kitty then went with Florence dressed as Mrs Pankhurst out of the front door. Other members of The Bodyguard, including Sophia Duleep Singh and her friend and 1912 glassbreaker, Ada Cecile Granville Wright, were waiting. They formed a protective screen around Florence but were rushed resulting in Florence and Kitty falling and being crushed. Florence was arrested by the police and taken away to Notting Hill Police Station. There they realised that she was not Mrs Pankhurst. Meanwhile, Mrs Pankhurst was helped to escape into a car which took her to a safe house.

Kitty also led the escape of Mrs Pankhurst from 63 Glebe House, owned by Mr and Mrs Schutze. Again, Mrs Pankhurst spoke from their home which had a balcony and again the gathered crowd included numerous undercover police officers. The veiled Bodyguard once again formed a shield for Mrs Pankhurst as she was led out of the front of the house by Kitty. Mrs Pankhurst veiled, got into a waiting car and attempted to drive away. However, the crowd prevented a fast escape and men then managed to look into the car and see that it was not Mrs Pankhurst, but a decoy. The police remained at Glebe House and with no back exit, Mrs Pankhurst was trapped. Kitty returned home but received a call instructing her to collect four suffragette Bodyguard members and their Indian clubs and follow a blue car that would be waiting outside a Knightsbridge shop. The blue car led them to Glebe Place where they attacked the waiting police officers. Other Bodyguard members charged out of another taxi and the house itself. With this as a distraction, Mrs Pankhurst was able to escape and later accounted that:

> The police were between two fires. While the battle raged, I, with two others, dashed up the area steps and into the car. The big detective stood at the area door and was trying to block the car, and a girl engaged him single-handed with an Indian club; he had his umbrella, and she kept him off until I was away. All I regret is that I saw so little of the fight, being otherwise engaged myself.... As for our fighting women they are in great form and very proud of their exploits as you can imagine. The girl who had her head cut open and would not have it stitched as she wanted to keep the scar as big as possible. The real warrior spirit![13]

An active Bodyguard member, Grace Roe, said of her time in this special group that they were 'under terrific strain all the time' because they didn't 'know what's going to happen next.'[14]

Sometimes Bodyguard members out on licence under the Prisoners (Temporary Discharge for Ill-Health) Act 1913 (nicknamed the 'Cat and Mouse Act') were still required for protection duties. Grace Roe recounted:

'There was a time when a warrant was out for my arrest and Annie [Kenney] would want me close to her when she was going into a meeting.... The only thing that saved me was my hat!'[15]

Stories relating to the Cat and Mouse Act and how the WSPU responded to protect, hide and escape their members released on licence are covered in the next chapter.

Chapter 13

Suffragette Surveillance and Suffragette Safe Houses

*'My speciality was escapes that is escapes from the
houses to which I had been taken when released under this
Cat and Mouse Act.'*[1]

Researching the Great Militant Protest of March 1912 has drawn out numerous references to buildings that were safe havens for suffragettes and stories of police surveillance of suffragettes. This chapter provides a brief insight into the role played by such properties and their owners as well as the police surveillance implemented. Particular reference has been made to stories involving March 1912 glassbreakers.

The Special Branch of the Metropolitan Police force was augmented in 1909 to protect cabinet ministers from the suffragettes. This undercover police force were later tasked with taking photographs of suffragettes. Many were reportedly taken in the exercise yard of Holloway prison. However, it is known for example that the best photograph of Annie Kenney was taken as she left Maidstone prison in Kent under licence.[2] Photographs were used to identify militant suffragettes attempting to enter public buildings such as museums or art galleries. This followed a number of attacks on art and displays by suffragettes. An example was 1912 glassbreaker Mary Ann Aldham who in 1913 slashed a painting of Henry James in the Royal Academy. When arrested she gave her alias name, Mary Wood, saying 'I have tried to destroy a valuable picture because I wish to show the public that they have no security for their property nor for their art treasures until women are given the political freedom.'[3]

Mary Ann's name and photograph were included on the New Scotland Yard Criminal Record sheet dated 16 May 1914 alongside Ethel Cox which stated:

In continuation of the Memorandum of 24th April 1914, special attention is also drawn to the undermentioned SUFFRAGETTES who have committed damage to public art treasures or public offices, and who may at any time again endeavour to perpetrate similar outrages[4]

Front Hall

CRIMINAL RECORD OFFICE,

NEW SCOTLAND YARD, S.W.

16th May, 1914.

In continuation of the Memorandum of 24th April, 1914, special attention is also drawn to the undermentioned SUFFRAGETTES who have committed damage to public art treasures or public offices, and who may at any time again endeavour to perpetrate similar outrages.

MARY ALDHAM.

ETHEL COX.

OVER]

Mary A. Aldham and Ethel Cox by the Criminal Record Office, 1914. (© National Portrait Gallery)

Above and below: Surveillance photographs of militant suffragettes by the Criminal Record Office, 1914. (© National Portrait Gallery)

Below is the key to these numbered photographs:

Number	Name	March 1912 Glass Breaker
1	Margaret Gertrude Schencke (alias: Margaret Scott)	No
2	Olive Leared (née Hockin)	No
3	Margaret McFarlane	Yes[5]
4	Mary Ellen Taylor	Yes
5	Annie Bell	No
6	Jane Short	No
7	Gertrude Mary Ansell	No
8	Maud Mary Brindley	No
9	Verity Oates	No
10	Evelyn Manesta	No
11	Mary Raleigh Richardson	No
12	Lilian Lenton	Yes
13	Kitty Marion (Katherina Maria Schäfer)	Yes
14	Lillian Forrester	No
15	Miss Johansen	No
16	Clara Elizabeth Giveen	Yes
17	Jennie Baines	No
18	Miriam Pratt	No

Lillian Forrester and Evelyn Manesta refused to have their photographs taken whilst serving a prison sentence so the above photographs were taken without their knowledge or consent. Evelyn's photograph was altered to remove the arm of a police officer from around her neck. He was holding her still so that the photograph could be taken.

As part of their surveillance of suffragettes, police forces around the country watched houses and premises. For example, when a suffragette prisoner was released on licence under the Prisoners (Temporary Discharge for Ill-Health) Act 1913 (nicknamed the 'Cat and Mouse Act') the police would escort them to a house or premises and then have them watched around the clock. According to suffragette Grace Roe, 'detectives guarding safe houses were known to be sleepy in the early hours.'[6] This was clearly beneficial to the WSPU when they were helping their 'mice' members escape. However, they did not always choose the early hours for the escape to take place. Sometimes it worked best in broad daylight!

Illustrating this first-hand are the accounts given by March 1912 glassbreaker and active militant suffragette Lilian Lenton (alias Ida Inkley and Miss May Denis/ Dennis). She 'resolved to commit arson and, with Olive Wharry, who had the same idea, she embarked on a series of terrorist acts. She was arrested in February 1913, suspected of having set fire to the tea pavilion in Kew Gardens. After hunger striking for two days she was forcibly fed, and then quickly released from prison seriously ill, suffering from pleurisy after food had entered her lungs...She was sent, accompanied by a doctor, to friends at 34 Harrington Square. Once she had recovered she managed to evade recapture, although for some of the time the police certainly knew her whereabouts, until in June she was arrested in Doncaster and charged as "May Dennis", with being on the premises of "Westfield", an unoccupied house at Balby, which had been set on fire.'[7] Police records show that Lilian had been staying at the Doncaster home of suffragette Miss Violet Key-Jones (150 Osbourne Road). There were other suffragettes staying there and also at Doncaster's Albany Hotel. These were Mrs Annie Seymour Pearson, Miss Augusta Mary Ann Winship and Miss Kathleen Brown. Miss Violet Key-Jones was a founder organiser of the York WSPU. Mrs Annie Seymour Pearson lived in York and set up her own safe house there for suffragettes and supporters. Miss Augusta Mary Ann Winship (known as 'Tinie') was a servant from Scarborough and Miss Kathleen Brown was from Newcastle.

Having been arrested in Doncaster in June 1913, Lilian went on hunger strike. She was not forcibly fed but after several days released from Armley prison in Leeds. Lilian tells her account of events after this in a 1960 BBC interview. In this Lilian was referred to as the '*elusive Pimpernel*':

> My speciality was escapes that is escapes from the houses to which
> I had been taken when released under this Cat and Mouse Act. These
> houses were surrounded by detectives whose job it was to prevent
> my getting out before the day on which the police would have the
> right to come and take me back to prison. I haven't time to detail
> even one of them but I will give a kind of general idea of the sort
> of tricks that we played. The first one of any importance was I think
> when I was released from Armley Gaol in 1913. I was taken to the
> house of a local suffragette in Leeds.

She was discharged to the care of Mrs Rutter at 7 Westfield Terrace, Chapel Allerton[8]. Her husband was the prominent art critic Frank Rutter and in 1912 he was the Director of Leeds Art Gallery and a member of the MPU.

> When I arrived I found large numbers of detectives both at the front
> and at the back door – it was a terraced house – whose job it was as

I say not to let me get away. Nevertheless within a few hours I was out. The way we did it was that another girl named Elsie Duval came in the back door dressed as an errand boy carrying a heavy hamper and chewing an apple.[9] [Elsie Duval was] about 22 years of age and ....[had] been residing with the Rutters for the past ten months.[10]

She was the daughter of March 1912 glassbreaker Jane Emily Duval and sister to glassbreaker Norah. Her brother, Victor, was Honorary Organising Secretary for the MPU. As outlined in chapter one, if Elsie was at the March 1912 protest she evaded arrest.

The van driver, Harry Barker, 'identified a well known suffragette named Mrs Lucy J. Malcolm who [resided] at 12 Lodge View, New Wortley, Leeds, as the person who opened the back door at 7 Westfield Terrace when he arrived with his van and said "All right. It's here" and admitted Miss Duval into the house carrying the grocer's basket.'[11] Lilian then 'went out carrying that self-same hamper but now emptied and chewing the self-same apple.'[12] She escaped 'and the surrounding detectives that were watching never suspected anything.'[13] 'At about 8.30pm which would be about ten minutes after the van left the house, Acting Detective Inspector Dalton who was watching the front of 7 Westfield Terrace, saw Mrs Malcolm leave the house and board a tram car proceeding towards the city.'[14]

Lilian's escape from the Rutter's was not easy. Lilian explained that, 'a very elaborate escape scheme had been worked out but so many things went wrong at the beginning that the police were soon on my track and it was days before I was

Elsie Duval. (© LSE Women's Library Collection)

able to shake them off and finally reach safety in the house of some suffragettes near Edinburgh.'[15] It is understood that a friend of Lilian's called Miss Woods was also involved in her escape. Miss Woods had apparently arrived at 7 Westfield Terrace a few days before Lilian was released from prison and then left on the escape day. Charles Christopher Bell, 32, employed by Leeds based firm Messrs Roses, a retail provision merchant, was alleged to have organised the cab that took Lilian and another woman from Leeds to Harrogate. His brother was the manager at Roses and when questioned by the police, refused to say where Charles was.[16] Lilian was tracked to Harrogate, then to Scarborough and next 'a farm a few miles from the town'.[17] Leeds City Police noted that they knew Lilian then went to Scotland but had not ascertained her exact whereabouts. Dundee was one town she visited as was a house near Edinburgh.

From Scotland, Lilian travelled to Cardiff, Wales where she was nearly caught. Lilian escaped by disguising herself as an infirm old lady'.[18]

> Made up to resemble an aged woman, with a black shawl pinned tightly over her head, and attired almost in rags, she hobbled through the streets of Cardiff on Tuesday morning and took the train to London, her ticket being obtained for her by a trustworthy member of the Union, who accompanied her on the journey, but travelled in an adjoining compartment. The "old lady," of whom she had charge, travelled third class. Whether or not the disguise was changed on reaching London is not known, but it may have been taken for granted that no risks were run. The militant women are clever in the matter of makeup and with the resources at their command it would be comparatively easy for the fugitive to avoid suspicion and travel unnoticed by the boat train to Dover. Instead however, of crossing the Channel to Calais by steamer, Miss Lenton was conveyed some distance along the South Coast, and embarked upon one of those private yachts, which at this season are always to be seen in the Channel. Having got so far he disguise could now be thrown aside, and she reached the French shore in the evening.[19]

At this time the Criminal Record Office issued a 'wanted' photograph of her, (see image 12 in Criminal Record Office image earlier in this chapter) 'in which she looks very pretty, with her hair loose. She is described as 5' 2" with brown eyes and brown hair.'[20]

Wealthy supporters of the WSPU would lend suffragettes needing to escape 'rather fine grand clothes'[21] including cloaks and hats. The AFL were also known to help dress the suffragettes in disguises for missions. Grace Roe recounted her and glassbreaker Charlie Marsh being dressed as chorus girls for one secret mission,

'She was fair and she had a black wig. I had a red wig.'[22] March 1912 glassbreaker Winifred Mayo helped establish the AFL and as well as giving elocution lessons to WSPU speakers, advised suffragettes about make-up and costume so that they were better equipped to evade capture by the police.

It is not clear if Lilian Lenton and those that helped her escape received such support but Lilian was clearly a master of escape. She documented that 'on another occasion I came out of Holloway in London and went to the house of a suffragette in Barnes.'[23] It is believed that this was the time Lilian was released on licence for 5 days (on 15 October 1913) to Mrs Diplock at The Limes, Putney Park Avenue, London SW.[24] Lilian had been wanted since escaping to France in July 1913 and 're-arrested in October 1913, while reclaiming a bicycle from the left luggage office of Paddington Station. She went on hunger-and-thirst strike while on remand and was forcibly fed. Her condition caused some alarm and she was eventually released under the "Cat and Mouse" Act on 15 October, on licence for five days.'[25] Despite having abstained from food for nearly a week, Lilian's general condition was described by the prison doctor on 14 October 1913 as 'so far fairly satisfactory – she is cheerful – has a good colour and her voice is strong'.[26] Her release is documented by the prison staff and they stated 'the Police have been instructed to make every effort to keep her under their supervision, but that, judging from past experience, ... will be a difficult one.'[27] Lilian's explanation of this escape continued:

> This time I was out sooner than they expected me and no plans whatsoever had been thought out for my getaway and we really did not see how it was going to be possible for me to get away with all those detectives round the place until at last we decoyed them off by means of another girl pretending to be me who went away in an ambulance. When all was quiet and no police were in sight I made a sudden dash across the road in front of a rapidly approaching omnibus, swung round and sprang onto it. The two or three detectives who had been left behind hiding in the bushes dashed after me shouting but of course the bus did not stop. They had not slowed down for me and they had doubtless not heard the shouts.[28]

Lilian remained on the run until 22 December when she was 'arrested on a charge of setting fire to a house in Cheltenham. She was identified from police photographs, went on hunger-and-thirst strike, and was released at 11am on Christmas Day to the care of Mrs Impey, Cropthorne, Middletonhall Road, Kings Norton, Birmingham.'[29] Mrs Ethel Impey's maiden name was Adair-Roberts. Just 4ft 9in tall, she came from a family with strong pro-suffrage beliefs. Two of her sisters in particular, Muriel and Winifred, were involved in the WSPU. In her 1974 interview, Winifred recalled that her sister Ethel helped suffragettes hide and escape using her married home in Birmingham and that she 'was wonderful at hiding them and walking under the nose of the policemen.... When she'd bring out a suffragette.... Ethel would go down the street out from the front door and chat up the policemen at the corner... the suffragette and a friend ... went out of the back kitchen door... Ethel was wonderful... She loved fooling the police.'[30]

In her 1960 interview, Lilian Lenton continued: 'The Cheltenham police took me to the house and deposited me there and by a supreme bit of good luck there was a gap of a few minutes before the Birmingham police arrived. In that few minutes I was away and when they did come they surrounded the house watching for the mouse who had already escaped.'[31]

Lilian 'evaded the police until early May 1914 when she was re-arrested in Birkenhead.'[32] She was out for a walk 'dressed in a yellow jersey, a blue dress and brown stockings, and had a large broad-brimmed hat and a veil'[33]. She was recognised by a detective named Gordon Hughes, who went up to her and said, "Good afternoon, Miss Lenton."

> "I am not Miss Lenton," was the reply.
> "Oh, yes, you are," the officer replied. Miss Lilian then confessed to her identity.'[34]

'She was then remanded, to await trial ... [in] Leeds prison where she again went on hunger-and-thirst strike until she was released on 12 May. Lilian Lenton had not been recaptured by the time that the WSPU brought an end to militancy in August 1914.'[35]

There were many other safe houses, rest houses and nursing homes used by suffragette prisoners seeking refuge and recuperation. Some of these are detailed below.

Leonora Cohen and her husband, Henry established a vegetarian boarding house in Harrogate and used it to give refuge to suffragettes evading the police. It was called '*Pomona*' and was in Harlow Moor Drive. They advertised it in *The Suffragette* as 'Pomona, a Reform Food Establishment. Excellent catering by specialist in Reform diets. Late dinners. Separate Tables.'[36] Lilian Lenton was taken to this house from Armley gaol on another occasion. Lilian recounted that:

> We were told by the press that as the procession of police cars passed along with me in the middle one there was betting as to my chances of escaping again. At first odds were even as it were but when it was realised that I should be up against the very same police who had lost me the previous year they became 100 to 1 but I went the following day. The detectives surrounding the place not knowing

this continued to watch and in fact increased their precautions until the day before that on which I was due to return to prison. On the morning of that day they saw 50 heavily veiled women draw up at the front door and be admitted one by one when suddenly the door opened and all fifty rushed out and scattered in all directions. There were not 50 detectives at that front door. They took it for granted that I was one of them but they did not know which. There was simply confusion until all the women had disappeared and the detectives had returned dejectedly to their posts no doubt realising now that their time was being wasted. However they couldn't be sure. I might still be in the house. They didn't know.[37]

Leonora, 39, was a member of the elite Bodyguard, helping to protect the WSPU leaders (see chapter twelve). Elizabeth Crawford refers to Leonora, 39, being a March 1912 glassbreaker who evaded arrest.[38] According to Leonora in her 1974 interview[39] her husband Henry and son Reg had to put up with what others said about her beliefs and actions. Other men said if she were their wife, 'they'd tie her to a table leg'[40]. Young Reg was at college and during the time that Lilian Lenton was hiding at his home and he would be questioned by the detectives watching the house. They would ask how Lilian Lenton was and he would reply, 'not my business'. Then at school his headmaster would ask the same and he would say 'not my business nor yours.' According to Leonora in her interview, the Harrogate branch of the WSPU gave Reg a cricket bat (he was a keen cricketer) and called it 'the Lenton bat'. This was in recognition of his support of the cause.

As detailed in chapter eight, a property used as an office was 12 Dalmeny Avenue which overlooked Holloway prison. The house was rented by the WSPU for housing and interviewing suffragettes who had just left the prison.

Three houses with nicknames referring to mice were '*Mouse Castle*', '*Mouse Hole*' and a house for '*country mice*'. Believed to be the eldest March 1912 glassbreaker was Hilda Brackenbury, aged 79. Her home at 2 Campden Hill in London, W8 was nicknamed '*Mouse Castle*'. Suffragettes released from prison were welcomed there. Annie Kenney, who continued to lead the WSPU in 1912 whilst Mrs Emmeline Pankhurst was imprisoned, was taken there from Maidstone prison in 1913. Welsh suffragette Rachel Barrett, who in March 1912 helped continue to run the WSPU national campaign whilst the leaders and glassbreakers were imprisoned, had spent time at '*Mouse Castle*'. She was taken there in 1913 after being released from prison on licence. On one occasion she was smuggled out in disguise so she could speak at meetings, only to then be rearrested. Rachel then went to '*Mouse Hole*' in St John's Wood, owned by her friend Ida Wylie. Ida was an author and a member of the WSPU who provided a suffragette safe house. Mrs Emmeline Pankhurst had used it when hiding from the police. Rachel Barrett, using pseudonym Miss Ashworth, also spent time hiding from the police in Ida Wylie's Aunt Jane's Edinburgh home.

Elizabeth Robins who had attended the 1911 deputation to see Mr Asquith (see the introductory chapter) owned a farmhouse, Backsettown in Henfield, West Sussex. It was known amongst the WSPU members as for 'country mice' seeking to evade arrest or recover from hunger striking and forcible feeding. In March 1912 the police searched for Christabel Pankhurst there. It is believed however that Christabel was hiding in Wimbledon at Dorset Hall, the home of WSPU member Rose Lamartine Yates. She was reputedly disguised in a nurse's uniform supplied by the London Pembury Gardens nursing home (often frequented by recovering suffragette prisoners) and fled to France. It is known that Dorset Hall was used by suffragettes recovering from hunger strike with March 1912 glassbreakers Gertrude Wilkinson and sisters Edith Begbie and Florence Macfarlane going there.

Dorset Hall was home for one of the first suffragette prisoners to be forcibly fed (1909), Mary Leigh, for six months. It was also frequently visited by Emily Wilding Davison who spent the afternoon there visiting Rose and collecting some 'Votes for Women' flags the day before she went to the Epsom Derby, where she was fatally injured. Emily was already in Holloway prison when the March 1912 glassbreakers arrived. She was serving time for setting fire to pillar boxes in Westminster in

Suffragette garden party believed to be at Dorset Hall, belonging to Rose Lamartine Yates. (© LSE Women's Library Collection)

Above left: Mary Leigh, c.1910. (© LSE Women's Library Collection)

Above right: Emily Wilding Davison, c.1905. (© LSE Women's Library Collection)

December 1911.The last poem in 'Holloway Jingles' was 'L'Envoi' by Emily Wilding Davison. The poem is described as 'a rallying cry to the suffragettes to march "fearless through the darkness" as "the glorious dawn is breaking".[41] Emily Wilding Davison died in June 1913 after running in front of the King's horse at the Epsom Derby clutching a 'Votes for Women' rosette.

Like Mary Leigh, glassbreaker, Evaline Hilda Burkitt was one of the first suffragette prisoners to be forcibly fed in 1909. In 1913 after another period in prison, Evaline was released into the care of Mrs Whitehead at 297 Killinghall Road, Bradford.

A village in Surrey was described as 'rather a nest of suffragettes.'[42] In addition to their London home, known as '*Mouse Castle*', the Brackenbury family had a home in Peaslake, Surrey. This second home was called 'Brackenside' and was another known safe house for suffragette prisoners. In 1912 and according to one resident, Edwin Waterhouse, a founder member of the accountancy firm Price Waterhouse:

> .... there are fourteen ladies of very advanced views, among them Mrs Brackenbury and her two daughters, all of whom were convicted recently of breaking shop windows in London for the purposes of advertising themselves and their cause.[43]

Ethel Smyth's Surrey home, *Coign* (now renamed *Brettanby Cottage*), in Hook Heath, Woking had been the resting place for Mrs Emmeline Pankhurst in May 1913. She had been released on licence to recuperate following hunger striking.

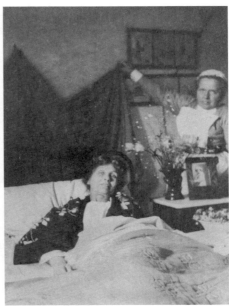

Above left: Dr Flora Murray. (© LSE Women's Library Collection)

Above right: Nurse Catherine Pine nursing Mrs Emmeline Pankhurst c.1913. (© LSE Women's Library Collection)

On 26 May 1913 she was rearrested at the garden gate of Smyth's home. With Mrs Emmeline Pankhurst was Ethel shielding her with an umbrella, Dr Flora Murray who always cared for her after periods of hunger strike and nurse Catherine Pine.

Also, in Surrey but this time the home of the Pethick-Lawrences, was *The Mascot*, now called the *Dutch House*, in South Holmwood, Dorking. This was where Lady Constance Lytton was shielded.

The nursing home at 9 Pembridge Gardens, Notting Hill was run by nurses Catherine Pine and Gertrude Townend. Both trained at St Bartholomew's Hospital and were also WSPU members. Nurse Townend had been 'injured in a tussle with police in 1913 at Bow Baths Hall'.[44] Nurse Pine did not take any militant action. She was known to always comply with the law and so whilst she would take care of suffragettes recuperating from hunger strike and forcible feeding, she would not help them hide or escape.[45] In 1913 Mrs Emmeline Pankhurst had been released from prison and she and other suffragettes went to Pembridge Gardens. There was significant police and press interest so Mrs Emmeline Pankhurst was cared for by nurse Pine in other safe houses in London and Surrey.[46]

Suffragette Ellen Pitfield, also a nurse, was taken to Pembridge Gardens in May 1912 after serving part of her six month sentence for setting fire to a basket containing shavings and smashing a window in a Post Office on 3 March. Ellen diagnosed with terminal cancer before her arrest, was nursed and cared for by Catherine Pine and Gertrude Townsend until her death in August 1912.

In 1913 and 1914, Detective Inspector Kitchener trailed March 1912 glassbreaker, Kitty Marion, who was a 'mouse' on the run. In January 1914 she travelled to Charing Cross station and was met by a WSPU member. Kitty Marion passed some information to this member before she was accosted by the police. She was taken to Holloway, went on hunger strike and was forcibly fed. When released under the Cat and Mouse Act again and still being trailed by the police, Kitty Marion was taken to safe house, Mouse Castle in Campden Hill Square where her escape was engineered. Whilst her friends shadow played her being tended to behind a closed curtain, Kitty was in fact helped out of the back of the house to a motorcycle. 'It was my first and only sidecar ride and with the excitement and romance of escaping the police once more, quite enjoyable despite my wretched weak physical condition and the miraculous avoidance of a collision.'[47] At the end of May 1914, Kitty, still a 'mouse', was taken to Paris. She was disguised in a dark wig and heavy veil and accompanied by Mary Leigh, Dr Violet Jones and glassbreaker Mrs Alice Green.

On 14 July 1913, glassbreaker Nellie Taylor travelled to her usual Monday WSPU meeting in the London Pavilion. There she was surprised to see Mrs Pankhurst and Annie Kenney who were out of Holloway on licence under the Cat and Mouse Act. 'When I left my children and started from home yesterday to attend the Meeting at the Pavilion I had not the slightest knowledge that Mrs Pankhurst would be present. In coming out I saw the Police all round and realised that she was to be arrested. I was so struck with the horror of the thought of such a magnificent woman being taken back to prison to be [locked up] under the Cat and Mouse Act that I tried by my presence to support her to her carriage.'[48]

Nellie was arrested but gave her alias name, Mary Wyan. The police officer arresting her, Metropolitan Police Constable Lee recorded that he was assisting 'plain clothes officers in trying to get a woman into a cab'.[49] This woman was Annie Kenney. Mrs Pankhurst was apparently left alone and escaped re-arrest. PC Lee claims that Mary Wyan 'pushed me with her hand to try and get me away. I then turned to disperse the crowd. She then got in front of me and pushed me again with her hand saying "I am one of the leaders. I won't go away". She then slapped me on the right side of the face. When I made my statement at the station she said "I must protest against that."'[50] Nellie denied hitting the officer, saying, 'I did not smack the Constable in the face. It would be beneath my dignity to do so to anyone.'[51] Nellie was sentenced to fourteen days' imprisonment and taken to Holloway where she was 'determined to protest in every possible way'[52] including smashing the windows of her cell and refusing both food and water. She was released on licence on 18 July and stayed with her sister, Dr Elizabeth Wilks, at 47 Upper Clapton Road, London. She voluntarily returned to Holloway a day late, on 25 July 1913, again went on hunger strike and was released under licence on 29 July with a date to return on 6 August. Nellie became very unwell and was taken to a nursing home in Campden Hill Terrace – near Kensington High Street. Reported in *The Suffragette* was the following account:

> Three or four wardresses dressed me. They took me in a taxi cab to the nursing home. One of the wardresses rang the bell and another pushed me out of the cab... I am very weak and have had nothing for four days and I sank to the pavement. Someone placed a chair for me by the gateway and left me.[53]

Nellie did not go inside but instead was taken to the workhouse and then prison again.

Another rest home available between 1908 and 1912 to suffragettes needing somewhere to rest and recuperate was the Blathwayt's family home, Eagle House, near Bath in Somerset. It was nicknamed 'Suffragette's Rest' and made available by owners, the Blathwayt family. Linley Blathwayt was born in 1839 and married Emily Marion. They had two children, Mary and William. When Linley retired from the British Indian Army he bought Eagle House which was large and set in four acres

Emmeline Pethick-Lawrence planting a tree, watched by Annie Kenney and Constance Lytton, 1909. (© LSE Women's Library Collection)

(From the right) Annie Kenney, Mary Blathwayt, Marion Wallace Dunlop and Florence Haig standing round a tree, Florence Haig (glassbreaker) holding a spade; Kitty and Jessie Kenney in the background (Jessie in a wheelchair). Jessie Kenney had recently had an operation at the Blathwayts' house. 11 Jun 1910. (© LSE Women's Library Collection)

Sisters Georgina and Marie Brackenbury planting a tree at Eagle House. (© LSE Women's Library Collection)

Georgina Brackenbury. (© LSE Women's Library Collection)

VOTES FOR WOMEN.

Miss ADELA PANKHURST,
Organiser, National Women's
Social and Political Union,
4, Clement's Inn, Strand, W.C.

Adela Pankhurst. (© LSE Women's Library Collection)

of land. Emily Marion and Mary Blathwayt were pro-women's suffrage and it was decided to open up the house to suffragette prisoners. Between 1910 and 1912, a commemorative orchard was created and sixty-eight ex-prisoners planted an evergreen or holly bush. These ex-prisoners included March 1912 glassbreakers, Mrs Emmeline Pankhurst, Georgina and Marie Brackenbury, Miss Ellen (Nellie) Crocker, Charlie Marsh, Maud Joachim, Vera Wentworth and Elsie Howey.

The Kent teenager glassbreaker, Ethel Violet Baldock's partner, Violet Ann Bland (Annie) had owned a fifteen-bedroom house in Henley Grove, Bristol. She ran it as a hotel and it was definitely open to WSPU visitors as her guests included Mary Blathwayt, Mary Phillips, Annie Kenney, Mary Sophia Allen and March 1912 glassbreakers Lettice Floyd, Elsie Howey and Vera Wentworth. It is known that in 1909 she had organised a fundraising reception there to honour suffragette hunger strikers Lillian Dove-Wilcox and Mary Allen.

When Adela Pankhurst needed a place to hide she used another suffragette's house. This was the home of Edith Key, Honorary Secretary and Organiser for Huddersfield WSPU. Edith was married to Frederick, a blind musician. Their home was above their music shop at 68 Regent Street, Huddersfield and reputedly served as the Huddersfield WSPU headquarters.

WSPU member Miss Winifred Adair-Roberts (nicknamed *Winks*) of Hampstead took hot meals, that she'd cooked at her Hampstead home, to Mrs Pankhurst when she was hiding in the Lincoln's Inn WSPU offices. According to reports relating to suffragette Rachel Barrett, there was a bedsit room in Lincoln's Inn that was used for recuperating released prisoners. In an interview, Winks said:

And then when Mrs Pankhurst came out of Holloway after being forcibly fed ... they took her to Lincoln Inn House in Kingsway and there were two policemen always at the door and – this whole building was offices and the WSPU had two rooms I think at the top and they got in Nurse Pine and Mrs Pankhurst was nursed back to health in the office of the WSPU – I don't know how they got her in there I've forgotten that but the difficulty was to feed her and I used to come from Hampstead to Kingsway with Mrs Pankhurst's hot dinner and in those days we didn't have handbags. We had ......
bags with run of string, like a hot water bottle cover more or less and I used to cover a hot dinner. She loved pigeons and cherries and peas in a thick gravy. I [would] carry a hot dish ... from Hampstead to Kingsway by tube...might have been bus... and I'd say good morning to the policemen at the door you see and they had not idea what I had in this bag. I would go up and they didn't know what office I went into you see.[54]

Disabled suffragette and March 1912 glassbreaker, Rosa May Billinghurst, lived in Lewisham and her home was reputedly a safe house. Rosa May had broken a window in Henrietta Street during the March 1912 protests. She 'refused to enter into recognisances and was sentenced to one month's imprisonment'[55]. Rosa

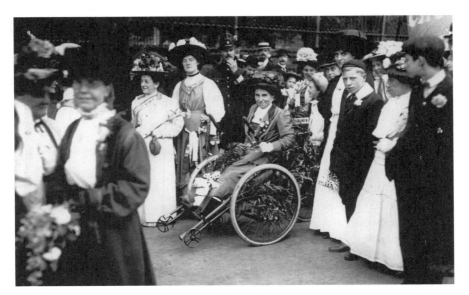

Rosa May Billinghurst. (© LSE Women's Library Collection)

Above: Rosa May Billinghurst being arrested. (© LSE Women's Library Collection)

Left: Rosa May Billinghurst. (© LSE Women's Library Collection)

May was an active, experienced suffragette who was wheelchair bound owing to paralysis caused by contracting polio as a child. She escaped on a WSPU tour to Kent in 1913 whilst a 'mouse' travelling with in a caravan.[56]

The Casey family offered their home up to suffragettes on the run. Isabella Casey and her daughter Eileen were March 1912 glassbreakers arrested with Olive Walton for breaking windows in Oxford Street. Isabella's husband, Dr Casey, was fully supportive of his family's involvement with the WSPU. In 1913, the police gained a warrant to enter Dr and Mrs Casey's home at 25 West Park Road, Kew searching for suffragettes (and 1912 glassbreakers) Kitty Marion and Clara Giveen.

They had been followed by a policeman on their mission to set fire to Hurst Park. Clara had asked Mrs Isabella Casey if she could stay over with a friend if they missed the last train. Isabella had not previously met Kitty but gave Clara a key. Isabella appeared as a witness to this case and was challenged over her decision to allow someone she had never met before come into her home. However, Isabella was adamant that as fellow suffrage campaigners they were both welcome.

Eileen Casey continued with militant action after the March 1912 glass-breaking. In Autumn 1913 she was imprisoned in Armley prison, went on hunger strike and was forcibly fed. Released on licence, Eileen went into the care of Mr and Mrs Bowers of Frizinghall, Bradford in West Yorkshire and escaped. She was on the run until spotted in June 1914 at her lodgings by a police officer from Bradford. He recognised her and surveillance began. She was arrested at a grandstand that had been erected in preparation for a Royal visit. In the suitcase she was carrying was found explosives, fuse, matches, firelighters, flash lamps, maps and suffragette literature.

Annex 1

List of March 1912 Glassbreakers

N.B. This list is in order of offence, location and surname. Where a glassbreaker damaged more than one property there is an entry for that glassbreaker for each location targeted.

Date of offence	Street name	Street Number	Name of Owner	Glass-breaker Surname	Glass-breaker First Name	Ailas used when arrested	Suffrage Society Branch	Travelled from	Glass-breaker(s) arrested with	Sentence	Prison
1-Mar-1912	Bond Street			Hutchinson	Anna Ada			Unknown. In 1913 she was in Nottingham		4 months	Aylesbury
1-Mar-1912	Brompton Road		Lazarus Phillips	Callender	Mary		Liverpool WSPU	Liverpool		Discharged	
1-Mar-1912	Charing Cross	62 - 65	Canadian Pacific Railway Company	Hicks	Amy Maud		Hampstead WSPU	Hampstead		4 months	Aylesbury

176

Date	Street	Number	Target	Surname	First name	WSPU role	Address/origin	Sentence	Prison
1-Mar-1912	Cockspur Street	15-16	Hamburg America Line	MacFarlane	Maggie/Margaret	In 1911 Secretary for WSPU Dundee and East Fife but by March 1912 had moved to London	Scottish but living in London by March 1912	4 months	Holloway
1-Mar-1912	Cockspur Street	17 and 19	Canadian National Railway	MacFarlane	Maggie/Margaret	In 1911 Secretary for WSPU Dundee and East Fife but by March 1912 had moved to London	Scottish but living in London by March 1912	4 months	Holloway
1-Mar-1912	Coventry Street	13	Straker Ltd	Forsyth	Lall		Unknown. In 1913 she was at: Cleveland Court Hotel, 17 Leinster Gardens, Lancaster Gate, London		
1-Mar-1912	Coventry Street	25	Messrs. Lockhart's restaurant	White	Florence			4 months	Aylesbury
1-Mar-1912	Coventry Street	10 - 11 - 12	Lambert and Co. Silversmiths, Jeweller and Antique Dealer	Haslam	Ethel	Ilford WSPU (Honorary Secretary)	Ilford, Essex	2 months hard labour	

Date of offence	Street name	Street Number	Name of Owner	Glass-breaker Surname	Glass-breaker First Name	Alias used when arrested	Suffrage Society Branch	Travelled from	Glass-breaker(s) arrested with	Sentence	Prison
1-Mar-1912	Downing Street	10	Official residence and office of the Prime Minister	Marshall	Emily Katherine Willoughby (Kitty)			York Street, Buckingham Gate, London	Mabel Tuke & Emmeline Pankhurst	2 months & 21 days	Holloway
1-Mar-1912	Downing Street	10	Official residence and office of the Prime Minister	Pankhurst	Emmeline		Leader of WSPU		Mabel Tuke. Kitty Marshall	2 months for glass breaking & 9 months for conspiracy to incite others	Holloway
1-Mar-1912	Downing Street	10	Official residence and office of the Prime Minister	Tuke	Mabel				Kitty Marshall & Emmeline Pankhurst	21 days. Also charged with conspiracy to incite others but dismissed from the case 4 April 1912.	Holloway
1-Mar-1912	Haymarket	4	Hill and Sons	Proctor	Zoe		Chelsea WSPU	Chester Terrace, Chelsea		6 weeks	Holloway
1-Mar-1912	Haymarket	11 - 12	Dewer and Sons	Branson	Grace						Aylesbury
1-Mar-1912	Haymarket	24	Randall Ltd	Branson	Grace						Aylesbury
1-Mar-1912	Haymarket	31	Burberry Ltd	Garrett	Eliza						

List of March 1912 Glassbreakers

Date	Place	No.	Target	Surname	First name	Role	Address	Name	Sentence	Prison
1-Mar-1912	Haymarket	54	Sinclair and Co., Photographic and Scientific Instrument Makers	Winter	Amy					
1-Mar-1912	Haymarket	55 - 56	Underwood and Farrant	Winter	Amy					
1-Mar-1912	Haymarket	60	H. Elkins	Jacob	Edith					
1-Mar-1912	Holles Street	18, 19, 20		Collier	Constance Louise	Hampstead WSPU	65 King Henry's Road, Hampstead	Margaret Eleanor Thompson	4 months	Holloway
1-Mar-1912	Holles Street	18; 19; 20		Thompson	Margaret Eleanor	Hampstead WSPU	Stanley Gardens, Hampstead	Constance Louise Collier	6 months	Holloway
1-Mar-1912	India Office		India Office	Marshall	Emily Katherine Willoughby (Kitty)			Mabel Tuke & Emmeline Pankhurst	2 sentences to run consecutively: 2 months & 21 days	Holloway
1-Mar-1912	India Office		India Office	Pankhurst	Emmeline	Leader of WSPU		Mabel Tuke. Kitty Marshall	2 months for glass breaking & 9 months for conspiracy to incite others	Holloway

Date of offence	Street name	Street Number	Name of Owner	Glass-breaker Surname	Glass-breaker First Name	Ailas used when arrested	Suffrage Society Branch	Travelled from	Glass-breaker(s) arrested with	Sentence	Prison
1-Mar-1912	India Office		India Office	Tuke	Mabel				Kitty Marshall & Emmeline Pankhurst	21 days.. Also charged with conspiracy to incite others but dismissed from the case 4 April 1912.	Holloway
1-Mar-1912	Kensington High Street		Barkers	Mitchell	Lilias		Aberdeen (organiser)			4 months	Holloway
1-Mar-1912	New Bond Street	1	Mr W Truefitt, hairdresser	Ward	Florence		Walsall WSPU (organiser from 1913)	Walsall		4 months	Birmingham
1-Mar-1912	New Bond Street	12	Muhlenkamp Bros.	Miles	Mary Louisa						
1-Mar-1912	New Bond Street	22	Phillips Morris and Co.	Ryland	Bertha		Birmingham & Midlands WSPU (paid organiser)			6 months	Birmingham
1-Mar-1912	New Bond Street	27	Richard Jules	Cardo	Kate	Catherine Swaine				4 months	Holloway
1-Mar-1912	New Bond Street	32	Jes. Marsus	Cardo	Kate	Catherine Swaine				Charge not proceeded with.	Charged for damaging 27 & 33 New Bond Street. Sentenced to serve in Holloway - see above & below.

List of March 1912 Glassbreakers

Date	Address	No.	Business	Surname	Forename		Organisation	City	Sentence	Prison
1-Mar-1912	New Bond Street	33	Alfred Clark	Cardo	Kate	Catherine Swaine			4 months	Holloway
1-Mar-1912	New Bond Street	47	Maison Pinett	Humphreys	Annie					Aylesbury
1-Mar-1912	New Bond Street	50	Chappell and Co.	Evans	Dorothy Elizabeth		Birmingham & Midlands WSPU (paid organiser)	Birmingham	4 months	Aylesbury
1-Mar-1912	New Bond Street	51	Whitehouse Linen Specialists	Humphreys	Annie					Aylesbury
1-Mar-1912	New Bond Street	53	Carlton White	Evans	Dorothy Elizabeth		Birmingham & Midlands WSPU (paid organiser)	Birmingham	4 months	Aylesbury
1-Mar-1912	New Bond Street	54	Rimell and Allsop	Evans	Dorothy Elizabeth		Birmingham & Midlands WSPU (paid organiser)	Birmingham	4 months	Aylesbury
1-Mar-1912	New Bond Street	90	Walpole Bros	Benson	Dorothea					
1-Mar-1912	New Bond Street	92	J.A. Cooling	Benson	Dorothea					
1-Mar-1912	New Bond Street	102	Long and Sons	Burkitt	Evaline Hilda		Birmingham & Midlands WSPU (paid organiser)	Birmingham	4 months	Holloway
1-Mar-1912	New Bond Street	103	Archibald Ramsden	Burkitt	Evaline Hilda		Birmingham & Midlands WSPU (paid organiser)	Birmingham	4 months	Holloway

Date of offence	Street name	Street Number	Name of Owner	Glass-breaker Surname	Glass-breaker First Name	Atlas used when arrested	Suffrage Society Branch	Travelled from	Glass-breaker(s) arrested with	Sentence	Prison
1-Mar-1912	New Bond Street	105	W. Coulsen and Son	Burkitt	Evaline Hilda		Birmingham & Midlands WSPU (paid organiser)	Birmingham		4 months	Holloway
1-Mar-1912	New Bond Street	107	London Soap and Candle Co.	Crees	Sarah						
1-Mar-1912	New Bond Street	126	Aerated Bread Co.	Humphreys	Annie						Aylesbury
1-Mar-1912	New Bond Street	129	London City and Midland Bank	Wilde	Adeline Redfern		Active in Birmingham - founding member in 1907. Founded Stoke-on-Trent WSPU in 1908.	Stoke-on-Trent		4 months	
1-Mar-1912	New Bond Street	130	National Linen Co.	Fern	Emily					4 months	Birmingham
1-Mar-1912	New Bond Street	133	F. Smythson Ltd	Fern	Emily					4 months	Birmingham
1-Mar-1912	New Bond Street	134	J. P. White	Fern	Emily					4 months	Birmingham
1-Mar-1912	New Bond Street	155	A. Tooth and Sons	Markwick	Charlotte Malcolm Lester					None as charge for no.155 discharged at 5 March hearing	

Date	Street	No.	Business	Surname	Forename					Sentence	Prison
1-Mar-1912	New Bond Street	158b	E.M. Hodgkins, Fine Art Dealer	Markwick	Charlotte Malcolm Lester					verdict of "not guilty" reached	
1-Mar-1912	New Bond Street	160	Hudson Brothers	Bodell	Mrs E	Miss Emma Bowen				4 months	Birmingham
1-Mar-1912	New Bond Street	165; 166; 167	Asprey and Co. Ltd	Hazel	Gladys Mary					2 months hard labour	Holloway
1-Mar-1912	New Bond Street			Jones	May Riches		Birmingham & Midlands WSPU	Birmingham		2 months	
1-Mar-1912	Old Bond Street	1	Scotts Ltd	O'Kell	Kathleen					4 months	Birmingham
1-Mar-1912	Old Bond Street	2	Klackners	Smith	Maud					4 months	Birmingham
1-Mar-1912	Old Bond Street	3 - 4	Hill Bros.	Haley	Margaret						Aylesbury
1-Mar-1912	Old Bond Street	6	Hummel & Co	Haley	Margaret						Aylesbury
1-Mar-1912	Old Bond Street	21	Duveen Brothers, Antique Dealers	Smith	Maud					4 months	Birmingham
1-Mar-1912	Old Bond Street	22	Messrs. Creighton / Crichton Brothers, Silversmiths	Smith	Maud					4 months	Birmingham
1-Mar-1912	Oxford Street	180		Wylie	Barbara Franny		Scotland	Scotland	Emma Wylie		

Date of offence	Street name	Street Number	Name of Owner	Glass-breaker Surname	Glass-breaker First Name	Alias used when arrested	Suffrage Society Branch	Travelled from	Glass-breaker(s) arrested with	Sentence	Prison
1-Mar-1912	Oxford Street	180		Wylie	Emma		Scotland	Scotland	Barbara Wylie		
Likely 1 March 1912	Oxford Street	236		Arton	Eveleen Boyle Anna			Kensington Gate	Alice Green		
Likely 1 March 1912	Oxford Street	236		Green	Alice			Lambeth, London	Eveleen. Arton	4 months	Holloway
Likely 1 March 1912	Oxford Street	238		Arton	Eveleen Boyle Anna			Kensington Gate	Alice Green		
Likely 1 March 1912	Oxford Street	238		Green	Alice			Lambeth, London	Eveleen Arton.	4 months	Holloway
Likely 1 March 1912	Oxford Street	240		Arton	Eveleen Boyle Anna			Kensington Gate	Arrested with Alice Green. Janie Terrero also broke window at no. 240.		
Likely 1 March 1912	Oxford Street	240		Green	Alice			Lambeth, London	Arrested with Eveleen Arton Janie Terrero also broke window at no. 240.	4 months	Holloway

List of March 1912 Glassbreakers

Date	Street	Number	Shop	Surname	First name	Branch	Place	Notes	Sentence	Prison
1-Mar-1912	Oxford Street	240; 242; 244; 246		Terrero	Janie	Pinner WSPU (Honorary Secretary)	Pinner, Middx	Alice Green and Eveleen Boyle Anna Arton also smashed window at no. 240	4 months	Holloway
1-Mar-1912	Oxford Street	251 - 253	Jays Ltd	Conway	Kate Cecilia					
1-Mar-1912	Oxford Street	264		Neave	Nellie				6 months	Maidstone
1-Mar-1912	Oxford Street	278		Collier	Constance Louise	Hampstead WSPU		Margaret Eleanor Thompson	4 months	Holloway
1-Mar-1912	Oxford Street	278		Thompson	Margaret Eleanor	Hampstead WSPU	Hampstead	Constance Louise Collier	6 months	Holloway
1-Mar-1912	Oxford Street	288		Collier	Constance Louise	Hampstead WSPU		Margaret Eleanor Thompson	4 months	Holloway
1-Mar-1912	Oxford Street	288		Thompson	Margaret Eleanor	Hampstead WSPU	Hampstead	Constance Louise Collier	6 months	Holloway
1-Mar-1912	Oxford Street	290	DH Evans	Boyd	Janet Augusta			Florence Eliza Haig	6 months	Holloway
1-Mar-1912	Oxford Street	290	DH Evans	Haig	Florence Eliza	Chelsea WSPU (Honorary Secretary)		Janet August Boyd	4 months	Holloway
1-Mar-1912	Oxford Street	320		Boyd Janet	Janet Augusta			Florence Eliza Haig	6 months	Holloway

Date of offence	Street name	Street Number	Name of Owner	Glass-breaker Surname	Glass-breaker First Name	Alias used when arrested	Suffrage Society Branch	Travelled from	Glass-breaker(s) arrested with	Sentence	Prison
1-Mar-1912	Oxford Street	320		Haig	Florence Eliza		Chelsea WSPU (Honorary Secretary)		Janet August Boyd	4 months	Holloway
1-Mar-1912	Oxford Street	334 - 348	Marshall & Snellgrove	Casey	Eileen Mary			25 West Park Road, Kew, London	Olive Walton	4 months	Holloway
1-Mar-1912	Oxford Street	334 - 348	Marshall & Snellgrove	Walton	Olive Grace		Tunbridge Wells (Honorary Secretary)	Tunbridge Wells, Kent	Eileen Casey	4 months	Aylesbury
1-Mar-1912	Oxford Street	351	Mr. Archibald White, brush manufacturer	Casey	Isabella			25 West Park Road, Kew, London		2 months hard labour	Holloway
1-Mar-1912	Piccadilly	9 - 13		Bowker	Dorothy Agnes		WSPU paid organiser: 1910-1912 Leicester; 1912 Hastings.		Edith Lane, Helen Creiggs	4 months	Aylesbury
1-Mar-1912	Piccadilly	9 - 13		Creiggs	Helen				Edith Lane, Dorothy Bowker		
1-Mar-1912	Piccadilly	9 - 13		Lane	Edith				Helen Creiggs, Dorothy Bowker		

List of March 1912 Glassbreakers

Date		No.	Business	Surname	Forename		Chelsea WSPU	Chelsea	Sentence	Prison
1-Mar-1912	Piccadilly	16	Drew & Co	Blacklock	Charlotte				4 months	Birmingham
1-Mar-1912	Piccadilly	38 - 39	Cook and Sons	Friedlander	Violet Helen				4 months	Birmingham
1-Mar-1912	Piccadilly	43	Messrs. Southern and Co. Booksellers	O'Kell	Agnes	Oonah Caillagh				Aylesbury
1-Mar-1912	Piccadilly	44 - 45	Thomas Wing	O'Kell	Agnes	Oonah Caillagh				
1-Mar-1912	Piccadilly	65 - 66	De Castro and Sons	Buckton	Agnes					Aylesbury
1-Mar-1912	Piccadilly	68	Randall Ltd	Farmer	Alice				1 month hard labour	Holloway
1-Mar-1912	Piccadilly	69	Boucheron and Co.	Stevenson	Geraldine Phyllis	Grace Stuart			4 months	Birmingham
1-Mar-1912	Piccadilly	157	Barret and Sons	Sheppard	Genie				6 months	Aylesbury
1-Mar-1912	Piccadilly	163	Messrs. Andre and Co. Hatters	Cowen	Molly				2 months hard labour	
1-Mar-1912	Piccadilly	163a	Messrs. Whitmore and Bailey, Cigar Merchants	Cowen	Molly					
1-Mar-1912	Piccadilly	198	Mr R. J. Dobbie	Ede	Frances					Aylesbury
1-Mar-1912	Piccadilly	200	Whitmore and Bailey	Ede	Frances					

Date of offence	Street name	Street Number	Name of Owner	Glass-breaker Surname	Glass-breaker First Name	Alias used when arrested	Suffrage Society Branch	Travelled from	Glass-breaker(s) arrested with	Sentence	Prison
1-Mar-1912	Piccadilly	210	Moreal Bros, Cobbett and Sons Ltd	Lane	Catherine						
1-Mar-1912	Piccadilly	227	Herman Appenrodt	Young	Elizabeth						
1-Mar-1912	Piccadilly	228 - 229	Manfield and Sons	Young	Elizabeth						
1-Mar-1912	Regent Street	3	Dorland Advertising Agency	Lackey	Norah Kathleen					4 months	
1-Mar-1912	Regent Street	21	Post Office	Hull	Florence Jessie	Mary Gray	Letchworth WSPU (Honorary Secretary)		Hazel Inglis	1 month hard labour	Holloway
1-Mar-1912	Regent Street	21	Post Office	Inglis	Hazel	May Morrison	Croydon WSPU		Florence Jessie Hull	Bound over to keep the peace for 12 months' Only served short time on remand	
1-Mar-1912	Regent Street	33 - 37	Drew & Sons	Leo	Rosa			Elgin Avenue, London			

List of March 1912 Glassbreakers

Date	Street	No.	Business	Surname	Forename(s)	WSPU notes	Address	Co-accused	Sentence	Prison
1-Mar-1912	Regent Street	39 - 55	Swan and Edgars	Bowker	Dorothy Agnes	WSPU paid organiser: 1910-1912 Leicester; 1912 Hastings.		Edith Lane, Helen Creiggs	4 months	Aylesbury
1-Mar-1912	Regent Street	39 - 55	Swan and Edgar	Creiggs	Helen			Edith Lane, Dorothy Bowker		
1-Mar-1912	Regent Street	39 - 55	Swan and Edgars	Lane	Edith			Helen Creiggs, Dorothy Bowker		
1-Mar-1912	Regent Street	59	Messrs. Skinner and Grant, Tailors	Gurney	Agnes Brita Lingen				6 months	Aylesbury
1-Mar-1912	Regent Street	63	Messrs. Gaffin and Co., monumental sculptors	Gurney	Agnes Brita Lingen				6 months	Aylesbury
1-Mar-1912	Regent Street	73 - 81	Stewart Dawson and Co.	Cook	Grace M.			Winifred Mayo	4 months	Birmingham
1-Mar-1912	Regent Street	73 - 81	Stewart Dawson and Co.	Mayo	Winifred Monck Mason	Kensington WSPU & founding member of AFL	Chelsea, London	Grace Cook		
1-Mar-1912	Regent Street	74	Callard and Co.	Joachim	Maud Amalia Fanny	Chelsea WSPU			6 months	Maidstone

Date of offence	Street name	Street Number	Name of Owner	Glass-breaker Surname	Glass-breaker First Name	Alias used when arrested	Suffrage Society Branch	Travelled from	Glass-breaker(s) arrested with	Sentence	Prison
1-Mar-1912	Regent Street	76 - 78	Packer and Co.	Fargus	Henrietta, Helen, Olivia Robarts						
1-Mar-1912	Regent Street	95a	Mable Todd & Co	Diederichs Duval	Jane Emily			Wandsworth, London		6 months	Birmingham
1-Mar-1912	Regent Street	97	Samuel Henson	Diederichs Duval	Jane Emily			Wandsworth, London		6 months	Birmingham
1-Mar-1912	Regent Street	100	Aquascutum Ltd	Jarvis	Kathleen					6 weeks hard labour.	
1-Mar-1912	Regent Street	103	Simpson and London	Benett	Sarah			Finchley Road, London		3 months. with hard labour	Holloway
1-Mar-1912	Regent Street	105	Sir John Bennett	Benett	Sarah			Finchley Road, London		3 months' with hard Labour	Holloway
1-Mar-1912	Regent Street	106 - 108	London Stereoscopic Company	Bray	Winifred Edith		Willesden and Kensal Rise WSPU	Willesden, London		4 months	Birmingham
1-Mar-1912	Regent Street	111	Johnson and Co.	Julian	Peggy					1 month hard labour	Holloway
1-Mar-1912	Regent Street	130	Carrington and Co.	Connor-Smith	Aileen					6 months	Aylesbury
1-Mar-1912	Regent Street	134	Jewellers and Silversmiths Association	Marion	Kitty (born Katherine Maria Schafer in Westphalia, Germany)					6 months	Birmingham

List of March 1912 Glassbreakers

Date	Street	No.	Premises	Surname	Forename			Sentence	Notes	Prison
1-Mar-1912	Regent Street	136	Sainsbury and Sons	Marion	Kitty (born Katherine Maria Schafer in Westphalia, Germany)			6 months		Birmingham
1-Mar-1912	Regent Street	149	Post Office	Freeth	Lilian				Margaret Wallace; Ena Shallard	
1-Mar-1912	Regent Street	149	Post Office	Shallard	Ena				Margaret Wallace; Lilian Freeth	
1-Mar-1912	Regent Street	149	Post Office	Wallace	Margaret				Ena Shallard; Lilian Freeth	
1-Mar-1912	Regent Street	155	Messrs. Hedges and Butler, wine merchants	Hyams	Rebecca	Janet Green		6 months		Birmingham
1-Mar-1912	Regent Street	156 - 170	Robinson and Cleaver Ltd	Hudleston	Evelyn		London	6 months	Not listed as arrested with Isabella Potbury, Molly Ward, Olive Wharry but targetted same building	Birmingham
1-Mar-1912	Regent Street	156 - 170	Robinson and Cleaver Ltd	Potbury	Isabella Claude			6 months	Molly Ward; Olive Wharry.	Holloway

Date of offence	Street name	Street Number	Name of Owner	Glass-breaker Surname	Glass-breaker First Name	Alias used when arrested	Suffrage Society Branch	Travelled from	Glass-breaker(s) arrested with	Sentence	Prison
1-Mar-1912	Regent Street	156 - 170	Robinson and Cleaver Ltd	Ward	Molly				Isabella Potbury; Olive Wharry.	Discharged	
1-Mar-1912	Regent Street	156 - 170	Robinson and Cleaver Ltd	Wharry	Olive				Isabella Potbury; Molly Ward.	6 months	Birmingham
1-Mar-1912	Regent Street	159 - 161	Messrs. Edwards and Sons, Jewellers	Hyams	Rebecca	Janet Green				6 months	Brimingham
1-Mar-1912	Regent Street	163 - 165	International Fur Stores	Aldham	Mary Ann					6 months	Holloway
1-Mar-1912	Regent Street	167	Isadore Goss	Aldham	Mary Ann					Discharged for the charge at this location.	Charged for damaging 163-165 Regent Street. Sentenced to serve in Holloway - see above.
1-Mar-1912	Regent Street	169	American Shoe Co.	Carwin	Sarah Jane			Tavistock Mansions, London		6 months	Birmingham
1-Mar-1912	Regent Street	173	Kodak Ltd	Carwin	Sarah Jane			Tavistock Mansions, London		6 months	Birmingham

Date	Street	Number	Shop/Company	Surname	First name	Organisation/Role	Address	Sentence	Prison
1-Mar-1912	Regent Street	175	Buttericks Publishing Co.	Carwin	Sarah Jane		Tavistock Mansions, London	6 months	Birmingham
1-Mar-1912	Regent Street	178	Garrads and Co. Jewellers	Guthrie	Joan Lavender Baillie	Laura Grey			
1-Mar-1912	Regent Street	179, 181, 183	J.C. Vickery	Carwin	Sarah Jane		Tavistock Mansions, London	6 months	Birmingham
1-Mar-1912	Regent Street	184 - 186	Brooks & Son	Wentworth	Vera (Born Jessie Spinks)	London and then worked in Bristol		6 months	Holloway
1-Mar-1912	Regent Street	189	A.E. Hawley & Company	Bryer	Constance	Islington North WSPU (Honorary Secretary)	49 Tufnell Park, London	4 months	Birmingham
1-Mar-1912	Regent Street	195 - 197	Raoul Shoe Company	Bryer	Constance	Islington North WSPU (Honorary Secretary)	49 Tufnell Park, London	4 months	Birmingham
1-Mar-1912	Regent Street	198	Burnett and Co.	Durham	Alice Lilla		Hartfield, East Sussex		
1-Mar-1912	Regent Street	201	Morney Frères	Ayrton-Gould	Barbara	WSPU paid organiser	London	Remanded. Then bound over to keep the peace	Holloway
1-Mar-1912	Regent Street	202	Hamley Bros. Ltd	MacRae	Helen		Edenbridge, Kent	4 months	Holloway
1-Mar-1912	Regent Street	205	Burgess and Dercy	Monck-Mason	Alice	Kensington WSPU			

Date of offence	Street name	Street Number	Name of Owner	Glass-breaker Surname	Glass-breaker First Name	Atlas used when arrested	Suffrage Society Branch	Travelled from	Glass-breaker(s) arrested with	Sentence	Prison
1-Mar-1912	Regent Street	206	Fuller Ltd	MacRae	Helen			Edenbridge, Kent		4 months	Holloway
1-Mar-1912	Regent Street	208	Liberty and Co. Ltd	Field	Louisa				Elsie Howey	4 months	Holloway
1-Mar-1912	Regent Street	208	Liberty and Co. Ltd	Howey	Rose Elsie Neville		WSPU paid organiser		Louisa Field	4 months	Aylesbury
1-Mar-1912	Regent Street	210	Maison Lewis	Field	Louisa				Elsie Howey	4 months	Holloway
1-Mar-1912	Regent Street	211	Messrs. Pound and Company, trunk makers	Outerbridge	Frances Olive	Frances Williams	Sydenham and Forest Hill WSPU	Bow, London		4 months	Holloway
1-Mar-1912	Regent Street	221	Tiffany and Co.	Downing	Caroline Lowder		Chelsea WSPU	Bow, London		4 months	Birmingham
1-Mar-1912	Regent Street	227	Elphinstone and Co.	Downing	Edith Elizabeth		Chelsea WSPU			6 months	Holloway
1-Mar-1912	Regent Street	227a	Gladwell and Co.	Downing	Edith Elizabeth		Chelsea WSPU			6 months	Holloway
1-Mar-1912	Regent Street	245 - 247	Jays Ltd, clothing shop	Aitken	Marion Violet		Editor of WSPU magazine *The Suffragette*		Clara Giveen.	4 months	Birmingham
1-Mar-1912	Regent Street	245 - 247	Jays Ltd, clothing shop	Giveen.	Clara Elizabeth			Unknown. In 1913 she was in Oxford	Violet Aitken	4 months	Birmingham

List of March 1912 Glassbreakers

Date	Street	Number	Establishment	Surname	First name		Address	Other name	Sentence		Prison
Likely 1 March 1912	Regent Street	255		Arton	Eveleen Boyle Anna		Kensington Gate	Alice Green			
Likely 1 March 1912	Regent Street	255		Green	Alice			Eveleen. Arton	4 months		Holloway
Likely 1 March 1912	Regent Street	257		Arton	Eveleen Boyle Anna		Kensington Gate	Alice Green	4 months		
Likely 1 March 1912	Regent Street	257		Green	Alice			Eveleen. Arton	4 months		Holloway
1-Mar-1912	Strand		Messrs. E.G. Reeve and Son, Tailors on the Strand	Adams	Martha A		Brecknock Road, Camden Road, N.W.		4 months		
1-Mar-1912	Strand		Messrs. Lyons restaurant	De Roxe	Mabel				4 months		
1-Mar-1912	Strand		Messrs. Bewlay and Co. tobacconists	De Roxe	Mabel						
1-Mar-1912	Strand		Messrs. Threshers and Glenny Outfitters	De Roxe	Mabel				4 months		
1-Mar-1912	Strand		Offices of London and North-Western Railway Company	Duval	Norah				4 months		

Date of offence	Street name	Street Number	Name of Owner	Glass-breaker Surname	Glass-breaker First Name	Alias used when arrested	Suffrage Society Branch	Travelled from	Glass-breaker(s) arrested with	Sentence	Prison
1-Mar-1912	Strand		Messrs. Downs and Co., outfitters, Strand	Green	Helen	Helen Collier	Croydon WSPU (Treasurer)	Croydon		Bound over to keep the peace for 12 months'. Only served short time on remand	
1-Mar-1912	Strand		Messrs. Samuel Smith & Sons (Limited), Tailors.	Lambert	Clara			Unknown. In 1913 she was in Catford, Lewisham		4 months	
1-Mar-1912	Strand		Mr C.B. Vaughan, pawnbroker	Marsh	Charlotte Augusta Leopoldine		Nottingham WSPU (paid organiser)	Unknown. In 1913 she was in Nottingham	Ada Cecile Granville Wright	6 months	Aylesbury
1-Mar-1912	Strand		Mr C.B. Vaughan, pawnbroker (believed Ada was arrested at same location as Charlotte Marsh)	Wright	Ada Cecile Granville			Westminster Mansions, London	Charlotte Augusta Leopoldine Marsh	6 months	Aylesbury
1-Mar-1912	Strand		West Strand Telegraph Office	Singer	Alice		Hampstead WSPU	18 Reynolds Close, Golders Green		Bound over to keep the peace for 12 months'. Only served short time on remand	

List of March 1912 Glassbreakers

Date	Location	Target	Surname	First Name		Address	Sentence	Prison
1-Mar-1912	Strand	Messrs. Morgan and Ball	Young	Cecilia			4 months (was arrested for damage to other premises (address unknown) but charges dropped)	Birmingham
1-Mar-1912	Strand		Begbie	Edith Marian	Wimbledon WSPU	107 Ridgeway, Wimbledon	4 months	
1-Mar-1912	Villiers Street (next to Strand)	Messrs. William Clowes and Sons Limited Printers	Stacey	Edith			4 months	
1-Mar-1912	Unknown	Southern Pacific Railway Company	Stacey	Edith			4 months	
1-Mar-1912	Whitehall	United Services Institution	Brackenbury	Hilda		2 Campden Hill Square, London W.	Offered choice of paying fine & being bound over to keep the peace for 12 months or 14 days imprisonment Chose 14 days.	Holloway

Date of offence	Street name	Street Number	Name of Owner	Glass-breaker Surname	Glass-breaker First Name	Alias used when arrested	Suffrage Society Branch	Travelled from	Glass-breaker(s) arrested with	Sentence	Prison
1-Mar-1912	Unknown			Adamson	Kate					Offered choice of paying fine & being bound over to keep the peace for 12 months or 14 days imprisonment Chose 14 days.	
1-Mar-1912	Unknown			Bartlett	Elsie					1 month	Holloway
1-Mar-1912	Unknown			Cairns	Ida					6 weeks	
1-Mar-1912	Unknown			Craggs	Helen Millar		Organiser in London			Acquitted	
1-Mar-1912	Unknown			Edwards	Blanche					2 months	Holloway
1-Mar-1912	Unknown			Fernie	Emily						
1-Mar-1912	Unknown			Franklin	Florence					Offered choice of paying fine & being bound over to keep the peace for 12 months or 14 days imprisonment Chose 14 days.	

List of March 1912 Glassbreakers

Date		Surname	First Name		Branch	Location	Sentence	Prison
1-Mar-1912	Unknown	Fussell	Emily Victoria			Unknown. In 1913 she was in Newcastle-Upon-Tyne	6 months	Aylesbury
1-Mar-1912	Unknown	Gargett	Laura Amelia Allan		Possibly Palmers Green WSPU, North London	Palmers Green, North London	2 months	Holloway
1-Mar-1912	Unknown	Gibb	Ellison			Glasgow	6 months	Aylesbury
1-Mar-1912	Unknown	Gould	Elizabeth Finlayson					
1-Mar-1912	Unknown	Hall	Jeannie				Offered choice of paying fine & being bound over to keep the peace for 12 months or 14 days imprisonment Chose 14 days.	
1-Mar-1912	Unknown	Hicks	Lilian Martha		Hampstead WSPU	Hampstead		
1-Mar-1912	Unknown	Joseph	Lily Delissa	Leah Joseph			1 month	Holloway
1-Mar-1912	Unknown	Kelly	Agnes A.		Palmers Green WSPU (organiser)		4 months	

Date of offence	Street name	Street Number	Name of Owner	Glass-breaker Surname	Glass-breaker First Name	Alias used when arrested	Suffrage Society Branch	Travelled from	Glass-breaker(s) arrested with	Sentence	Prison
1-Mar-1912	Unknown			Kelly	Kathleen					4 months	
1-Mar-1912	Unknown			Martin	Mary Sophia					1 month	Holloway
1-Mar-1912	Unknown			McCarthy	Adelaide					Discharged	
1-Mar-1912	Unknown			McKenzie	Lizzie		Lewisham WSPU (Honorary Secretary)	Baring Road, Lewisham, London		2 months	Holloway
1-Mar-1912	Unknown			Medd-Hall	Leonie						
1-Mar-1912	Unknown			Morris	Lily					2 months hard labour	Holloway
1-Mar-1912	Unknown			Parker	Frances Mary (Fanny)		West of Scotland WSPU (organiser)	Scotland		4 months	Holloway
1-Mar-1912	Unknown			Pascoe	Jane					1 month	Holloway
1-Mar-1912	Unknown			Shipley	Alice Maud		Edinburgh WSPU	Edinburgh		4 months (refused to be bound over to keep the peace)	Holloway
1-Mar-1912	Unknown			Startup	Dorothy Wonfor			Dorset Square, Mayfair, London		Discharged due to insufficient evidence	

1-Mar-1912	Unknown		Stevenson	Ella	Ethel Slade					
1-Mar-1912	Unknown		Wallis	Margaret						
1-Mar-1912	Unknown		Wharton	Dorothy					1 month	Holloway
1-Mar-1912	Unknown		Wilson	Amy						
1-Mar-1912	Unknown		Wilson	Joan					Offered choice of paying fine & being bound over to keep the peace for 12 months or 14 days imprisonment Chose 14 days.	
1-Mar-1912	Unknown		Wilson	Margaret					14 days	
1-Mar-1912	Unknown		Woodburn	Amy			West Hampstead			
3-Mar-1912	Roman bath Street, Newgate Street	Post Office	Pitfield	Ellen			Skove House, Harkwell Heath, Buckingham-shire		6 months	Holloway
4-Mar-1912	Baker Street	Post Office	Bennett	Blanche		Irish Women's Suffrage Society	Belfast	Mary Nesbit	2 months hard labour	Holloway

Date of offence	Street name	Street Number	Name of Owner	Glass-breaker Surname	Glass-breaker First Name	Alias used when arrested	Suffrage Society Branch	Travelled from	Glass-breaker(s) arrested with	Sentence	Prison
4-Mar-1912	Baker Street		Post Office	Nesbit	Mary			Hyde Park Mansions	Blanche Bennett	2 monhs hard labour	Holloway
4-Mar-1912	Berkeley Square	14	Home of Right Honourable L. Harcourt M.P.	Lowy	Henrietta				Vera Swann Note: Ethel Smyth attacked same building.	Offered choice of fine and bound over to keep the peace for 12 months or 1 month. Not known which she chose.	
4-Mar-1912	Berkeley Square	14	Right Honourable L. Harcourt, M.P.	Smyth	Dame Ethel Mary				Note: Henrietta Lowy; Vera Swann attacked same building	2 months hard labour	Holloway
4-Mar-1912	Berkeley Square	14	Right Honourable L. Harcourt, M.P.	Swann	Vera				Henrietta Lowy. Note: Ethel Smyth attacked same building.	Offered choice of fine and bound over to keep the peace for 12 months or 1 month. Not known which she chose.	

List of March 1912 Glassbreakers

Likely to be 4-Mar-1912	Bow Street		Bow Street Police Station	Brackenbury	Georgina Agnes		2 Campden Hill Square, London		Offered choice of fine and bound over to keep the peace for 12 months or 1 month. Not known which she chose.	
4-Mar-1912	Brompton Road	47, 49, 90, 92 & 112		Heliss	Mary	Liverpool WSPU	Liverpool	Helena de Reya	Discharged	
4-Mar-1912	Brompton Road	87 - 135	Harrods	Abraham	Dorothy Foster	Liverpool WSPU	Liverpool.		Released on grounds of insufficient evidence.	
4-Mar-1912	Brompton Road	87 - 135	Harrods	Ker	Dr Alice Jane Shannon Stewart	Liverpool WSPU	Birkenhead		3 months	Holloway
4-Mar-1912	Church Place, Piccadilly		Post Office	Harvey	Violet			Mary Hewitt		
4-Mar-1912	Church Place, Piccadilly		Post Office	Hewitt	Mary Graily			Violet Harvey	4 months	Holloway
4-Mar-1912	Dover Street	30a	Post Office	Aimler	Audrey			Gertrude Wilkinson - not sure if arrested with but did break window in same property as Gertrude Wilkinson	2 months hard labour	Holloway

Date of offence	Street name	Street Number	Name of Owner	Glass-breaker Surname	Glass-breaker First Name	Alias used when arrested	Suffrage Society Branch	Travelled from	Glass-breaker(s) arrested with	Sentence	Prison
4-Mar-1912	Dover Street	30a	Post Office	Wilkinson	Gertrude Jessie Heward	Jessie Howard	Sheffield WSPU & in 1913 became Literature Secretary for WFL.		Audrey Aimler - not sure if arrested with but did break window in same property as Audrey Aimler	4 months	Holloway
4-Mar-1912	Edgware Road	36	Messrs. Cozen's Shop	Rowlett	Margaret			Finchley Road		6 months	Holloway
4-Mar-1912	Edgware Road	74	Post Office	Beach	Ivy Constance			Brighton	Mabel Norton; Catherine Green; Marie Brown		
4-Mar-1912	Edgware Road	74	Post Office	Brown	Marie			Brighton	Mabel Norton; Ivy Constance Beach; Catherine Green		
4-Mar-1912	Edgware Road	74	Post Office	Green	Catherine			Reading	Mabel Norton; Ivy Constance Beach; Marie Brown		

List of March 1912 Glassbreakers

Date	Street	No.	Court	Surname	First name			Address	Notes	Sentence	Prison
4-Mar-1912	Edgware Road	74	Post Office	Norton	Mabel	Mabel North		Gave address as WSPU Headquarters at Clement's Inn	Ivy Constance Beach; Catherine Green; Marie Brown		
4-Mar-1912	Great Marlborough Street		Marlborough Street Court and Police Station	Fontaine	Olive M		Newport, Wales briefly Co-Secretary with Margaret Mackworth	Newport, Wales	Broke windows at same location as Mary Fraser and Evelyn Scott.	1 month hard labour	Holloway
4-Mar-1912	Great Marlborough Street		Marlborough Street Court and Police Station	Fraser	Mary				Arrested with Evelyn Scott. Also in same location was Olive Fontaine	Offered choice of paying fine & being bound over to keep the peace for 12 months or 1 month hard labour. Chose 1 month hard labour.	Holloway
4-Mar-1912	Great Marlborough Street		Marlborough Street Court and Police Station	Scott	Evelyn				Arrested with Mary Fraser. Also in same location was Olive Fontaine	Offered choice of fine and bound over to keep the peace for 12 months or 1 month hard labour. Not known which she chose.	

Date of offence	Street name	Street Number	Name of Owner	Glass-breaker Surname	Glass-breaker First Name	Atlas used when arrested	Suffrage Society Branch	Travelled from	Glass-breaker(s) arrested with	Sentence	Prison
Likely 4-Mar-1912	Buckingham Palace Road		Gorringer department store	Cheffins	Georgina Fanny			Hythe, Kent		4 months	Holloway
Likely 4 March 1912	Hertford Street	8	Mr Pease M.P., President of Board of Education	Crawfurd	Helen	Helen Jack		Glasgow	Glasgow	1 month	
4-Mar-1912	Home Office		Home Office	Brown	Jeanie					1 month hard labour	Holloway
4-Mar-1912	Home Office		Home Office	Du Sautoy-Newby	Kathleen Marie Anstice		Ilfracombe WSPU	Ilfracombe, Devon		two months hard labour	Holloway
4-Mar-1912	Home Office		Home Office	Harrison	Marie					2 months hard labour	Holloway
4-Mar-1912	Home Office		Home Office	Morris	Caroline					2 months hard labour	Holloway
4-Mar-1912	Home Office		Home Office	Rix	Winefride Mary			Tonbridge, Kent		2 months hard labour	Holloway
4-Mar-1912	Kensington High Street	19	Messrs Yeats and Company	Moorhead	Ethel Agnes Mary			Dundee		Case dismissed	
4-Mar-1912	Kensington High Street	Various shops		Allan	Janie			44 Prestwick, Ayrshire		4 months	Holloway
4-Mar-1912	Kensington High Street		Messrs Sanders and Company Jewellers	MacFarlane	Florence Geraldine			Dundee	61 Nethergate, Dundee	4 months	Aylesbury

List of March 1912 Glassbreakers

4-Mar-1912	Kensington High Street		Thomas Cook & Sons	Moorhead	Ethel Agnes Mary		Dundee		Case dropped	
4-Mar-1912	Knightsbridge	109 to 125	Harvey Nichols	De Reya	Helena	Liverpool WSPU	Liverpool	Helena de Reya	3 months	
4-Mar-1912	Knightsbridge	109 to 125	Harvey Nichols	Heliss	Mary	Liverpool WSPU	Liverpool	Mary Heliss	Discharged	
4-Mar-1912	Mansion House		Lord Mayor's residence	Chappelow	Grace	Essex	Hatfield Peverel, Essex	Grace Chappelow	2 months hard labour	
4-Mar-1912	Mansion House		Lord Mayor's residence	Rock	Dorothea		Ingatestone, Essex	Dorothea Rock	2 months hard labour	Holloway
4-Mar-1912	Mansion House		Swordbearer's office	Pease	Fanny			Fanny Pease	2 months hard labour	
4-Mar-1912	Mansion House		Swordbearer's office	Rock	Madeline			Madeline Rock	2 months hard labour	Holloway
4-Mar-1912	Northumberland Avenue	1	Commercial Cable Company	Baldock	Ethel Violet		Tunbridge Wells, Kent	Ethel Violet Baldock	Fined and bound over to keep the peace for 12 months	
4-Mar-1912	Northumberland Avenue	1	Commercial Cable Company	Bland	Violet Ann (Annie)			Violet Bland	4 months	Aylesbury
4-Mar-1912	Oxford Street	70	Post Office	Inglis	Isabel			Arrested with Lilian Lenton. Mary Selkirk and Edith Prier also there as pair.	2 months	Holloway

Date of offence	Street name	Street Number	Name of Owner	Glass-breaker Surname	Glass-breaker First Name	Alias used when arrested	Suffrage Society Branch	Travelled from	Glass-breaker(s) arrested with	Sentence	Prison
4-Mar-1912	Oxford Street	70	Post Office	Lenton	Lilian Ida	Ida Inkley			Arrested with Isabel Ingliss. Mary Selkirk and Edith Prier also there as pair.	2 months	Holloway
4-Mar-1912	Oxford Street	70	Post Office	Prier	Edith				Arrested with Mary Selkirk. Lilian Lenton and Isabel Inglis also there as a pair.	2 months	
4-Mar-1912	Oxford Strret	70	Post Office	Selkirk	Mary				Arrested with Edith Prier. Lilian Lenton and Isabel Inglis also there as a pair.	2 months	
Likely 4-Mar 1912	Palace Yard			Brackenbury	Marie Venetia Caroline			2 Campden Hill Square, London W.		Offered choice of paying fine & being bound over to keep the peace for 12 months or 14 day. Chose 14 days.	Holloway

List of March 1912 Glassbreakers

Date	Location	No.	Property	Surname	Forename	Branch	Address	Associated names	Sentence	Prison
4-Mar-1912	Palace Yard			Clarence	Edith	Axminster branch (Honorary Secretary from 1910)	Coaxdon Hall, Axminster, Devon		Offered choice of fine and bound over to keep the peace for 12 months or 1 month. Not known which she chose.	
4-Mar-1912	Rutland Gate	46	House of General Robb	Thomas	Ellen		Gave address as WSPU Headquarters at Clement's Inn		6 weeks hard labour	Holloway
4-Mar-1912	Rutland Gate	47	House of Mr George P. Fuller	Garrett-Anderson	Louisa		Harley Street		6 weeks with hard labour	Holloway
4-Mar-1912	Sloane Square		Post Office	Crocker	Ellen (Nellie)	Nottingham WSPU	Nottingham	Gladys Roberts and Mrs Mary Ellen Taylor	Served 1 month on remand after magistrate refused bail. Then on 28 March 1912 sentenced to 3 months.	Holloway
4-Mar-1912	Sloane Square		Post Office	Taylor	Mary Ellen (Nellie)	Nottingham WSPU	Nottingham	Gladys Roberts and Miss Nellie Crocker	Served 1 month on remand after magistrate refused bail. Then on 28 March 1912 sentenced to 3 months.	Holloway

209

Date of offence	Street name	Street Number	Name of Owner	Glass-breaker Surname	Glass-breaker First Name	Alias used when arrested	Suffrage Society Branch	Travelled from	Glass-breaker(s) arrested with	Sentence	Prison
4-Mar-1912	Sloane Square/Kings Road		Post Office	Roberts	Gladys		Nottingham WSPU (organiser)	Nottingham	In window smashing party with Mary Ellen Taylor and Miss Nellie Crocker	Served 1 month on remand after magistrate refused bail. Then on 28 March 1912 sentenced to 3 months.	Holloway
4-Mar-1912	Westbourne Grove		Post Office	Beedham	Dora			Knebworth	Constance Moore	2 months hard labour	
4-Mar-1912	Westbourne Grove		Post Office	Dorien	Daphne			Gave address as WSPU headquarters at Clement's Inn	Alison Martin	2 months hard labour	Holloway
4-Mar-1912	Westbourne Grove		Post Office	Martin	Alison			Gave address as WSPU headquarters at Clement's Inn	Daphne Dorien	2 months	Holloway
4-Mar-1912	Westbourne Grove		Post Office	Moore	Constance			South Croydon	Dora Beedham	2 months hard labour	Holloway
Likely 4-Mar-1912	Westbourne Grove		Lilley and Skinner	Lewis	Ethel					6 months	Maidstone
4-Mar-1912	Westminster		The Local Government Board	Barrowman	Janet		Glasgow WSPU	Glasgow	McPhuns, Nancy A John	2 months hard labour	Holloway

Date	Location	Target	Surname	First name	Other name	Organisation	Place	Associates	Sentence	Prison
4-Mar-1912	Westminster	Local Government Board	Evans	Kate Williams			Wales	Jane Lomax	2 months hard labour	
4-Mar-1912	Westminster	The Local Government Board	John	Nancy A.		Glasgow WSPU	Glasgow	Barrowman, McPhuns	2 months hard labour	Holloway
4-Mar-1912	Westminster	Local Government Board	Lomax	Jane				Kate Evans	2 months hard labour	Holloway
4-Mar-1912	Westminster	The Local Government Board	McPhun	Frances Mary	Fanny Campbell	Glasgow WSPU (Honorary Sec)	Glasgow	Barrowman, Nancy A John, Margaret McPhun	2 months hard labour	Holloway
4-Mar-1912	Westminster	Local Government Board	McPhun	Margaret Pollock	Margery Campbell	Glasgow and West of Scotland WSPU (Press Secretary)	Glasgow	Barrowman, Nancy A John, Frances McPhun	2 months hard labour	Holloway
4-Mar-1912	Whitehall	Agricultural Offices	Hughes	Morrie		Harrogate WSPU (organiser)	Harrogate	Alice Agnes Wilson	Offered choice of fine and bound over to keep the peace for 12 months or 1 month. Not known which she chose.	Holloway
4-Mar-1912	Whitehall	Agricultural Offices	Wilson	Alice Agnes			Harrogate	Morrie Hughes	2 months hard labour	

Date of offence	Street name	Street Number	Name of Owner	Glass-breaker Surname	Glass-breaker First Name	Alias used when arrested	Suffrage Society Branch	Travelled from	Glass-breaker(s) arrested with	Sentence	Prison
4-Mar-1912	Whitehall		United Services Institution	Ball	Lillian		Balham WSPU	12 Holderness Road, Tooting	Norah Yorke, Elizabeth Herrick	2 months hard labour	Holloway but transferred to Reading for own protection
4-Mar-1912	Whitehall		United Services Institution	de Cadiz	Leila Gertude Garcias	Margaret (Maggie) Murphy			Rosalind de Cadiz, Margaret Spanton	2 months hard labour	Holloway
4-Mar-1912	Whitehall		United Services Institution	de Cadiz	Rosalind Mary Garcias	Jane Murphy			Leila de Cadiz, Margaret Spanton	2 months hard labour	Holloway
4-Mar-1912	Whitehall		United Services Institution	Herrick	Elizabeth			Possibly Kensington (ran hat shop in High Street Kensington)	Lilian Ball and Norah Yorke	2 months hard labour	Holloway
4-Mar-1912	Whitehall		United Services Institution	Spanton	Helen Margaret				Rosalind de Cadiz, Leila de Cadiz	2 months hard labour	Holloway
4-Mar-1912	Whitehall		United Services Institution	Yorke	Norah		Balham WSPU		Lillian Ball, Elizabeth Herrick	6 weeks hard labour.	Holloway
4-Mar-1912	Whitehall		War Office	Fowler	Emma					2 months hard labour	Holloway

List of March 1912 Glassbreakers

Date	Location	No.	Target	Surname	First name	Organisation	Place	Name	Sentence	Prison
4-Mar-1912	Whitehall		War Office	Lilley	Louise	Clacton WSPU (Honorary Treasurer), Grafton Street, Clacton-on-Sea	Clacton-on-Sea	Kate Lilley	2 months hard labour	Holloway
4-Mar-1912	Whitehall		War Office	Lilley	Kate	Clacton WSPU (Honorary Secretary) Grafton Street, Clacton-on-Sea	Clacton-on-Sea	Louise Lilley	2 months hard labour	Holloway
4-Mar-1912	Whitehall		War Office	McAlpin	Caxton		Scotland		2 months hard labour	Holloway
4-Mar-1912	Whitehall		War Office	Richmond	Katherine Mary			Myra Sadd Brown	2 months hard labour	
4-Mar-1912	Whitehall		War Office	Sadd-Brown	Myra			Mary Richmond	2 months hard labour	
4-Mar-1912	Whitehall		War Office	Simmons	Victoria	Bristol WSPU			2 months hard labour	Holloway
4-Mar-1912	Wimpole Street	36	House of Lord Cromer	Keller	Phyllis		Woking		1 month	Holloway
4-Mar-1912	Wimpole Street		Western District Post Office	Boyle	Dinah/Diana		Brighton	Katie Gliddon	2 months hard labour	Holloway

213

Date of offence	Street name	Street Number	Name of Owner	Glass-breaker Surname	Glass-breaker First Name	Alias used when arrested	Suffrage Society Branch	Travelled from	Glass-breaker(s) arrested with	Sentence	Prison
4-Mar-1912	Wimpole Street		Western District Post Office	Gliddon	Katie Edith	Catherine (or Katherine) Susan Gray	Croydon WSPU	Croydon	Diana Boyle	2 months hard labour	Holloway
4-Mar-1912	Young Street, Kensington		Post Office	Lindsay	Lily			Germany	Alice Morgan Wright, Enid Renny	2 months hard labour	Holloway
4-Mar-1912	Young Street, Kensington		Post Office	Renny	Enid Marguerite			'Ava Bank', Broughty Ferry, Scotland	Lily Lindsay, Alice Morgan Wright	2 months hard labour	Holloway
4-Mar-1912	Young Street, Kensington		Post Office	Wright	Alice Morgan			United States of America	Lily Lindsay, Enid Renny	2 months hard labour	Holloway
4-Mar-1912	Unknown		Lord Chancellor's house	Corner	Sara (also known as Sara Wilson)			Scotland (possibly Bothwell)		2 months hard labour	Holloway
4-Mar-1912	Unknown		Lord Chancellor's house	Jacobs	Agnes, Eleanor			Loughton, Essex		1 month hard labour	Holloway
4-Mar-1912	Unknown			Allen	Doreen			London		4 months	Holloway
4-Mar-1912	Unknown			Archibold	Louise			Richmond		4 months	Birmingham
4-Mar-1912	Unknown			Cather	Joan	Josephine Carter		London		2 months hard labour	Holloway

List of March 1912 Glassbreakers

Date	Source	Surname	First name	Alias	WSPU	Address	Arrested with	Sentence	Prison
4-Mar-1912	Unknown	Floyd	Lettice Annie		Berkswell WSPU (West Midlands)		Annie Williams	2 months hard labour	Holloway
4-Mar-1912	Unknown	Gatty	Katherine		Ealing WSPU	96 Churchfield Road, Acton, London		6 months	Holloway
4-Mar-1912	Unknown	Lees	Edith Anne	Annie Baker		8 Ebers Grove, Nottingham			
4-Mar-1912	Unknown	Thomson	Elizabeth		Edinburgh WSPU	Edinburgh		Offered choice of fine and bound over to keep the peace for 12 months or 1 month. Not known which she chose.	Holloway
4-Mar-1912	Unknown	Tollemache	Grace		Bath WSPU (joint secretary with sister Aethel).	Bath		2 months hard labour	Holloway
4-Mar-1912	Unknown	Williams	Annie		Appointed as WSPU organiser in Wales in 1912	Newquay, Cornwall	Lettice Annie Floyd	Offered choice of fine and bound over to keep the peace for 12 months or 1 month. Not known which she chose.	
Likely 4-Mar 1912	Unknown	Lowy	Gertrude Golda					2 months hard labour	Holloway

215

Date of offence	Street name	Street Number	Name of Owner	Glass-breaker Surname	Glass-breaker First Name	Alias used when arrested	Suffrage Society Branch	Travelled from	Glass-breaker(s) arrested with	Sentence	Prison
4-Mar-1912	Unknown			Solomon	Georgina Margaret		Hampstead WSPU	Hampstead		1 month hard labour	Holloway
Likely 4-Mar 1912	Unknown			Thomson	Agnes Colquhoun		Edinburgh WSPU	Edinburgh		Evaded arrest	
5-Mar-12	N/A			Pethick-Lawrence	Emmeline					9 months for conspiring to incite others	Holloway
5-Mar-12	N/A			Pethick-Lawrence	Frederick					9 months for conspiring to incite others	Holloway
Unknown	Henrietta Street			Billinghurst	Rosa May			Lewisham, London		1 month	
Unknown	Lower Thames Street	101	Customs House	Emerson	Kathleen		Irish Women's Suffrage Society	Dublin, Ireland		2 months hard labour	Holloway
Unknown	Unknown			Bardsley	Kathleen Blanche	Kate Bard				4 months	Holloway
Unknown	Unknown			Barker	Elsie						
Unknown	Unknown			Bray	Constance		Willesden and Kensal Rise WSPU	Willesden, London		Offered choice of fine and bound over to keep the peace for 12 months or 1 month. Not known which she chose.	

List of March 1912 Glassbreakers

Surname	First name	Other name	Branch	Location	Notes	Sentence	Prison			
Bristy	Alice					4 months	Holloway	Unknown	Unknown	Unknown
Chambers	Constance					Fined and bound over to keep the peace for 12 months		Unknown	Unknown	Unknown
Cohen	Leonora		Harrogate WSPU	Harrogate		Evaded arrest		Unknown	Unknown	Unknown
Craig	Constance I			Possibly Penzance, Cornwall	May have known/travelled with Anne Rachael Perks	2 months hard labour		Unknown	Unknown	Unknown
Crawley	Ethel	Mary Carlyn	Balham WSPU			2 months hard labour	Holloway	Unknown	Unknown	Unknown
Daring	Joan					6 weeks hard labour	Holloway	Unknown	Unknown	Unknown
Davies	Alice		Liverpool WSPU (branch organiser)	Liverpool		3 months	Holloway	Unknown	Unknown	Unknown
Dodgson	Mary Boyd					2 months hard labour		Unknown	Unknown	Unknown
Eldridge	Clara					Discharged		Unknown	Unknown	Unknown
Eldridge	Martha					Discharged		Unknown	Unknown	Unknown
Evans	Elsie					2 months hard labour		Unknown	Unknown	Unknown
Gordon	Ailsie							Unknown	Unknown	Unknown
Gough	Theresa		Glasgow WSPU	Glasgow		2 months hard labour	Holloway	Unknown	Unknown	Unknown

Date of offence	Street name	Street Number	Name of Owner	Glass-breaker Surname	Glass-breaker First Name	Alias used when arrested	Suffrage Society Branch	Travelled from	Glass-breaker(s) arrested with	Sentence	Prison
Unknown	Unknown			Grant	Georgina Helen					2 months hard labour	
Unknown	Unknown			Grieve	Marion		Edinburgh WSPU	Edinburgh		2 months hard labour	Holloway
Unknown	Unknown			Hanson	Marie						
Unknown	Unknown			Hilliard	Mary Ann					2 months hard labour	Holloway
Unknown	Unknown			Hudson	Edith		Edinburgh WSPU	Edinburgh		6 months	Holloway
Unknown	Unknown			Ireland	Charlotte					Offered choice of fine and bound over to keep the peace for 12 months or 1 month. Not known which she chose.	
Unknown	Unknown			Jeffcott	Olivia					2 months hard labour	Holloway
Unknown	Unknown			Jones	Hope					6 months	Maidstone
Unknown	Unknown			Laing	Jessie Jane					2 months hard labour	Holloway
Unknown	Unknown			Martin	Ethel					Discharged under Indictable Offences Act.	

		Surname	First name		Location	Sentence	Prison
Unknown	Unknown	McDonald	Agnes			2 months hard labour	Holloway
Unknown	Unknown	McMurdo	Leslie	Leslie Lawless	Unknown. In 1913 she was in Chelsea, London	1 month hard labour	
Unknown	Unknown	Mills	Katey			2 months hard labour	Holloway
Unknown	Unknown	Moore	Mrs E				
Unknown	Unknown	Myer	Annie		Liverpool	2 months hard labour	Holloway
Unknown	Unknown	Myers	Louise May			Discharged	
Unknown	Unknown	Palethorpe	Fanny Davison		Ainsdale, Lancashire	4 months	
Unknown	Unknown	Perks	Anne Rachael		Unknown. In 1913 she was in Cornwall		
Unknown	Unknown	Raya	Elena				
Unknown	Unknown	Sandau-Van	Elsie Wolf			2 months hard labour	
Unknown	Unknown	Smart	Nancy				
Unknown	Unknown	Swan	Annie		Scotland	2 months hard labour	Holloway
Unknown	Unknown	Till	Flora			2 months hard labour	Holloway
Unknown	Unknown	Tyson	Leonora	WSPU Streatham (Honorary Secretary)		2 months hard labour	Holloway

Date of offence	Street name	Street Number	Name of Owner	Glass-breaker Surname	Glass-breaker First Name	Atlas used when arrested	Suffrage Society Branch	Travelled from	Glass-breaker(s) arrested with	Sentence	Prison
Unknown	Unknown			Weller	Marie Louise			Towcester, Northamptonshire		Fined and bound over to keep the peace	
Unknown	Unknown			Watson	Dorothy						
Unknown	Unknown			Whitlock	Winifred					Offered choice of fine and bound over to keep the peace for 12 months or 1 month. Not known which she chose.	
Unknown	Unknown			Wilson	Elsie					6 weeks hard labour	Holloway
Unknown	Unknown			Wilson	Eva					2 months hard labour	Holloway
Unknown	Unknown			Wilson	Louisa					Offered choice of fine and bound over to keep the peace for 12 months or 1 month. Not known which she chose.	Holloway
Unknown	Unknown			Wyatt	Aubrey					2 months hard labour	
Unknown	Unknown			Young	E. Phoebe						

Annex 2

List of signatories embroidered onto cloth/handkerchiefs by suffragette prisoners in Holloway in 1912

Full name	March 1912 glass breaker (Yes/No)	Signature on Janie Terrero handkerchief (Yes/No)	Signature on West Hoathly handkerchief dated March 1912 (Yes/No)	Signature on The LSE Women's Library Panel (1912) (Yes/No)
Aldham, Mary Ann	Yes	Yes	Yes	Yes
Allan, Janie	Yes	No	Yes	Yes
Allen, Doreen	Yes	Yes	Yes	Yes
Arton, Eveleen B.A.	Yes	No	No	Yes
Bardsley, Kathleen	Yes	No	Yes	Yes
Bennett, Blanche	Yes	No	No	Yes
Billinghurst, Rosa May	Yes	No	No	Yes
Boyd, Janet	Yes	No	Yes	Yes
Burkitt, Evaline Hilda	Yes	Yes	Yes	Yes
Capel, Gladys	No	No	No	Yes

Full name	March 1912 glass breaker (Yes/No)	Signature on Janie Terrero handkerchief (Yes/No)	Signature on West Hoathly handkerchief dated March 1912 (Yes/No)	Signature on The LSE Women's Library Panel (1912) (Yes/No)
Cardo, Kate	Yes	No	Yes	Yes
Casey, Eileen	Yes	No	Yes	Yes
Casey, Isabella	Yes	No	Yes	Yes
Chappelow, Grace	Yes	No	Yes	Yes
Cheffins, Georgina Fanny	Yes	No	Yes	Yes
Collier, Constance Louise	Yes	No	Yes	Yes
Craig, Constance	Yes	Yes	Yes	Yes
Crawley, Ethel M.	Yes	No	Yes	Yes
Crocker, Ellen (Nellie)	Yes	No	Yes	Yes
Davies, Alice	Yes	No	Yes	Yes
de Reya, Helena	Yes	Yes	Yes	Yes
du Sautoy- Newby, Marie	No	No	Yes	Yes
Downing, Edith	Yes	No	Yes	Yes
Ellenbogen, Jeanette S.	No	No	No	Yes
Floyd, Lettice	Yes	Yes	Yes	Yes
Follit, Beatrice	No	No	No	Yes
Fowler, Emma	Yes	No	Yes	Yes
Gatty, Katherine	Yes	No	Yes	Yes
Grant, Georgina Helen	Yes	Yes	Yes	Yes

List of signatories embroidered onto cloth/handkerchiefs

Name				
Green, Alice	Yes	Yes	Yes	Yes
Guthrie, Joan Lavender Bailie	Yes	No	No	Yes
Haig, Florence Eliza	Yes	No	No	Yes
Haslam, Ethel C.	Yes	No	No	Yes
Hatfield, Louise	No	Yes	Yes	Yes
Hazel, Gladys M.	Yes	Yes	No	No
Herrick, Elizabeth	Yes	No	No	Yes
Hewitt, Mary Graily	Yes	No	Yes	Yes
Hilliard, Mary	Yes	No	Yes	Yes
Hudson, Edith	Yes	Yes	Yes	Yes
Jeffcott, Olivia	Yes	Yes	Yes	Yes
Jocke, Barbara S.	No	No	No	No
Jones, May R.	Yes	Yes	Yes	Yes
Laing, Jessie	Yes	Yes	Yes	Yes
Lambert Clara or Lane Catherine (initials 'C.L.' included)	Yes	No	Yes	No
Lehmann, Caroline (initials 'C.E.L' included)	No	No	Yes	Yes
Lenton, Lilian Ida	Yes	No	No	Yes
Lilley, Kate	Yes	No	Yes	Yes
Lilley, Louise	Yes	No	Yes	Yes

Full name	March 1912 glass breaker (Yes/No)	Signature on Janie Terrero handkerchief (Yes/No)	Signature on West Hoathly handkerchief dated March 1912 (Yes/No)	Signature on The LSE Women's Library Panel (1912) (Yes/No)
Lindsay, Lily (appears as 'Lindesay, Lillie')	Yes	No	Yes	Yes
Lowy, Gertrude	Yes	No	Yes	Yes
MacFarlane, M (Maggie, Margaret)	Yes	Yes	Yes	Yes
MacRae, Helen	Yes	No	Yes	Yes
Marshall, Emily Katherine	Yes	No	Yes	Yes
McKenzie, Lizzie	Yes	No	Yes	Yes
McPhun, Frances	Yes	No	Yes	Yes
McPhun, Margaret	Yes	No	Yes	Yes
Mitchell, Lilias	Yes	No	Yes	Yes
Morgan Wright, Alice	Yes	No	Yes	Yes
Myer, Annie	Yes	No	Yes	Yes
Nesbit, Mary (Cassie Nesbit included)	Yes	No	Yes	Yes
Palethorpe, Fanny Davison	Yes	No	Yes	Yes
Parker, Frances	Yes	No	Yes	Yes
Pease, Fanny	Yes	Yes	Yes	Yes

List of signatories embroidered onto cloth/handkerchiefs

Potbury, Isabella	Yes	Yes	Yes
Proctor, Zoe	Yes	No	Yes
Remny, Enid M.	Yes	No	Yes
Roberts, Gladys	Yes	No	Yes
Rock, Dorothea Howlett	Yes	No	Yes
Rock, Madeleine	Yes	No	Yes
Rowlatt, Margaret	Yes	No	Yes
Sheppard, Genie	Yes	No	No
Shipley, Alice Maud	Yes	No	Yes
Simmons, Victoria	Yes	No	Yes
Stewart Ker, Alice J.	Yes	No	No
Terrero, Janie	Yes	Yes	Yes
Tollemache, Grace	Yes	No	Yes
Tyson, Leonora	Yes	Yes	Yes
Wentworth, Vera	Yes	Yes	Yes
Davison, Emily Wilding	No	No	Yes
Gertrude Jessie Heward Wilkinson	Yes	No	No
Williams, Frances	Yes	No	Yes
Wilson, Eva	Yes	No	Yes
Yorke, Norah	Yes	No	Yes

Endnotes

Introduction

1. Referred to by WSPU in their various promotional materials for this protest.
2. Following the March 1912 hammer attacks, *Votes for Women* reported that *The Globe* newspaper had coined a new word by describing the suffragettes who were smashing windows as 'vitrifragists' or 'glassbreakers'.
3. Pankhurst, Emmeline, *My Own Story*, Vintage Books, 2015, p.197.
4. The National Archives, HO/144/1193/220196, Charge Sheet states aged 20 but birth certificate shows that Ethel Violet Baldock was born 20 January 1893.
5. This cannot be categorically verified as some of the ages of glassbreakers were not recorded and have not all yet been traced.
6. Pankhurst, Emmeline, *My Own Story*, Vintage Books, 2015, p.182.
7. Old Bailey Online, https://www.oldbaileyonline.org, May 1912, Trial of Emmeline Pankhurst, Frederick William Pethick-Lawrence (40, Barrister), Emmeline Pethick-Lawrence, t19120514-54, p.2.
8. Pankhurst, Emmeline, *My Own Story*, Vintage Books, 2015, p.189.
9. Pankhurst, Emmeline, *My Own Story*, Vintage Books, 2015, pp.190–191.
10. Old Bailey Online, https://www.oldbaileyonline.org, t19120514-54.
11. Pankhurst, Emmeline, *My Own Story*, Vintage Books, 2015, p.197.

Chapter 1

1. Speech by Mrs Emmeline Pankhurst, *The Standard*, 17 February 1912.
2. Old Bailey Online, https://www.oldbaileyonline.org, May 1912, Trial of Emmeline Pankhurst, Frederick William Pethick-Lawrence (40, Barrister), Emmeline Pethick-Lawrence, t19120514-54, p.5.
3. Proctor, Zoe, *Life and Yesterday*, The Favil Press, 1960, p.99.
4. *The Standard*, 17 February 1912.
5. *The Standard*, 17 February 1912.
6. The National Archives, HO/144/1193/220196.
7. Crawford, Elizabeth, *The Women's Suffrage Movement: A Reference Guide 1866–1928*, Routledge, 2001, p.615.
8. *Votes for Women*, 29 March 1912, p.407.
9. *Votes for Women*, 29 March 1912, p.407.
10. The National Archives, HO/144/1194/220196, Statement by Lillian Ball, dated 23 March 1912, to the Metropolitan Police Criminal Investigation Department.
11. The National Archives, DPP1-23 Ex153, Letter from nurse Ellen Pitfield, 1912.
12. Butler, Simon, *Land Girl Suffragette: The Extraordinary Story of Olive Hockin, Author, Artist, Arsonist*, Halstar Ltd, 2016, p.16.
13. Votes for Women, 8 March 1912, p. 363.

14. Votes for Women, 8 March 1912, p. 363.
15. Mapping Women's Suffrage entry (online) for Ellen Pitfield, provided by The National Archives.
16. The Women's Library, LSE, Letters from the Taylor family and their relations during Mrs Taylor's first imprisonment, 1912.
17. The National Archives, DPP1-23 Ex 142, Letter from Amy Woodburn to Mrs Pankhurst, 26 February 1912.
18. The National Archives DPP1-23 Ex 147, Letter from Lady Constance Lytton regarding schoolteacher Miss Avery, 19 February 1912.
19. Quotation from The National Archives blog called 'Suffragettes, 1912: "Rather broken windows than broken promises"', (part of 'Suffrage 100 – Archives at Night: Law Breakers, Law Makers'), dated Friday, 9 March 2018, by researchers Vicky Iglikowski-Broad, Katie Fox and Rowena Hillel.
20. Meaning 'a confused struggle or fight' according to *Oxford English Dictionary*.
21. Overton, Jenny and Mant, Joan, *A Suffragette Nest: Peaslake, 1910 and After*, Hazeltree Publishing, 1998, p.30.
22. Overton, Jenny and Mant, Joan, *A Suffragette Nest: Peaslake, 1910 and After*, Hazeltree Publishing, 1998, p.20.
23. Overton, Jenny and Mant, Joan, *A Suffragette Nest Peaslake, 1910 and After*, Hazeltree Publishing, 1998, p.20.
24. Witness Statement by Lillian Ball to the Metropolitan Police Criminal Investigation Department, 23 March 1912.
25. The National Archives, SM DPP1-23 Ex 92, Instructions to Volunteers, 28 February 1912.
26. LSE Library, Elsie Duval and Hugh Franklin, A tragic story of love, pain and death, with the women's suffrage movement as a backdrop.
27. Pankhurst, Emmeline, *My Own Story*, Vintage Books, 2015, pp.194–195.
28. *Votes for Women*, 29 March 1912, p.407.
29. Proctor, Zoe, *Life and Yesterday*, The Favil Press, 1960, p.100.
30. 8SUF – Oral Evidence on the Suffragette and Suffragist Movement: The Brian Harrison Interviews. Interview with Miss Hazel Inglis, 8SUF/B/069 & 8SUF/B/073, dated 21 February 1976.
31. Edited by Viv Gardner and Diane Atkinson, Kitty Marion Autobiography, Manchester University Press, 2019, p. 159.
32. Crawford, Elizabeth, *The Women's Suffrage Movement: A Reference Guide 1866–1928*, Routledge, 2001, p.135.
33. The National Archives, HO/144/1193/220196, According to police estimates.
34. Purvis, Jane, *Women's History Review*, 'The prison experiences of the suffragettes in Edwardian Britain', Routledge, 1995, 4:1, 103–133, DOI: 10.1080/0961202950 0200073.

Chapter 2

1. Pankhurst, Emmeline, *My Own Story*, Vintage Books, 2015, p.195.
2. Pankhurst, Emmeline, *My Own Story*, Vintage Books, 2015, p.195.
3. The National Archives, HO/144/1193/220196.
4. Edited by Viv Gardner and Diane Atkinson, Kitty Marion Autobiography, Manchester University Press, 2019, p. 159.
5. Pankhurst, Emmeline, *My Own Story*, Vintage Books, 2015, p.195.
6. The Women's Library, Grace Roe, 8SUF/B/13, 4 October 1974.
7. The Women's Library, Grace Roe, 8SUF/B/13, 4 October 1974.

8. Atkinson, Diane, *Rise Up Women!: The Remarkable Lives of the Suffragettes*, Bloomsbury, 2018, pp.272–273. Her source: Emily Katherine Willoughby Marshall, 'Suffragette Escapes And Adventures', typescript memoir, Museum of London Suffragette Collections, pp.57–58.

9. Overton, Jenny and Mant, Joan, *A Suffragette Nest: Peaslake, 1910 and After*, Hazeltree Publishing, 1998, p.30.

10. Pankhurst, Emmeline, *My Own Story*, Vintage Books, 2015, p.195.

11. *The Daily Graphic*, 2 March 1912.

12. Crawford, Elizabeth, *The Women's Suffrage Movement: A Reference Guide 1866–1928*, Routledge, 2001, p.76.

13. Crawford, Elizabeth, *The Women's Suffrage Movement: A Reference Guide 1866–1928*, Routledge, 2001, p.76.

14. Proctor, Zoe, *Life and Yesterday*, The Favil Press, 1960, p.100.

15. Proctor, Zoe, *Life and Yesterday*, The Favil Press, 1960, pp.100–101.

16. Proctor, Zoe, *Life and Yesterday*, The Favil Press, 1960, p.101.

17. Crawford, Elizabeth, *The Women's Suffrage Movement: A Reference Guide 1866–1928*, Routledge, 2001, pp.175–176.

18. Crawford, Elizabeth, *The Women's Suffrage Movement: A Reference Guide 1866–1928*, Routledge, 2001, p.176.

19. Proctor, Zoe, *Life and Yesterday*, The Favil Press, 1960, p.102.

20. Pankhurst, Emmeline, *My Own Story*, Vintage Books, 2015, pp.195–196.

21. Crawford, Elizabeth, *The Women's Suffrage Movement: A Reference Guide 1866–1928*, Routledge, 2001, p.377.

22. Edited by Viv Gardner and Diane Atkinson, Kitty Marion Autobiography, Manchester University Press, 2019, p. 159.

23. 8SUF – Oral Evidence on the Suffragette and Suffragist Movement: The Brian Harrison Interviews. Interview with Miss Hazel Inglis, 8SUF/B/069 & 8SUF/B/073, dated 21 February 1976 and with Mrs Helen Green, 8SUF/B/074, dated 16 March 1976.

24. It is likely that Rosa Leo acted on 1 March 1912. However it has not been possible to confirm this.

25. Crawford, Elizabeth, The Women's Suffrage Movement, A Reference Guide 1866-1928, Routledge, 2001, p. 142.

26. It is likely that Rebecca Hyams acted on 1 March 1912. However it has not been possible to confirm this.

27. Crawford, Elizabeth, Woman and her Sphere, 'Suffrage Stories/Campaigning for the Vote: Selfridge's and Suffragettes', 16 May 2013.

28. Crawford, Elizabeth, Woman and her Sphere, 'Suffrage Stories/Campaigning for the Vote: Selfridge's and Suffragettes', 16 May 2013.

29. Crawford, Elizabeth, Woman and her Sphere, 'Suffrage Stories/Campaigning for the Vote: Selfridge's and Suffragettes', 16 May 2013.

30. Pethick-Lawrence, Emmeline, *Votes for Women*, February 1909.

31. Pankhurst, Emmeline, *My Own Story*, Vintage Books, 2015, p.196.

32. Proctor, Zoe, *Life and Yesterday*, The Favil Press, 1960, p.105.

33. BBC Broadcast, 1958, Also included in: The militant campaign of the suffragettes, Meet the suffragettes who smashed windows and started fires to raise awareness for their cause, #100years, By BBC News, Facebook.

34. *The Times*, 14 March 1912.

35. The book is called *They Couldn't Stop Us!: Experiences of Two (Usually Law-Abiding) Women in the Years 1909–1913* published by W.E. Harrison & Sons Ltd in 1957 by

Margaret Eleanor Thompson and her sister, Mary D. Thompson. Mary was never a prisoner although she was arrested once.

36. Thompson, Margaret Elenor and Thompson, Mary D., *They Couldn't Stop Us!: Experiences of Two (Usually Law-Abiding) Women in the Years 1909–1913*, W.E. Harrison & Sons Ltd, 1957, pp.34–35.
37. Pankhurst, Emmeline, *My Own Story*, Vintage Books, 2015, p.196.
38. Atherton, Kathryn, *Suffragette Planners and Plotters: The Pankhurst, Pethick-Lawrence Story*, Pen & Sword Books Ltd, 2019, p.82.
39. *Birmingham Gazette and Express*, Monday, 11 March 1912.

Chapter 3

1. *Votes for Women*.
2. Pankhurst, Emmeline, *My Own Story*, Vintage Books, 2015, p.197.
3. *Votes for Women*, 29 March 1912, p.407.
4. Pankhurst, Emmeline, *My Own Story*, Vintage Books, 2015, pp.204–205.
5. Pankhurst, Emmeline, *My Own Story*, Vintage Books, 2015, p.205.
6. The National Archives.
7. Jenkins, Jess, The Smeeton Westerby Suffragette, p.261.
8. Nottingham Women's Group and Mapping Women's Suffrage website: https://www.mappingwomenssuffrage.org.uk/suffrage-map
9. Ball, Lillian, Witness Statement taken by the Metropolitan Police Criminal Investigation Department, 23 March 1912.
10. The National Archives, SM HO/144/1119/203651, Letter from Lillian Ball.
11. The National Archives, SM HO/144/1119/203651, Letter from Lillian Ball.
12. The National Archives, SM HO/144/1119/203651, Letter from Lillian Ball.
13. Ball, Lillian, Witness Statement taken by the Metropolitan Police Criminal Investigation Department, 23 March 1912.
14. *Votes for Women*, 15 March 1912, p.381.
15. LSE Library, 7KGG/1/1, Katie Gliddon's diary.
16. Home Office charge sheets and diaries of Katie Gliddon refer to 'Dinah'. However other sources refer to 'Diana'.
17. LSE Library, 7KGG/1/1, Katie Gliddon's diary.
18. Women's Suffrage History & Citizenship resources for schools, https://www.suffrageresources.org.uk/database/2262/mrs-edith-ruth-mansell-moullin.
19. LSE Women's Library GB106 7KGG/21
20. LSE Library, 7KGG/1/1, Katie Gliddon's diary.
21. The Women's Library, Mrs Leonora Cohen, 8SUF/B/18, 26 October 1974.
22. Edited by Viv Gardner and Diane Atkinson, Kitty Marion Autobiography, Manchester University Press, 2019, p. 160.
23. *The Times*, 6 March 1912.
24. Godfrey, Jennifer, *Suffragettes of Kent*, Pen & Sword Books Ltd, 2019, p.8, using source *Votes for Women*, 15 March 1912, p.361.
25. Suffragettes/WALLACE, http://thechartists.org.
26. Called Annie according to her great nephew Dr Eamonn Butler as quoted in his blog, '100 years since winning the vote: a tribute to Violet Ann Bland', published by the Adam Smith Institute.
27. Godfrey, Jennifer, *Suffragettes of Kent*, Pen & Sword Books Ltd, 2019, p.8, using source *Votes for Women*, 15 March 1912, p.381.

28. *The Times*, 6 March 1912.
29. Godfrey, Jennifer, *Suffragettes of Kent*, Pen & Sword Books Ltd, 2019, p.9, using source The National Archives, 7LGA/1/2, Record of Louisa Garrett Anderson's trial on 5 March 1912.
30. *The Times*, 6 March 1912.
31. Proctor, Zoe, *Life and Yesterday*, The Favil Press, 1960, pp.98–99.
32. The Women's Library, Mrs Leonora Cohen, 8SUF/B/18, 26 October 1974.
33. The People's Voice website, Database of Poems, *Newington butts were lively* by Dr Alice Jane Shannon Stewart Ker.
34. *The Times*, 13 March 1912.
35. *The Times*, 13 March 1912.
36. Overton, Jenny and Mant, Joan, *A Suffragette Nest: Peaslake, 1910 and After*, Hazeltree Publishing, 1998, p.30.
37. www.exploringsurreyspast.co.uk.
38. 8SUF – Oral Evidence on the Suffragette and Suffragist Movement: The Brian Harrison Interviews. Interview with Miss Hazel Inglis, 8SUF/B/069 & 8SUF/B/073, dated 21 February 1976 and with Mrs Helen Green, 8SUF/B/074, dated 16 March 1976.
39. The National Archives, HO/144/1194/220196, Home Office note, dated 2 April 1912.
40. The National Archives, HO/144/1194/220196, Home Office note, dated 2 April 1912.
41. *Woking News and Mail*, 26 April 1912.
42. BBC Broadcast, 1968, Also included in: The militant campaign of the suffragettes, Meet the suffragettes who smashed windows and started fires to raise awareness for their cause, #100years, By BBC News. Facebook.
43. The National Archives, HO/144/1193/220196.

Chapter 4
1. Pankhurst, Emmeline, *My Own Story*, Vintage Books, 2015, p.205.
2. Atherton, Kathryn, *Suffragette Planners and Plotters: The Pankhurst, Pethick-Lawrence Story*, Pen & Sword Books Ltd, 2019, p.20.
3. John, Angela V., *Evelyn Sharp: Rebel Woman, 1869–1955*, Manchester United Press, 2009, p.67.
4. The Women's Library, Grace Roe, 8SUF/B/13, 4 October 1974.
5. John, Angela V., *Evelyn Sharp: Rebel Woman, 1869–1955*, Manchester United Press, 2009, p.67.
6. John, Angela V., *Evelyn Sharp: Rebel Woman, 1869–1955*, Manchester United Press, 2009, p.68.
7. John, Angela V., *Evelyn Sharp: Rebel Woman, 1869–1955*, Manchester University Press, 2009, page 67.
8. John, Angela V., *Evelyn Sharp: Rebel Woman, 1869–1955*, Manchester United Press, 2009, p.67.
9. ESNP, MSS. Eng. Misc. E636, 22 December 1944, as cited in *Evelyn Sharp: Rebel Woman 1869–1955* by Angela V. John, Manchester University Press, 2009, p.68.
10. The National Archives, HO/144/1193/220196.
11. The National Archives, HO/144/1193/220196.
12. The National Archives, HO/144/1193/220196.
13. The National Archives, HO/144/1193/220196.
14. Old Bailey Online, https://www.oldbaileyonline.org, t19120514-54.

15. *The Times*, 27 March 1912.
16. *The Times*, 27 March 1912.
17. *The Times*, 27 March 1912.
18. 'D of P P' means Director of Public Prosecution Service.
19. 'H.L' means Hard Labour.
20. See chapter seven for further information on Rule 243A and its' application.
21. The National Archives, HO/144/1194/220196, Home Office note, dated 28 March 1912.
22. The National Archives, HO/144/1194/220196, Home Office note, dated 30 March 1912.

Chapter 5

1. The National Archives, HO/144/1193/220196, Letter from David Wilkie, Manager for Scotland of Joseph Watson & Sons Ltd to his solicitor, Mr James T. Orr of 174 West George Street, Glasgow, dated 11 March 1912.
2. As referred to by Ethel Agnes Mary Moorhead and accounted in Elizabeth Crawford's *The Women's Suffrage Movement: A Reference Guide 1866–1928*, Routledge, 2001, P.425.
3. Not all information is available for the March 1912 glassbreakers so there may be more Scottish suffragettes not mentioned here.
4. *Votes for Women*, 8 March 1912.
5. Website www.ualresearchonline.arts.ac.uk
6. ualresourceonline.arts.ac.uk in article entitled 'Smashing Handkerchief'.
7. www.madeinperth.org
8. National Records of Scotland website, https://www.nrscotland.gov.uk/files/exhibitions/women-suffrage/edith-hudson.html.
9. Gough, Theresa, Karmie M.T. Kranich, Holloway Jail, 28 April 1912 cited in *Literature of the Women's Suffrage Campaign in England*, edited by Carolyn Christensen Nelson Broadview Press, 2004, p.158.
10. Jones, Rebecca, Kate Evans…and Kate Evans!, Glasgow Women's Library, 21 September 2018.
11. *Daily Record*, 18 November 2012.
12. Keys, Karen, descendant of the McPhun sisters. Letter from Frances McPhun to Miss Laura Underwood, smuggled out of Holloway prison, March 1912.
13. Keys, Karen, descendant of the McPhun sisters. Letter from Frances McPhun to Miss Laura Underwood, smuggled out of Holloway prison, March 1912.
14. Keys, Karen descendant of the McPhun sisters. Letter written on an envelope from Frances McPhun to Miss Laura Underwood, smuggled out of Holloway prison, March 1912.
15. The National Archives, HO/144/1193/220196, Letter from David Wilkie, Manager for Scotland of Joseph Watson & Sons Ltd to his solicitor, Mr James T. Orr of 174 West George Street, Glasgow, dated, 11 March 1912.
16. Edited by Viv Gardner and Diane Atkinson, Kitty Marion Autobiography, Manchester University Press, 2019, p. 160.
17. The National Archives, HO/144/1193/220196, Letter to Sir Henry Craik from Una MacKinnon, Jemima Downie, Catherine S. Thomson and S.C. Logan, dated 16 March 1912.
18. The National Archives, HO/144/1193/220196, Letter to Sir Henry Craik from Una MacKinnon, Jemima Downie, Catherine S. Thomson and S.C. Logan, dated 16 March 1912.
19. A record of arrests in the 8 March 1912 Votes for Women newspaper (p.363) refers to Janie Allan receiving 5 weeks' hard labour.
20. Held by the Museum of London.
21. *The Times*, 7 March 1912.
22. Henderson, Mary, *Ethel Moorhead: Dundee's Rowdiest Suffragette*, 15 March 2020.

23. *The Times*, 7 March 1912.
24. The Women's Library, LSE.
25. *The Times*, 6 March 1912.
26. Godfrey, Jennifer, *Suffragettes of Kent*, Pen & Sword Books Ltd, 2019.
27. *The Advertiser*, 11 March 1912.
28. *The Advertiser*, 11 March 1912.

Chapter 6

1. The National Archives, HO/144/1194/220196, Notes on Home Office file, dated 28 March 1912.
2. The National Archives, HO/144/1193/220196.
3. The National Archives, HO/144/1194/220196, Letter from Mr Renny to the Right Honourable Secretary of State, Home Department, Letter dated 28 March 1912.
4. The National Archives, HO/144/1194/220196, Notes on Home Office file, dated 28 March 1912.
5. The National Archives, HO/144/1193/220196, Letter dated 6 March 1912 from Solicitors Messrs Watson Sons & Room to the Right Honourable Reginald McKenna, Secretary of State for Home Affairs.
6. The National Archives, HO/144/1193/220196, Letter dated 18 March 1912 from Miss Gladys Shedden to the Right Honourable Reginald McKenna.
7. Purvis, June, *Christabel Pankhurst*, Routledge, 2018, p.468.
8. The National Archives, HO/144/1194/200196, Letter from Mr Renny to the Right Honourable Secretary of State, Home Department, dated 28 March 1912.
9. The National Archives, HO/144/1194/220196, Letter from Mr Renny to the Right Honourable Secretary of State, Home Department, dated 28 March 1912.
10. The National Archives, HO/144/1194/220196, notes on Home Office file, dated 28 March 1912.
11. The National Archives, HO/144/1193/220196.
12. The National Archives, HO/144/1193/220196, Report by W.C. Sullivan.
13. The National Archives, HO/144/1193/220196, Letter dated 23 March 1912 from Home Office to Foreign Office.
14. The National Archives, HO/144/1194/220196, Letter dated 28 March 1912 to the Right Honourable Reginald McKenna from Mrs H.R. Wright.
15. The National Archives, HO/144/1194/220196, Petition Form completed by Alice Morgan Wright, 30 March 1912.
16. The National Archives, HO/144/1194/220196.
17. The National Archives, HO/144/1194/220196, Letter dated 3 April 1912 from Acting Governor of Holloway prison to the Commissioner.

Chapter 7

1. LSE Library, 7KGG/2.
2. Gliddon, Katie, March 1912 glassbreaker, cited in Caitlin Davies's, *Bad Girls: The Rebels and Renegades of Holloway Prison*, John Murray Publishers, 2018, p.79.
3. Proctor, Zoe, *Life and Yesterday*, The Favil Press, 1960, p.99.
4. The Women's Library, LSE, 7KGG/1/3, Katie Gliddon's secret prison diary, 1912.
5. The National Archives, HO/144/1194/220196, Letter dated 18 April 1912 from Chairman of the Newington Petty Sessional Division, County of London, to the Right Honourable Reginald McKenna.

6. Thompson, Margaret Elenor and Thompson, Mary D., *They Couldn't Stop Us!: Experiences of Two (Usually Law-Abiding) Women in the Years 1909–1913*, W.E. Harrison & Sons Ltd, 1957, p.35.
7. *The Times*, 6 March 1912.
8. *The Times*, 6 March 1912.
9. *The Times*, 6 March 1912.
10. Atherton, Kathryn, *Suffragette Planners and Plotters: The Pankhurst, Pethick-Lawrence Story*, Pen & Sword Books Ltd, 2019, p.75.
11. Crawford, Elizabeth, Woman and her Sphere, 'Suffrage Stories: Mrs Alice Singer, Miss Edith New and the Suffragette Doll', 2 May 2013.
12. *The Times*, 27 March 1912.
13. Atkinson, Diane, Rise Up Women – The Remarkable Lives of the Suffragettes, Bloomsbury, 2018 page 307.
14. The Times, 8 March 1912
15. Purvis, Jane, *Women's History Review*, 'The prison experiences of the suffragettes in Edwardian Britain', Routledge, 1995, 4:1, 116, DOI: 10.1080/09612029500200073.
16. Purvis, Jane, *Women's History Review*, 'The prison experiences of the suffragettes in Edwardian Britain', Routledge, 1995, 4:1, 117, DOI: 10.1080/09612029500200073, original source: undated letter (*c*.22 March 1912) written on dark brown lavatory paper From Myra Sadd Brown in Holloway to her children and Mademoiselle, Fawcett Library Autograph Letter Collection.
17. The National Archives, Instructions to governors in prisons on the treatment of first division and second division prisoners, 1912, Catalogue Ref: PCOM 8/228.
18. M.O. - Modus Operandi abbreviation referenced in chapter seven and this is the understood meaning but the original source did not define it.
19. McKenna, Reginald, Hansard, Commons, Volume 35, 21 March 1912.
20. Proctor, Zoe, *Life and Yesterday*, The Favil Press, 1960, p.107.
21. Proctor, Zoe, *Life and Yesterday*, The Favil Press, 1960, pp.107–112.
22. LSE Library, 7KGG/2.
23. Atkinson, Diane, *Rise Up Women!: The Remarkable Lives of the Suffragettes*, Bloomsbury, 2018, p.293. Her source: Emily Katherine Willoughby Marshall, 'Suffragette Escapes And Adventures', 61.218/2, Museum of London Suffragette Collections, pp.59–61.
24. Atkinson, Diane, *Rise Up Women!: The Remarkable Lives of the Suffragettes*, Bloomsbury, 2018, pp.293–294. Her source: Emily Katherine Willoughby Marshall, 'Suffragette Escapes And Adventures', 61.218/2, Museum of London Suffragette Collections, pp.61–64.
25. Proctor, Zoe, *Life and Yesterday*, The Favil Press, 1960, p.104.
26. Proctor, Zoe, *Life and Yesterday*, The Favil Press, 1960, p.105.
27. Proctor, Zoe, *Life and Yesterday*, The Favil Press 1960, pp.104–105.
28. The Women's Library, LSE, Letters from the Taylor family and their relations during Mrs Taylor's first imprisonment, Letter from Mary Ellen (Nellie) Taylor to Mr Taylor and her children, 7 March 1912.
29. Proctor, Zoe, *Life and Yesterday*, The Favil Press, 1960, p.109.
30. The National Archives, HO/144/1193/220196.
31. The National Archives, HO/144/1193/220196, Petition dated 8 March 1912 by Olive Fargus.
32. Purvis, Jane, *Women's History Review*, 'The prison experiences of the suffragettes in Edwardian Britain', Routledge, 1995, 4:1, 103–133, DOI: 10.1080/09612029500200073.

33. The National Archives, HO/144/1193/220196, Letter to the Right Honourable Reginald McKenna dated, 6 March 1912 by Genie Sheppard.
34. The National Archives, HO/144/1193/220196, Handwritten note from James Scott, Governor at Holloway, dated 9 March 1912, regarding Genie Sheppard letter of 6 March.
35. The National Archives, HO/144/1193/220196, Petition dated 9 March 1912 by Sara Corner.
36. The National Archives, HO/144/1193/220196, Letter dated 8 March 1912 by J.T. Wilson.
37. Ibid., Holloway Governor report, dated 18 March 1912.
38. The National Archives, HO/144/1194/220196, Letter from Kathleen Warne to Right Honourable The Home Secretary, dated 26 March 1912.
39. *The Advertiser*, 11 March 1912.
40. The National Archives, HO/144/1193/220196.
41. Purvis, Jane, *Women's History Review*, 'The prison experiences of the suffragettes in Edwardian Britain', Routledge, 1995, 4:1, 103–133, DOI: 10.1080/09612029500200073.
42. The National Archives, HO/144/1194/220196, Note, dated 28 March 1912.
43. The National Archives, HO/144/1194/220196, Report by the Assistant Surveyor Colonel J. Winn, dated 27 March 1912.
44. Purvis, Jane, *Women's History Review*, 'The prison experiences of the suffragettes in Edwardian Britain', Routledge, 1995, 4:1, 103–133, DOI: 10.1080/09612029500200073.
45. Purvis, Jane, *Women's History Review*, 'The prison experiences of the suffragettes in Edwardian Britain', Routledge, 1995, 4:1, 103–133, DOI: 10.1080/09612029500200073.

Chapter 8

1. Purvis, Jane, *Women's History Review*, 'The prison experiences of the suffragettes in Edwardian Britain', Routledge, 1995, 4:1, 103–133, DOI: 10.1080/09612029500200073.
2. Proctor, Zoe, *Life and Yesterday*, The Favil Press, 1960, p.115.
3. Davies, Caitlin, *Bad Girls: The Rebels and Renegades of Holloway Prison*, John Murray Publishers, 2018, p.79.
4. The Women's Library, Miss Winifred Adair Roberts, 8SUF/B/015, 8 October 1974.
5. LSE Library, 7KGG/1/1, Katie Gliddon's diary.
6. The National Archives, Codes used by the Women's Social and Political Union for secret messages. These were used as evidence in the conspiracy trials against the WSPU leaders, Catalogue Ref: DPP 1/23 f205.
7. Proctor, Zoe, *Life and Yesterday*, The Favil Press, 1960, p.114.
8. The Women's Library, LSE, Letters from the Taylor family and their relations during Mrs Taylor's first imprisonment, Letter from Dr Elizabeth Wilks, 1912.
9. Proctor, Zoe, *Life and Yesterday*, The Favil Press, 1960, p.109.
10. Purvis, Jane, *Women's History Review*, 'The prison experiences of the suffragettes in Edwardian Britain', Routledge, 1995, 4:1, 117, DOI: 10.1080/09612029500200073, original source: undated letter (*c.*22 March 1912) written on dark brown lavatory paper from Myra Sadd Brown in Holloway to her children and Mademoiselle, Fawcett Library Autograph Letter Collection.
11. The Women's Library, LSE, Letters from the Taylor family and their relations during Mrs Taylor's first imprisonment, Letter from Mr Taylor to Mr Edwin Richmond, 2 April 1912.
12. The Women's Library, LSE, Letters from the Taylor family and their relations during Mrs Taylor's first imprisonment, Letter from Mr Taylor to Miss Mary Barrowman, 25 April 1912.
13. Proctor, Zoe, *Life and Yesterday*, The Favil Press, 1960, pp.103–104.
14. Purvis, Jane, *Women's History Review*, 'The prison experiences of the suffragettes in Edwardian Britain, Routledge, 1995, 4:1, 103–133, DOI: 10.1080/09612029500200073.

15. Crawford, Elizabeth, The Women's Suffrage Movement, A Reference Guide 1866-1928, Routledge, 2001, p. 50
16. Purvis, Jane, *Women's History Review*, 'The prison experiences of the suffragettes in Edwardian Britain', Routledge, 1995, 4:1, 103–133, DOI: 10.1080/09612029500200073.
17. Purvis, Jane, Women's History Review, 'The prison experiences of the suffragettes in Edwardian Britain', Routledge, 1995, 4:1, 103–133, DOI: 10.1080/09612029500200073.
18. The People's Voice website, Database of Poems, *Oh! Who are these in scant array* by Kathleen Emerson, 1912.
19. Poem written by suffragette prisoner Kathleen O'Kell whilst in Winson Green prison, Birmingham, on 17 June 1912, Museum of London Collections Online, www.collections. museumoflondon.org.uk.
20. Poem written by suffragette prisoner Kathleen O'Kell whilst in Winson Green prison, Birmingham, on 17 June 1912, Museum of London Collections Online, www.collections. museumoflondon.org.uk.
21. The National Archives, HO/144/1193/220196.
22. NRO, MC 2165/1/23, 976X4, 1912, Diary of William Hay MacDowell Aitken, Canon of Norwich Cathedral.
23. The National Archives, HO/144/1195/220196.
24. Poem written by suffragette prisoner Kathleen O'Kell whilst in Winson Green prison, Birmingham, on 17 June 1912, Museum of London Collections Online, www.collections. museumoflondon.org.uk.
25. Bonhams website, https://www.bonhams.com.
26. Poem written by suffragette prisoner Kathleen O'Kell whilst in Winson Green prison, Birmingham, on 17 June 1912, Museum of London Collections Online, www.collections. museumoflondon.org.uk.
27. Poem written by suffragette prisoner Kathleen O'Kell whilst in Winson Green prison, Birmingham, on 17 June 1912, Museum of London Collections Online, www.collections. museumoflondon.org.uk.
28. Poem written by suffragette prisoner Kathleen O'Kell whilst in Winson Green prison, Birmingham, on 17 June 1912, Museum of London Collections Online, www.collections. museumoflondon.org.uk.
29. *Votes for Women*, 7 March 1912.
30. Poem written by suffragette prisoner Kathleen O'Kell whilst in Winson Green prison, Birmingham, on 17 June 1912, Museum of London Collections Online, www.collections. museumoflondon.org.uk.
31. Poem written by suffragette prisoner Kathleen O'Kell whilst in Winson Green prison, Birmingham, on 17 June 1912, Museum of London Collections Online, www.collections. museumoflondon.org.uk.
32. Included in Redfern autograph book.
33. Poem written by suffragette prisoner Kathleen O'Kell whilst in Winson Green prison, Birmingham, on 17 June 1912, Museum of London Collections Online, www.collections. museumoflondon.org.uk.
34. Poem written by suffragette prisoner Kathleen O'Kell whilst in Winson Green prison, Birmingham, on 17 June 1912, Museum of London Collections Online, www.collections. museumoflondon.org.uk.
35. Poem written by suffragette prisoner Kathleen O'Kell whilst in Winson Green prison, Birmingham, on 17 June 1912, Museum of London Collections Online, www.collections. museumoflondon.org.uk.

36. Daly Goggin, Maureen and Fowkes Tobin, Beth, *Women and Things, 1750–1950: Gendered Material Strategies*, Routledge, 2016.

Chapter 9

1. National Archives HO/144/1193/220196, Report from Holloway prison, dated 15 March 1912.
2. The National Archives, HO/144/1193/220196, Report from Holloway prison, dated 15 March 1912.
3. LSE Library, 7KGG/1/1, Katie Gliddon's diary.
4. *The Times*, 6 March 1912.
5. The National Archives, HO/144/1193/220196, Letter to the Right Honourable Reginald McKenna from Rabbi Cohen, dated 21 March 1912.
6. The National Archives, HO/144/1193/220196, Letter from Alan Garrett Anderson to Holloway prison, dated 1 April 1912.
7. The Women's Library, LSE, Letters from the Taylor family and their relations during Mrs Taylor's first imprisonment, Letter from Mary Ellen (Nellie) Taylor to Mr Taylor and Dr Elizabeth Wilks, 21 March 1912.
8. The National Archives, HO/144/1193/220196.
9. Proctor, Zoe, *Life and Yesterday*, The Favil Press 1960, p.115.
10. Purvis, Jane, *Women's History Review*, 'The prison experiences of the suffragettes in Edwardian Britain', Routledge, 1995, 4:1, 103–133, DOI: 10.1080/09612029500 200073.
11. 'Personal Experiences' article in *Votes for Women*, 5 July 1912, p.4.
12. 'Personal Experiences' article in *Votes for Women*, 5 July 1912, p.4.
13. The Story of Leonora Tyson a Streatham Suffragette.
14. Davies, Caitlin, *Bad Girls: The Rebels and Renegades of Holloway Prison*, John Murray Publishers, 2018, p.79.

Chapter 10

1. Gough, Theresa, Karmie M.T. Kranich, Holloway Jail, 28 April 1912 cited in *Literature of the Women's Suffrage Campaign in England*, edited by Carolyn Christensen Nelson, Broadview Press, 2004, p.158.
2. Atkinson, Diane, *Rise Up Women!: The Remarkable Lives of the Suffragettes*, Bloomsbury, 2018, p.106.
3. *The Advertiser*, 11 March 1912.
4. The National Archives, HO/144/1195/220196, Report from Holloway prison.
5. The National Archives, HO/144/1195/220196, Report from Holloway prison.
6. *The Times*, 12 March 1912.
7. The National Archives, HO/144/1193/220196.
8. Proctor, Zoe, *Life and Yesterday*, The Favil Press, 1960, p.102.
9. Crawford, Elizabeth, *The Women's Suffrage Movement: A Reference Guide 1866–1928*, Routledge, 1999, p.311.
10. *Votes for Women*, 1908.
11. Proctor, Zoe, *Life and Yesterday*, The Favil Press, 1960, p.95.
12. BBC Archives, 13 July 1958.
13. Crawford, Elizabeth.
14. National Museum Wales, online letter collection.

15. National Museum Wales, online letter collection.
16. Atkinson Diane, Rise UP Women, Bloomsbury, 2018, p. 458
17. Atkinson Diane, Rise UP Women, Bloomsbury, 2018, p. 410
18. Atkinson, Diane, Museum of London article, 7 March 2018.
19. *The Times*, 8 March 1912.
20. https://ualresearchonline.arts.ac.uk – article called 'Smashing Handkerchief'.
21. Proctor, Zoe, *Life and Yesterday*, The Favil Press, 1960, pp.107–108.
22. *The Times*, 6 March 1912.
23. Crawford, Elizabeth, Woman and Sphere, 'Suffrage Stories: "Laura Grey": Sex, Poison and Suicide'.
24. Crawford, Elizabeth, Woman and Sphere, 'Suffrage Stories: "Laura Grey": Sex, Poison and Suicide'.
25. *Votes for Women*, 1912.
26. *The Guardian*, 'A Suffragette Autograph Album – in pictures', 6 December 2012.
27. Votes for Women, 23 September 1910, p. 831
28. https://ualresearchonline.arts.ac.uk – article called 'Smashing Handkerchief'.
29. Crawford, Elizabeth.
30. Crawford, Elizabeth.

Chapter 11

1. 8SUF – Oral Evidence on the Suffragette and Suffragist Movement: The Brian Harrison Interviews. Interview with Miss Hazel Inglis, 8SUF/B/069 & 8SUF/B/073, dated 21 February 1976 and with Mrs Helen Green, 8SUF/B/074, dated 16 March 1976.
2. Records of US Immigration and Naturalisation Service. Letter from Emily Victoria Fussell to President Woodrow Wilson. 22/10/1913 51728/017

Chapter 12

1. Garrud, Edith, 'The World we live in: Self-defence', *Votes for Women*, March 1910.
2. The Women's Library, Grace Roe, 8SUF/B/13, 4 October 1974.
3. Godfrey, Emelyne, *Mrs Pankhurst's Bodyguard: On the Trail of 'Kitty' Marshall and the Met Police 'Cats'*, The History Press, 2023, p.48.
4. Garrud, Edith, 'The World we live in: Self-defence', *Votes for Women*, March 1910.
5. Women's Social and Political Union Eighth Annual Report Year Ending 28 February 1914, p.19.
6. *Women's History Review*, Speech by Barbara Wylie on 3 April 1913, quoted by Joan Sangster, 'Exporting Suffrage: British Influences on the Canadian Suffrage Movement', 28(4).566–586, Taylor & Francis, 5 July 2018.
7. The Women's Library, Grace Roe, 8SUF/B/13, 4 October 1974.
8. The Women's Library, Mrs Leonora Cohen, 8SUF/B/18, 26 October 1974.
9. Godfrey, Emelyne, *Mrs Pankhurst's Bodyguard: On the Trail of 'Kitty' Marshall and the Met Police 'Cats'*, The History Press, 2023, pp.169–170.
10. Godfrey, Emelyne, *Mrs Pankhurst's Bodyguards: On the Trail of 'Kitty' Marshall and the Met Police 'Cats'*, The History Press, 2023, Preface.
11. Held in the Suffragette Fellowship Collection at the Museum of London.
12. Godfrey, Emelyne, *Mrs Pankhurst's Bodyguard: On the Trail of 'Kitty' Marshall and the Met Police 'Cats'*, The History Press, 2023, Preface.
13. Smyth, Ethel, *Female Pipings in Eden*, London, Peter Davies, 1933, p.225, and quoted in Godfrey, Emelyne, *Mrs Pankhurst's Bodyguard: On the Trail of 'Kitty' Marshall and the Met Police 'Cats'*, The History Press, 2023, p.164.

14. The Women's Library, Grace Roe, 8SUF/B/13, 4 October 1974.
15. The Women's Library, Grace Roe, 8SUF/B/13, 4 October 1974.

Chapter 13
1. BBC Archives, Oral interview of Lilian Lenton (alias Ida Inkley and Miss May Denis), first broadcast 1 January 1960.
2. Godfrey, Jennifer, *Suffragettes of Kent*, Pen & Sword Books Ltd, 2019.
3. National Portrait Gallery quote this online at https://www.npg.org.uk.
4. National Portrait Gallery, online at https://www.npg.org.uk.
5. Spelt 'MacFarlane' elsewhere in this book because charge sheets and other archive material/sources use that spelling.
6. The Women's Library, Grace Roe, 8SUF/B/13, 4 October 1974.
7. Crawford, Elizabeth, *The Women's Suffrage Movement: A Reference Guide 1866–1928*, Routledge, 1999, p.341.
8. The National Archives, Part 2 1255/234788, Memo from Leeds City Police to S.S., Home Office, dated 25 June 1913.
9. BBC Archives, Oral interview of Lilian Lenton (alias Ida Inkley and Miss May Denis), first broadcast 1 January 1960.
10. The National Archives, Part 2 1255/234788, Memo from Leeds City Police to S.S., Home Office, dated 25 June 1913.
11. The National Archives, Part 2 1255/234788, Memo from Leeds City Police to S.S., Home Office, dated 25 June 1913.
12. BBC Archives, Oral interview of Lilian Lenton (alias Ida Inkley and Miss May Denis), first broadcast 1 January 1960.
13. BBC Archives, Oral interview of Lilian Lenton (alias Ida Inkley and Miss May Denis), first broadcast 1 January 1960.
14. The National Archives, Part 2 1255/234788, Memo from Leeds City Police to S.S., Home Office, dated 25 June 1913.
15. BBC Archives, Oral interview of Lilian Lenton (alias Ida Inkley and Miss May Denis), first broadcast 1 January 1960.
16. The National Archives, Part 2 1255/234788, Leeds City Police report, 20 June 1913.
17. The National Archives, Part 2 1255/234788, Memo from Leeds City Police to S.S., Home Office, dated 25 June 1913.
18. *South Wales Daily News*, 6 May 1914, DCONC/5/44, p.148.
19. *Western Mail*, 18 July 1913, DCONC/5/43, p.45.
20. Crawford, Elizabeth, *The Women's Suffrage Movement: A Reference Guide 1866–1928*, Routledge, 1999, p.341.
21. The Women's Library, Grace Roe, 8SUF/B/13, 4 October 1974.
22. The Women's Library, Grace Roe, 8SUF/B/13, 4 October 1974.
23. BBC Archives, Oral interview of Lilian Lenton (alias Ida Inkley and Miss May Denis), first broadcast 1 January 1960.
24. Crawford, Elizabeth, *The Women's Suffrage Movement: A Reference Guide 1866–1928*, Routledge, 1999, p.341.
25. Crawford, Elizabeth, *The Women's Suffrage Movement: A Reference Guide 1866–1928*, Routledge, 1999, p.341.
26. The National Archives, Part 1, 1255/234788, dated 15 October 1913, Ref: 234788/45.
27. Crawford, Elizabeth, *The Women's Suffrage Movement: A Reference Guide 1866–1928*, Routledge, 1999, p.341.

28. BBC Archives, Oral interview of Lilian Lenton (alias Ida Inkley and Miss May Denis), first broadcast 1 January 1960.
29. Crawford, Elizabeth, *The Women's Suffrage Movement: A Reference Guide 1866–1928*, Routledge, 1999, p.341.
30. The Women's Library, Miss Winifred Adair Roberts, BSUF/B/015, 8 October 1974.
31. BBC Archives, Oral interview of Lilian Lenton (alias Ida Inkley and Miss May Denis), first broadcast 1 January 1960.
32. Crawford, Elizabeth, *The Women's Suffrage Movement: A Reference Guide 1866–1928*, Routledge, 1999, p.341.
33. *Evening News*, 'Dramatic Arrest of a "Mouse"', 5 May 1915.
34. *Western Mail*, 6 May 1914, DCONC/5/44, p.146.
35. Crawford, Elizabeth, *The Women's Suffrage Movement: A Reference Guide 1866–1928*, Routledge, 1999, p.341.
36. Crawford, Elizabeth, *The Women's Suffrage Movement: A Reference Guide 1866–1928*, Routledge, 1999, p.135.
37. BBC Archives, Oral interview of Lilian Lenton (alias Ida Inkley and Miss May Denis), first broadcast 1 January 1960.
38. Crawford, Elizabeth, *The Women's Suffrage Movement: A Reference Guide 1866–1928*, Routledge, 1999, p.135.
39. The Women's Library, Mrs Leonora Cohen, 8SUF/B/019, 26 October 1974.
40. The Women's Library, Mrs Leonora Cohen, 8SUF/B/019, 26 October 1974.
41. The People's Voice website, Database of Poems, *L'Envoi* by Emily Wilding Davison.
42. Overton, Jenny and Mant, Joan, *A Suffragette Nest: Peaslake, 1910 and After*, Hazeltree Publishing, 1998, p.7.
43. Overton, Jenny and Mant, Joan, *A Suffragette Nest: Peaslake, 1910 and After*, Hazeltree Publishing, 1998, p.7.
44. Pine, Catherine, Mapping Women's Suffrage, https://www.mappingwomenssuffrage.org.uk.
45. Crawford, Elizabeth in article by Jessica Holland, *City Mag*, City University of London, 2007.
46. Crawford, Elizabeth, *The Women's Suffrage Movement: A Reference Guide 1866–1928*, Routledge, 1999.
47. Edited by Viv Gardner and Diane Atkinson, Kitty Marion Autobiography, Manchester University Press, 2019, p. 196.
48. The Women's Library, LSE, Account written in note book by Mrs Mary Ellen (Nellie) Taylor, alias Mary Wyan, 21 July 1913.
49. The Women's Library, LSE, Charge Sheet of Mary Wyan by PC Lee, 14 July 1913.
50. The Women's Library, LSE, Charge Sheet of Mary Wyan by PC Lee, 14 July 1913.
51. The Women's Library, LSE, Account written in note book by Mrs Mary Ellen (Nellie) Taylor, alias Mary Wyan, 21 July 1913.
52. The Women's Library, LSE, Draft letter written by Mrs Mary Ellen (Nellie) Taylor, alias Mary Wyan to the Right Honourable Reginald McKenna, 21 July 1913.
53. *The Suffrage*, 1 August 1913, p.724.
54. The Women's Library, Miss Winifred Adair Roberts, BSUF/B/015, 8 October 1974.
55. *The Times*, 13. March 1912.
56. Godfrey Jennifer, *Suffragettes of Kent*, Pen & Sword Books Ltd, 2018.

Index